WALES AND THE ALL BLACKS

An off-field history

ROGER G.K. PENN

Wales and the All Blacks

AN OFF-FIELD HISTORY

Originally Published in 2013 by Gomer Press
titled *Three Feathers and a Silver Fern*

This new updated edition published by Y Lolfa
in 2022

ISBN 978-1-80099-258-0

Originally published with the Financial
Support of the Books Council of Wales

Printed and bound in Wales at
Y Lolfa, Talybont, Ceredigion, SY24 5HE
www.ylolfa.com

This book is dedicated to the late

John Sinclair

*founder member of the New Zealand Rugby Museum,
who greatly enhanced the fellowship between
his countrymen and the Welsh.*

*In the course of arranging spectator tours to Wales and
welcoming visiting parties to his homeland, John enjoyed
bringing people together for the social side of rugby.*

Contents

Thanks and Acknowledgements

This book would not have been possible without the help of many, many people. To them all I offer my sincere thanks.

To every newspaper which formed a major part of my research, I offer my gratitude. Although each source is listed in the Bibliography, the *Western Mail* and the *New Zealand Herald* must be thanked especially.

I wish to thank the staff of the central libraries of Swansea, Auckland and Dunedin; the town libraries of Carmarthen, Haverfordwest, Llanelli and Neath; the reference libraries of Aberdare, Aberdeen, Cardiff, Exeter, Port Talbot and Newport; the National Library of Wales; the Glamorgan Archives in Cardiff; the West Wales Archives in Swansea; and the Pembrokeshire Records Office in Haverfordwest.

My five weeks research visit to New Zealand in late 2012 was an absolute pleasure. I am so grateful to everyone I met and spoke to, many being All Blacks. I wish to thank Stephen Berg and his team at the New Zealand Rugby Museum in Palmerston North, Ron Palenski and colleagues at the New Zealand Sports Hall of Fame in Dunedin, and Graham Walton at the International Hall of Fame, Eden Park.

On returning home I have been helped by historians and dedicated men of Welsh rugby. I refer to Mike Dams of Newport; Les Williams of Llanelli; Roy Lewis of Ebbw Vale; Mike Price of Neath; Ray Ruddick of Pontypool; Mike Thomas and Dave Dow of Swansea; Gordon Eynon, Pembrokeshire's Welsh Rugby Union representative; Phil McGowan of the

World Rugby Museum, Twickenham; Graham Ireland of the Scottish Rugby Union, Murrayfield; and Peter Owens of the Welsh Rugby Union, Cardiff. Thank you all sincerely.

In New Zealand, Dr Michael Bowen introduced me to Sir Colin Meads and Sir Brian Lochore, now both sadly departed, by telephone – so my thanks go to Michael and his wife, Diana, for these choice introductions, also to Michael's brother and wife, John and Valmai, and Elizabeth and Ken Bevan (my sister and her late husband).

Meeting Sir Colin Meads, a larger-than-life personality, at the Maldron Hotel, Cardiff, before the All Blacks clash in November 2012, was a great privilege. It was at this same venue that I also met our own J. P. R. Williams of Bridgend, a man who achieved remarkable success against the All Blacks and who agreed to provide a Foreword for this book. Thank you John, sincerely, for your kindness and support.

To all who provided a photograph and who are credited in the usual way, I thank you sincerely. Each of the following will also recognise their particular contributions to this story: John and Jenny Hornblow, Jim and Janet Moody, Alan Jones (Blaenavon), Steve Hopkins (in Australia), Brian Cook, Glenys Evans, John Langdon, Robin Meikle, Eirianwen Stanford, Charlie Rodea, Peter Griffiths, Barb Wright, Carolyn Griffin, and my wife, Celeste.

Finally, I wish to thank Dylan Williams for his help and guidance throughout; Jonathan Lewis and his team at Gomer Press; Garmon Gruffudd and colleagues at Y Lolfa, particularly Richard Pritchard, and the Welsh Books Council.

Now, I sincerely hope you enjoy the story.

ROGER PENN
Dolycwrt Cottage
July, 2022

Foreword by J. P. R. Williams

From the first game in 1905 the fixtures between Wales and New Zealand have had a charisma all of their own. Undoubtedly this began with the knowledge and belief that the best are always beatable, although every team that squares up to the All Blacks has to accept this. Yet when the Welsh face the haka one somehow senses a difference.

Could it be the mutual recognition of a proud temperament shared by two small nations making their way in the world, or just the single-mindedness of rugby men determined to win? In this publication Roger Penn reviews over a century of such fixtures but focuses more on the context of the occasions rather than the playing itself. And again one senses a difference and a different type of rugby history book.

The determination to win on the field is a clear aptitude in a player, but the determination to spend hours in archives in Wales and in New Zealand, to unearth and put together a convincing story and a personal perspective is quite another. The result is an account that rugby enthusiasts and historians will want to read and talk about afterwards. Roger's tour amongst the libraries, devotees, officials and players of the game on both sides of the world has given this book an assured appeal and authenticity. *Wales and the All Blacks* presents and celebrates a very special rugby relationship that combines drama, passion, intensity and *hwyl*. It is one I recognise well.

Preface

I am thrilled to be invited by Y Lolfa to write one last chapter for my off-field history of 'Wales and the All Blacks', which was previously published under the title *Three Feathers and a Silver Fern*. I have always believed that when Wales next triumph over our mighty friends from New Zealand, a reprint will be merited. Sadly, this mountain of a task remains work-in-progress, but how we yearn for the day. It need not be the most scintillating of rugby performances and a one-point victory will suffice, perhaps on a dark wet November night in beer-soaked Cardiff and with a lucky bounce – but, wouldn't this exhilarate the Welsh?

As we contemplate the day, we would be wise to reflect upon the 1905 first match between the two nations and the factors that determined Welsh success. That day the talented, rip-roaring home team were carried across the finishing line by the singing and fanatical support of spectators lucky enough to be inside the ground, and by many more viewing from lofty trees, roof-tops and wherever else they could catch a glimpse of the action. Indeed, it was a case of a country and its neighbouring nations closing ranks on a nigh-unbeatable All Black team.

For a repeat performance, I sense that Wales must replicate the swift ball-handling running that ignited the British Lions' series win in New Zealand in 1971, besides bringing two further All Black triumphs for Llanelli and the Barbarians, under the guidance of our own late Carwyn James.

But, neither must we forget our neighbours the Irish. Up

until 2016, they had never beaten the All Blacks. But just look at them now. In the last six years they have tucked five great victories under their belts which includes a test series win in New Zealand. Incredible! This will surely focus Welsh minds and help our cause.

So, I have much to share, and I sincerely hope you enjoy my presentation.

ROGER PENN
July, 2022

PART I
A WELCOME TO WALES
FOR THE 1905 'ORIGINALS'

All aboard the
Great Western Railway to Cardiff

There was a rousing reception when the all-conquering New Zealand 'Originals' pulled into Cardiff's packed train station in the early evening of Thursday December 14th 1905. Arriving a few minutes late in the rear carriage of the scheduled 6.50 p.m. passenger service from Leeds, the victors of every one of their twenty-seven matches in the British Isles stepped forward onto a packed platform amidst the great excitement and noise of a welcome to Wales. And, as they looked around to register the feel of the new surroundings, their easy manner and unassuming nature gave the distinct impression that the shouts and cheers were meant for others of far greater importance.

These masters of the game of rugby football were now universally recognised as being the world's best. Having travelled from Exeter to Edinburgh, and then throughout the Emerald Isle, undefeated, having scored 801 points and conceded only 22 – they were, without doubt, a special group of men. Led by the valiant Dave Gallaher, Irish born, Kiwi-bred and a Boer War fighter for Queen, King and Country – they were on a mission. They were too talented to ignore, too clever to underestimate, too amiable, by far, to dislike and ready for the biggest rugby showdown of the new century.

At a time when the game's status was growing, these New Zealanders were having a profound effect on rugby's popularity both on and off the field, and it was hardly surprising that they were foremost amongst the day's celebrities. Smartly dressed in shirts and ties, they were big and powerful, fleet of foot and steadfast in spirit. The game as they played it reflected the battles in their motherland of times past; and they played to win.

The Welshmen of this era were no mishits either: men of strength and fearless rank who packed coal, steel, emotion and pride into their national game. Besides drawing the crowds, rugby filled beer-flowing hostelries well into winter nights, ventilating the feelings and emotions of inter-town and village rivalry across the country. A quarter of a century earlier, Wales had been on the wrong end of a thirteen-try mauling against England, but that was then and lessons had been learnt.

Indeed, rugby football in Wales was a social winner, offering relief and respite to those who toiled above or below the ground. In a real way its communal bond gave reason, meaning, hope, enjoyment, also the togetherness and tribal delight of promoting the jersey of one's own team. It lit up the dark, cold, miserable winter afternoons with a glow that carried into the next week's play. Riding the waves of this powerful social force, the Welsh national team was reaping the benefit of its first successes. Earlier that same year, 1905, Wales' coordinated forward rushes and dribbles downfield had flattened the English Rose, the Scottish Thistle, and the Irish Shamrock, to earn the much-coveted Triple Crown. With some of the country's greatest players such as Rhys Gabe, Willie Llewellyn and Teddy Morgan having sailed to New Zealand a year earlier on a British tour, Welshmen knew their opponents well, recognising every capability and threat. And everybody who cared – and most did – knew that the Wales–New Zealand match of 1905 would be a game to remember. The Welsh prophets were correct.

As the chugging locomotives belched smoke and steam into the winter air, George Dixon, tour manager, Dave Gallaher, captain, and their men from the land of the long white cloud, were welcomed by a reception party of dignitaries led by the Lord Mayor of Cardiff, his councillors and officials of the Welsh Football Union (the equivalent of today's Welsh Rugby Union). Then, stepping outside the station, they walked into a huge wide audience: a sea of thousands of open, happy cheering faces, whilst hands and hats were held aloft, all excited to see the arrival of true sporting giants.

To the Welsh public, these scenes represented the weigh-in of a world heavyweight contest, confirming beyond all doubt that the stage was set, the fight was on. Gesturing with warmth and friendliness, the rugby footballers jumped aboard open horse-drawn carriages that ventured through the narrow man-made corridors dividing the crowds, leading the short distance into St Mary Street. With horses at half pace, and all eyes cast upon these sporting giants, the slow procession inched towards the Queen's Hotel, one of Cardiff's finest providers of good food, drink and accommodation and now a safe haven for the New Zealand party for these defining days of this demanding tour.

The *Western Mail* of December 15th 1905 reports that in the stately atmosphere of the sober coffee room, the tourists were shielded from the extravagance of the welcome, but time would show that this Cardiff greeting was no isolated occasion; these first impressions would count. The bonding of two rugby nations whose shared love of the national game eclipsed all else had been witnessed. This was a lasting fellowship that would walk down the years.

By now, these Colonial friends, or brother members of the British Empire as viewed in Edwardian days, had been christened with a new name that was destined to stay: All Blacks. We are led to believe that this name emerged from detailed newspaper reports in England describing the early stages of the tour. The New Zealand Sports Hall of Fame, Dunedin, quotes the opinion of Billy Wallace, a true rugby innovator and legend of the time, that the name came from a reporter's view that the entire team could run like 'Backs' – All *Backs* although wrongly spelt as All *Blacks* – and it is certain that the impact of their sharp strips also carried the name.

In fact, even before a ball was kicked in their first tour match at Exeter on September 16th, the reporter for *The Express and Echo* was seemingly sowing the first seed, describing 'the All Blacks as they are styled by reason of their sable and unrelieved costumes'. It is known that J. Buttery of the *Daily Mail* gave the name greater coverage in later matches, whilst the fact that these men were wreaking havoc on British teams, sweeping aside worthy opponents with relative ease and by considerable margins – helped the term to rise to the fore.

The welcome to Wales on that Thursday evening in 1905 had been extraordinary yet it continued to increase in depth and fervour on the pages of Friday's *Western Mail*, the recognised voice of rugby in Wales. Indeed, only days earlier in this same daily paper was the telling news that some fifty excursion trains were travelling into Cardiff for the match. Each was scheduled to carry hundreds of passengers from as far away as Lancashire, London and southern England, whilst extra carriages were supporting the regular services of the country's local lines. In truth, heavy locomotives were arriving from all directions, as a groundswell of rising activity confirmed that this match, above all others, had exceptional appeal and was extra special.

For the seasoned New Zealanders, big match preparations were now taken in their stride, but the packed streets of Cardiff on international days were – and still are – an intimidating proposition for visitors, the more so when Wales measures its might against the world's best. Despite rattling up a run of confidence–boosting successes, these All Blacks were wise enough to realise that since crossing the border into rugby–roused Wales they had hit upon a storm, strong enough, potentially, to blow them off-course. Their unblemished win record could be in serious jeopardy and only New Zealand's best display would prevent their celebrated run from coming to an abrupt end. In all they had seen and heard on their travels, nothing had compared with Cardiff's ringing public declaration and its insatiable craving for rugby glory.

Just as worrying at this late stage of a demanding tour was the fact that five more difficult matches had to be played in quick succession within the Principality. Whilst this was a mouth-watering prospect for the motivated Welsh, it was a major predicament for their visitors who, desperately over-extended, had no means of escape. Ahead lay two strenuous weeks that would make or break their campaign; two weeks that might yet continue to silence the partisan crowds, as well as a nation of doubters back at home.

In earning such immense sporting acclaim they had, as outlined in Christopher Tobin's wonderful *The Original All Blacks 1905-1906*, essentially confounded the critics head on. After failing to impress in their warm-up matches before leaving New Zealand, genuine misgivings had been cast over the likely success of the tour and its ability, through drawing crowds, to pay its way. The New Zealanders' send-off at Wellington in late July was less than lukewarm; however, under the motivating leadership of manager George Dixon, originally from Huddersfield, and Dave Gallaher, their inspirational captain, the six weeks on-board RMS *Rimutaka* were channelled into strenuous deck training for physical fitness and blackboard work which gave rise to effective tactics and a deeper understanding of the game. By the time the men docked in Plymouth, England, via Montevideo and Tenerife, they were a fresh, eager outfit, motivated and ready for the first game of the tour.

This is when they met Devon on September 16th, a leading English county side who were expected to turn up and walk away with victory. But these men in stately black, some wearing casual hats during the game, and all standing defiant to the end of play, ran riot, winning 55–4 at a time of three-point tries. In the next match, against Cornwall, they registered another great victory, 41–0: a score that was repeated in the following fixture against much fancied Bristol. It was a start that was too good to be true, causing everybody to sit up and take note.

Now in the form of their lives and travelling from one rugby stronghold to the next, nobody was able to withstand their might, try as they did. On a freezing cold day in Edinburgh against a nation on top of its game, the New Zealanders managed a 12–7 victory that silenced the Scottish crowd and embarrassed the Scottish administrators. In truth, New Zealand's reception in Scotland was as cold and as unwelcoming as the weather. Not only had the Scots initially refused to recognise the fixture as a full international by not awarding caps, but also few officials had met the team on arrival, leaving them, to a great extent, to their own devices.

On the morning of the match, there was even doubt about the game proceeding, for no one had bothered to cover the field with straw overnight, leaving it hard and dangerous. This was far from ideal for such a clash, but the New Zealanders, well used to playing rugby in all weathers, did not wish to disappoint the spectators who, at this early hour, were already trickling through the gates. So the match went ahead and proved to be great entertainment, bringing urgent bellows of encouragement from members of the Scottish Union camped on the touchline. Then, afterwards, little changed in the way of fellowship, or the lack of it, for as the Scottish players sat down to dinner amongst themselves, their visitors, excluded, dined elsewhere.

It is difficult to associate such indifference with the usual bonhomie of the Scots but, on this occasion, events had passed them by. Before setting sail, the Scottish Union had refused the Originals a financial pledge that was generally given by host teams to cover touring expenses, whilst instead (and rather generously as it transpired) offering all ground takings to their visitors following deduction of expenses. Clearly the Scots had underestimated the success and draw and the moneymaking opportunity of these men from 'Down Under' so, doubtless, a degree of apathy had arisen on account of this financial miscalculation alone.

How different from the hospitality and well-intentioned hullabaloo extended by the Irish, who celebrated the New Zealander's arrival in style, a part of which was an outing to the famous Guinness factory. Throughout their stay, they were showered with well-wishes, especially from adoring women, whilst the game's ratings were boosted by making the international an 'all-ticket' affair, a novel idea at the time. The game, a boisterous forward battle in the wet, was gripping entertainment in the pleasant Irish setting of Lansdowne Road, Dublin, the New Zealanders holding on to triumph, the game closer than the 15–0 score suggests.

In London's fashionable Crystal Palace arena, the bandwagon rolled on, so also the army of spectators who, having apparently pushed past gatemen, swelled the estimated crowd to a considerable 50,000 but with vast numbers also viewing from other inclines overlooking the field. One of the spectators, according to *The Original All Blacks 1905–1906*, was the Prince of Wales sitting in the stand, who witnessed a dominant display by the New Zealanders in overcoming the mighty physical presence of the English by five tries, 15–0. So far, it was a Home Nations whitewash that few had foreseen.

But this had been a gruelling tour, highly demanding in terms of constant matches, physical demands and long hours of travelling. By now, many players were carrying injuries, dipping below their best, and certainly tired and weary. This small squad of twenty-seven players, plus manager and coach, had played on average a match every three days – notching up twenty-seven straight victories within three months and a mountain of hard-earned points. They had been universally praised for achieving the near impossible, and now had to face Wales.

Ever since their arrival, all aspects of New Zealand's play had been studied and painstakingly discussed. Rugby's technical experts in the British Isles were intrigued most by the way the touring team, seemingly, stole a march on opponents by putting two men, as opposed to three, in the front row of the 'scrimmages.' At this time, scrimmages, today's scrums, were generally formed by the first forwards onto the scene, all others packing down behind them as and when they arrived. But not for the New Zealanders, who were already playing permanent specialists in every position. And, as the seven forwards usually won the ball, the 'extra man' was free to lend another pair of hands to the 'backs.' These men had done their homework well and their inventiveness made them quietly confident of victory against the Welsh and their demanding, emotional followers.

In the *Western Mail* on the day before the match, a local reporter described the discussion he had with coach James Duncan, one of the most influential figures in New Zealand rugby. When asked about the British team's tour to his homeland a year earlier, when New Zealand won the test match 9–3, he praised the Welsh backs who had made a big impression and who were remembered for their courage, cleverness and speed, with Rhys Gabe, in particular, singled out. Likewise, he complimented his own captain, Dave Gallaher, one of the most competitive footballers in the game, as a man who would have a major bearing on this forthcoming encounter. When invited to give his opinion about New Zealand's chances, Mr Duncan replied: 'I will tell you candidly that I think we are going to win. I believe we shall be too clever for your men all round.' And when questioned about his backs, as compared to the Welsh players, he considered that the New Zealanders would be too quick; what is more, he thought them to 'be at least as clever, but probably much cleverer.'

The next question concerned 'the forwards,' to which the interviewee pointed out that British players 'seem to get into the squash [scrimmage] anyhow,' whilst in New Zealand 'forward play is a science.' 'Our seven forwards have been able to hold their opponents in the scrums,' said Mr Duncan, 'and generally to heel out' – before explaining that in open play his men were sharp enough to gather the ball and initiate moves which resulted in scores.

No doubt, ardent New Zealand followers had similar views, but, in terms of overall numbers, they represented a small minority, because all over Wales, the Welsh were convincing themselves that victory was theirs for the taking. Likewise, in every Home Nation, true men of rugby were relying on Wales to rescue the grim standing of the British game by arresting this seemingly unstoppable talent that had effectively relegated all teams to a lower league. To see the New Zealanders making a clean sweep of the four proud home countries was unthinkable. It was time for the interests of the home unions to merge as one, whilst leeks and Brains bitter and all things Welsh became the order of the day.

Among rugby correspondents, no one was better prepared to present the final countdown to the match than the *Western Mail's* own reporter, duly described as Forward. Writing on the morning of the contest, he believed that the Welsh were in the prime of their lives, physically prepared, well led by Gwyn Nicholls, and with a mobile, hungry pack. As regards the backs, he saw Dicky Owen, the pocket-sized dynamo from Swansea, a mere 5' 4" and nine-and-a-half stones, and Percy Bush, the dazzling runner from Cardiff, as being key players. Just as importantly, the writer sensed that the Welsh were fired by 'spirit' and resolve 'to fight to the last ditch.'

But surprisingly, having taken the time to speak to the New Zealanders, he had detected a sense of uneasiness in their attitude. Whilst applauding their achievements in overcoming all manner of opposition to date, he described a distinct awareness within their ranks that trouble lay ahead. Even so, most of the touring party still believed that they would be returning undefeated to their families. The reporter felt that many favoured 'the little silver fern,' although others were bold enough to suggest 'that the leek will be too strong a vegetable' for the gentle plant, meaning that the Welsh could well be the first of the four Home Nations teams to triumph at the expense of the All Blacks.

Then, after admitting the folly of making predictions, this same sporting scribe chose to predict that honours may well end up even 'when the hurly-burly's done, and the battle's lost or won.' Finally, delving deeper and sensing the mood, he remarked that the touring party had 'breathed quite a different football atmosphere in Cardiff,' when compared with different parts of the kingdom, for he (the reporter) had attended the tourists' fixture against the English at Crystal Palace. 'We have never had such a reception anywhere,' said an unnamed All Black player interviewed, 'and we have never seen such unmistakable sign of keenness.' 'This man,' said the *Western Mail* correspondent, '[had] read the signs aright.'

Into the Dragon's Den as the Welsh prepare to pounce

In the lead up to this momentous occasion, two full trial matches had been arranged in Cardiff at a time when 'trial caps' honoured those who had played in the final trial, the last hurdle before selection. And, anxious to make a strong statement of intent, the Welsh Football Union committee who met at the Royal Hotel, Swansea, to choose the two teams, stated in the *Western Mail* of November 27th 1905 that the players chosen for a 'trial or international match' who failed to provide 'the committee' with a good excuse for absence, would be 'debarred' from club matches for a four-week term.

However, these heroes did not need such reminders; their resolve was already hardened. They would have happily swum up and down the River Taff if it improved their chances of wearing the red of Wales. By the time the second trial had taken place, on the day that New Zealand eased to victory over England, everyone in Wales was heartened by the emergence of a settled 'Probables' team. More importantly, both matches had solved the dilemma as to whether seven or eight forwards would play. Over the past fortnight, this subject had been thoroughly aired, attracting comments from most corners of the Principality, all aimed at nullifying New Zealand's rather different scrimmage practice. One gentleman, described as 'Old Judge', was adamant that this was not the time to experiment with the tried and trusted Welsh formation. He knew that each of the other countries had tinkered with their own team structures, the same intention having been in their minds, and, in so doing, all had gone down like a pack of cards. He stated in the *Western*

Mail of December 2nd 1905 that it was not wise to 'swap horses in crossing the stream and so fall between two stools' – clearly emphasising his point with a magnificent mixed metaphor that we can all understand.

Another, a former player described as an 'old half-back', said that Wales did not have a suitable player to perform a Gallaher-type of role. The New Zealand captain was a wing-forward although permanently detached from the scrum and it was therefore unreasonable to ask someone to step forward to fill such an unknown role. This same person's next message was that Wales had a choice of three half backs who knew each other's game, these being Owen, Bush and Trew, and they were as good as any side could field. 'Why not play these?' he asked, 'with Owen to work the scrum, and Bush and Trew standing on either side?'

Dr Pryce Jenkins, a representative of the Welsh Union, said, 'It is not for me' to dictate that the Welsh should rely on seven front men. He thought that those responsible for the team would have the best ideas, while hardened forwards like Hodges, Joseph and Dai Jones would have their say. Dr Jenkins considered the team might also want to vary their pattern 'when their own territory is assailed,' as opposed to when the Welsh 'are acting on the aggressive.'

All of this was highly technical, but equally essential in getting this aspect of play correct for victory. The topic led next to the referee's interpretation of events – and who was the referee for such an important match, somebody of experience, no doubt? But how would he control the forwards? Would he let the action flow; would he keep abreast of the speed of the game? At a time when appointments were made with little time to spare, both sides needed these questions answered besides a lot more. This appointment would be critical to the chances of both teams.

Again, the *Western Mail* had the answer, two days before kick-off. It was to be Mr John Dewar Dallas, a former captain of Watsonians rugby club, a young man aged twenty-seven, a former international player who was representing the Scottish Union. His appointment had 'given complete satisfaction to the members of the Welsh Union.' He was fully versed with all of rugby's intricacies, but this was, however, his first international as a referee – and what a game to control. Mr Dallas would be arriving on one of the early trains, but little did he know what was in store for him.

During their final preparations, the Welsh players had taken the opportunity to tread the turf of Cardiff Arms Park, where the hard–working groundsman and his team had taken every precaution to protect the playing surface, part of which, according to the *Western Mail*, 'contained a lot of bone.' According to this same newspaper, 'the straw was removed at the river end' of the playing field, allowing for handling movements, kicking practice and scrimmages to take place. The practice had been worthwhile and it was heartening to see that the backs slotted into each other's pattern of play.

Through having read reports and spoken to former players and ardent spectators of the game, the Welsh team had been reminded of the only previous occasion when black-shirted New Zealanders had played the Welsh national rugby team, exactly seventeen years earlier, way back in December 1888. In an article in this same newspaper of December 16th, a reporter who was given the pen name 'Welsh Athlete' shared his reflections of the 'Natives' – this being almost entirely a Māori team – when they played Wales at St Helen's in Swansea. It had been a keen contest which saw the Welsh earning a goal-and-two-tries-to-nil victory in a feast of fast-flowing rugby that thrilled onlookers. The gentleman explained that the New Zealanders made their entrance 'with a sort of mat wrapped around their shoulders,' and that they were known to engage in a 'war yell' at the start of their bigger matches. It was 'Aka something or other' – similar, or so the reporter thought, to what the present 'Colonial team' were singing on this tour, but more concise, 'a yell instead of a song,' whilst spared 'the dramatic posturing' of the current side.

The writer also recalled the time the tourists were beaten by Cardiff a few weeks later, when '[Norman] Biggs,' a local hero, played against a Māori wearing 'red stockings,' who could really motor. But as the reporter can 'remember right well,' during times when 'Norman humped his shoulders, and went for the line,' it was obvious who was the quicker of the two, 'and it was not him of the red stockings.'

So, understandably, the city of Cardiff was braced for the day of all days, and, with such a story to tell, journalists and reporters of newspapers and magazines across Britain were spilling into the station. There, staff prepared to handle one train's arrival upon another with outpourings of people by the hundreds. Horses pulled carts, brakes and wagons full of spectators down the dusty lanes and byways leading towards the city. Innkeepers, hoteliers and catering proprietors stood in wait, as did the shops and stores, chock–full of stock, many offering basic food for the day: all eagerly awaiting an influx of people, an explosion of activity to boost the coffers of a bumper Christmas season. Although trade had been quiet in the lead-up to the event, on the day the jangling of coins would be unmistakable from early morning until late night.

At the Post Office, telegrams offering up-to-date match reports threatened to propel revenue into dizzy heights. There would be queues and crowds like never seen before, as match details – even progress reports – were demanded all over the country, all over New Zealand, and all over rugby parts in-between. As employers stretched resources, shutting offices early to allow staff to get to the game, an exercise of 'give and take' was put in place, so that skeleton staff did the bare essentials during crucial match-time hours. At Cardiff's busy docks it was not feasible to cease operations, although agreement was given for workers to set off early enough to see the action if they had received prior consent.[1]

As the tension continued to mount, central Cardiff was awash with people by 10 a.m., wave upon wave of happy, smiling faces, many sporting a leek from their pantry. They were all aware that one shilling gained admittance at the entrance near the Angel Hotel, two shillings at the County Club gate and three shillings for the enclosure beneath the grandstand. It was a case of 'first come first served' for standing room, and this method, having been well advertised, was fair to all. Understandably, large crowds gathered early, the long queues kept orderly by an army of policemen, many on horseback, whilst anxious gatekeepers were preparing for their biggest task of the year. Wisely deciding to open ahead of time, they allowed the crowd, most with a spot of lunch packed inside their pockets, to filter from the thoroughfares to the edge of the field of play. Indeed, two hours before kick-off, the stands were getting full, and, said the *Western Mail* reporter 'Forward': 'one could not help sympathising with the thousands of people who were outside the gates struggling valiantly to gain admission.'

Crowd control on this mid-winter's day was a huge responsibility. Only three years earlier in 1902, the Ibrox disaster had shaken soccer to the core when a stand collapsed, tragically claiming the lives of innocent spectators. With some sections of the swelling crowd already 'swaying', ground officials, guided by good judgement, chose to close the Arms Park gates well ahead of kick-off. Those fortunate

---

1   *Western Mail*, December 14th 1905.

to be inside rejoiced at their great luck: most determined to make their presence felt by singing, shouting and offering encouragement. And, yes, there would be criticism of New Zealand should ever they stray offside, or obstruct knowingly, gainfully, or deliberately.

Spectators had made a big effort, travelling long distances, walking many miles, some having thrown their last pennies into the day. In a tough, harsh world of monotonous grind, hard slog and often little reward, it was a struggle for most to survive. Many miners from the Western Valley pits in Monmouthshire who were at this time 'on strike,' walked considerable distances to see the match. Although coal output was still increasing, fluctuating or falling prices, as determined by demand, supply and competition, were having a cruel effect on the working man and his family.

But most heaved a huge sigh of relief as December 16th promised respite, a day to remember, hopefully, glory too, and excellent odds for those who wagered their shillings on a Welsh win. They had arrived to support their heroes. This was not a run-of the-mill game of rugby; it was a call to arms, a duty owed to one's country, a most serious obligation. There was a most definite movement in a south-easterly direction this day, courtesy of a close network of connecting trains.

Rightfully proud of Wales' own recent run of Triple Crowns, and confident that it was possible to knock the New Zealanders off their perch, here was a nation united in lifting its team and carrying it across the line. Early singing at the pitch side had been merry but this would strengthen considerably when the players entered the field. As the band of the Second Voluntary Battalion of the Welsh Regiment played *Tôn y Botel* and *Lead Kindly Light* as well as *The Boys of the Old Brigade* and *Blue Bell*, many rested their voices, saving their lungs and energy for the main event.

The *Western Mail* stated that amongst those who entered the ground early 'were many of the old warriors of other days,' as well as past Welsh internationals who collected in small circles 'and fought their battles over again.' Everybody was clearly fascinated by the home team's mix, wondering how they might fare: there being four players from Cardiff, three from London Welsh, two from both Newport and Swansea, and a sole representative from Penygraig, Pontypool, Pill Harriers and Aberdare. Prospects could not be more exciting and it was only hoped that the 'gallant little country', Wales, would rise to the occasion to enhance the status of British rugby in the eyes of the world.

With neutrals also pledging their full support to Wales, among them Scots as well as Irish who had arrived by ferry, it was going to be a daunting afternoon for the New Zealanders. 'They'll think our fellows have wings,' were the words of Tom Williams, a selector for the Welsh Football Union, when asked for one quick comment as he shuffled past spectators to his seat.[2] Now, a Welsh hearth had been prepared for igniting, by a nation fuelled by passion and pride that could not wait. All it needed next was a spark to set the atmosphere alight. And, as the minutes on the ticking clock summoned the warriors into the still winter air of this fine, overcast day, it was time to spare a thought for the New Zealanders. For the first time on this tour, they were stepping into a dragon's den, as a Welsh nation prepared to pounce.

---

2   *Western Mail*, December 18th 1905.

Forty-five thousand Voices
and the Great Rivalry begins

In treading the Cardiff Arms Park turf that afternoon, the New Zealanders, strong to a man and immersed in rugby's great story, carried onto the field the deep traditions and pride of an equally passionate country. Indeed, when the New Zealanders arrived days earlier in Cardiff, and ventured through the packed streets to the Queen's Hotel, they displayed at the front of their vehicle a black banner, complete with silver fern bearing the words 'Ake! Ake! Kia kaha!' meaning 'Forever, forever be strong!' It was stated by Billy Stead, team vice-captain, that this same banner would be prominent at all venues where the team played in Wales, its words having great meaning for men needing every bit of inspiration.

The words were attributed to Rewi Maniapoto, a Māori chief at the Battle of Ōrākau in March 1864, and spoken to the men of his tribe when facing the enemy and, ultimately, death. This was during the time of the Land Wars when the Māori were fighting to retain their territory and, despite Rewi's warriors being hopelessly fewer in number, he refused the British offer to surrender, preferring to fight with courage and honour, whilst persuading his people to do the same. The resulting conflict lasted three days, and came to a conclusion when Rewi's remaining fighters escaped from the grip of their assailants. But the chief's words lived on, now a much-needed boost for these footballers facing the consequences of defeat, the ending of a magnificent record and death of a kind. 'Ake, Ake, Kia kaha' reminded them to be strong.

As Dave Gallaher led his men into battle, closely followed by Welsh captain, Gwyn Nicholls, and his team, the *Western*

Mail continued its commentary once the band had marched away. This was the time for Rewi Maniapoto's message to take effect in a performance of the haka by the New Zealanders, delivered with heart and nerve. This traditional dance, which commemorates celebrations and official welcomes and is presented as a challenge to which others duly respond, also has its origins deeply entrenched in the more severe circumstances of bloody conflict. And it is a powerful delivery, performed as a rite before battles begin, preparing those involved mentally and physically for what lies ahead.

But this day, its usual cutting edge was dulled and drowned by a sea of Welshmen whose own players had a bigger weapon up their sleeves, unleashed for the first time at a major sporting occasion. Responding with the rousing Welsh words of *Hen Wlad fy Nhadau* (*Land of My Fathers*) was akin to carrying a flaming Olympic torch into the arena, igniting the atmosphere like never before. 'The old land of my fathers is dear to me,' are the first words as literally translated, followed by a mention of poets, musicians and warriors, but its crescendo eclipses all else: 'Gwlad, Gwlad, pleidiol wyf i'm gwlad' meaning, 'My country, my country, devoted am I to my country'.

It is this heart-rending anthem that the Welsh players started to sing in quick response to the haka. This was at the suggestion of Tom Williams, selector and administrator, and, so it is believed, Teddy Morgan[3] led the way, the words soon to be raised to the heavens by forty-five thousand strong voices. Many people present felt that the occasion was similar to an eisteddfod, even touched by reverence but, whatever it may have been likened to, it was surely a massive body blow

---

3   Willie Llewellyn's name has also been linked to this act: understandable given that the two wing three-quarters were of similar size and appearance.

for the men in black and an almighty morale-boosting Welsh victory – without a ball having been kicked.

When both teams are equally matched the first strike is often the telling one. Had it been New Zealand's, they may have silenced the crowd and moved on to victory, but as it belonged to Wales, Teddy Morgan's first–half try struck a damaging blow. It took the score to 3–0 and despite a valiant New Zealand fightback and Bob Deans' assertions, and those of his colleagues and others, that a perfectly good try had been scored, this is how it stood for ever more.

'Such a game had never been played before, and such a victory had never been won,' said the *Western Mail* on the following Monday, when providing the leading news, quotes and detailed action; the game was likened to being a battle of the giants of world rugby, as indeed it was. Emphasising the point that Wales was the better team, the reporter acknowledged how 'the Colonials, keenly as they must have felt their defeat' were sufficiently fair competitors to admit that they had eventually 'met a team superior to their own.'

This was a game remembered for fierce forward combat, hard-hitting tackles, fast and furious running and the hostile berating by vast numbers of Welsh fans of New Zealand captain Dave Gallaher, like he had never experienced in his life. At the close of play, battered and bruised, he was a weary warrior, having given his all in the face of a tirade of stinging criticism for his alleged tendencies to obstruct at scrimmages. But his beaten smile and off-field sportsmanship were a credit to him and his countrymen, and, as he exchanged his shirt with Welsh captain, Gwyn Nicholls, he was the first to congratulate the Welsh.

'Yes, we have met our Waterloo,' he said. 'Wales beat us at our own game, and all I can say is that the Welshmen ought to feel proud of their side.' Adding that Winfield played extremely well at fullback and that he had not come across a better 'old crock' in midfield than Nicholls, he ended his comments with the words: 'No, I can't say any more.'

By way of contrast, Gwyn Nicholls, Welsh captain, was flowing with happiness when leaving the field to a background of tremendous noise: 'Oh,' he stated, 'we were just as good as they were,' adding that his team took its big opportunity. Then, when asked if his pack of forwards adopted the right style of rugby, he agreed that this was so. 'But I am too much elated just now to go into details,' he explained, repeating that the Welsh prospered from seizing their main moment.

George Dixon, the New Zealand tour manager, was clearly disappointed but also generous with his words, saying 'I'm bound to say the better side won' – adding 'you'll agree that our fellows had hard lines.' He referred to this game as being, beyond all doubt, the best of the entire tour.

Meanwhile, Tom Williams, Llwynypia, mentioned earlier, whose stroke of genius led to the players singing *Hen Wlad fy Nhadau*, explained that New Zealand's demise was due to Welsh adventure. 'The Welshmen did not go on the field to keep the score down,' he said. The team was intent upon achieving a victory, adding that the betting odds 'of 5 and 6 to 1' favouring the New Zealanders were 'absurd.'

Apart from bookmakers, who, feeling the headaches of those disproportionate odds and silently ruing the day, many others were known to make a comment. Here is a selection from the *Western Mail* of December the 18th, starting with a gentleman who travelled from Scotland. He felt that Wales would hold on as the game drew to a close, yet he was equally aware of the sheer ability and flair of the New Zealanders. He praised the football of Billy Wallace when events were proving difficult for his team, and felt a score should have resulted: 'The great Colonial went through the back division like a mackerel through a shoal of herrings, and it looked as if nothing living would stop him.'

Charlie Neill, a referee and an earlier candidate to officiate the game who had set sail from Ireland, admired the two teams and believed – and he a good prophet – 'that it was a case of the side that got the first blow in' – and, with it being the Welsh, 'they were ahead at the finish.'

Another from Germany – on a rugby pilgrimage, perhaps – had his eyes opened by the Welsh, having never witnessed such a spectacle: 'They fought as if their lives depended upon victory . . . I was reminded of Rome in ancient days.'

Meanwhile, an excited man from Ogmore could not contain his delight, being the most contented of all souls at his home that night. Everybody had told him Wales would lose: 'I said "No." Result – you don't want any more.'

At 6.15 p.m. this same evening both teams were attending the post-match dinner, smartly attired, many in morning suits at the Queen's Hotel. In the packed, bubbling, beer-flowing atmosphere, the doors had to be locked early, crowds of all descriptions milling around outside, as the evening gave way to cordiality, mutual appreciation and sportsmanship. Many wore the expression of fatigued happiness for it had been a long day and, as Billy Stead, vice-captain of the All Blacks, said of Cardiff that same night, in his *Billy's Trip Home*, 'It was the outburst of a nation's joy: an occasion [when] every Taffy, male and female seemed, for the time, to go mad.'

By now the New Zealanders were more frequently being referred to as 'All Blacks,' although also called 'Colonial-brethren' within the buzzing Welsh city. After the formalities of the evening meal and speeches had been completed, these popular visitors walked the dimly-lit streets of Cardiff in small groups, happily stopping to enjoy the scenes, talking to Welsh fans along the way. Cardiff had never experienced such an occasion and, to everyone's relief and credit, there were no serious disturbances: far from it, there were tales of happy scenes from all corners. Shortly after the final whistle was blown, it was said that Cardiff market was inundated by requests for leeks, or even onions (the next best thing!), whilst a mile away at Cowbridge Road the locals waited at the end of the street for boys on bicycles to convey the latest news. Up the road in the valley town of Pontypridd, a newsagent was so overjoyed upon hearing the final score that he gave away his entire consignment of the night's *Evening Press*.

Understandably, drinking continued long into the night: celebrations of a sporting occasion that, beyond doubt, bound the Prince of Wales' three feathers to a rather special silver fern. In the changing world to come, both countries would preserve the proud traditions of this day, whilst remaining in each other's fellowship along rugby's global journey. And both camps would also appreciate the following tale about a Welsh hero's return to his home town at the end of the evening. This was Cliff Pritchard, a helping hand in the day's winning score, who upon arriving back in Pontypool on the 11.27 p.m. train, was met by hundreds of local well-wishers and 'shouldered high amid deafening cheers.' Then everybody accompanied him to his house 'to the singing of the *Land of My Fathers*, *Sosban Fach* and *Men of Harlech*.'

This day the Welsh sang to their heart's content, and this factor had played its part in the great victory. New Zealand captain, Dave Gallaher, was just one admirer of the singing performance of a united choir which set a trend for future matches, saying, 'I was never impressed so much in my life.' It had been an uphill task for his team from that moment and, for the man himself, it was a torrid afternoon throughout. Although this ferocious contest had been an even one and his forwards had fought manfully, the backs had fallen well short of usual standards, missing Billy Stead, outside half, who was not well enough to play, although active as a touch judge.

Besides this, Gallaher was pegged back by Mr Dallas in a manner that had not happened before on tour. Mr Dallas penalised the captain, time and again, especially in the scrums, but, being a lawyer and a stickler for the rules, control was of the essence this day, and, in fairness, Mr Dallas held the match firmly in his grasp. Here the *Cambria Daily Leader* cites the kind of battles that appeared before his eyes:

> It was one of the sights of the game to see Owen hit Gallaher over; it was not far from being positively ludicrous to see the two of them watching each other when the ball was in the scrum. Three times the little man [Owen] was laid out, and one wonders now that he was not broken to pieces.

Despite being perceived as the villain of the peace, Gallaher kept his composure, channelling every ounce of energy into the next movement of play. Then, when the day's rugby was over, his pleasant manner was a joy to behold. On a day of high drama he had been shocked and hurt by the criticism, yet his words bore no grudge, and this would be his way despite facing close newspaper scrutiny in the days to come.

The *Cambria Daily Leader* of December 23rd 1905 led with the headlines 'Are Gallaher's Methods Unfair,' relating to an earlier enquiry carried out on the subject by the *Daily Mail*. Referees and leading officials had been asked for their opinions and had offered a range of views whilst the reporter's belief was that he had never seen a team experience so much criticism and hostility. This unidentified reporter felt that the unfair media criticism of Gallaher's style was bringing his standards of fair play into serious question, before leaping to his defence when saying that he, the writer, was of the opinion that there would not be such a result again 'if the sides met one hundred times on neutral ground.'

This is rugby, full of thrust, endeavour, controversy and different opinions – all components of its great and enduring intrigue. For sure, Gallaher would soldier onward, the way he knew best, as would his close rival that day, Swansea's legendary captain Dicky Owen, a scrum half, who, in an interview two days after the match, said, 'Well, he is a most useful man to his inside half' – despite admitting to being impeded when trying to collect possession of the ball 'as a consequence of him [Gallaher] cutting in between, and preventing me getting to it.'[4]

The interviewer's next question sought confirmation that the New Zealander lacked fair play in his general game, to which Dicky Owen replied, 'No . . . He knew his work thoroughly well' and was a fine performer. Then, responding to a suggestion that Gallaher was gunning for him, he replied, 'Oh, no . . . He was on me' at every opportunity and he was precise as a tackler, this aspect of play being 'exceptionally keen.' Then, when invited to add one last comment, the Welshman said so much in his brief reply: 'Well, I think it was the most historic game in football history.' Then he added that he had never met a team as great as New Zealand, 'They are veritable giants.'

Who could doubt these words of Dicky Owen, a man who was as respectful and eloquent in conversation as he was resolute, strong and articulate on the field of play. But, setting aside his opinions and the Gallaher affair at large, it is surprising all these years later to hear little or no mention of an incident that has ever since gripped the interest and imagination of rugby enthusiasts, in Wales, New Zealand and

---

4   *Western Mail*, December 19th 1905.

worldwide. This concerns the Bob Deans 'try that never was,' surely an omission on the part of the day's scribes, yet, equally, understandable. This is what the *Western Mail* had to say on the subject, bearing not the slightest hint of controversy:

> A magnificent run by Wallace took play to the Welsh line and *Hunter* [sic], receiving from Wallace, looked to be going over in the corner, but he was held up yards outside, where a scrum was formed and the excitement was more intense than ever.

Bill Wallace never forgot this incident throughout his long life. With Wales hanging on to their narrow 3–0 lead, they won the ball at a line-out, near half-way, towards the end of the match, before kicking ahead. It is then that Wallace fielded the ball and set off on his amazing run as described by the Scottish spectator. But he heard the distinctive cry of Bob Deans calling for the ball (not Hunter, as the report states). A long pass found the centre, six-foot tall and 14 stones who had a clear run for glory of about 25 yards. But, alas, Deans decided to cut towards the posts for an easier conversion and, by so doing, he allowed Welsh defenders, desperately covering, to catch him near the line.

It is then that a grey mist descended on those concerned like a thick and heavy blanket, as one of three things appears to have happened: Deans (whilst being tackled) dived and scored . . . or Deans was pulled down short of the line . . . or Deans dived and scored, only to recoil under the opposite force of Rhys Gabe's tackle, before being pulled back further by Gabe and apparently by others too – so that it appeared to referee Dallas that Deans was short of the line. According to Wallace, at this juncture the crowd went silent as if reacting to a sudden shock, suggesting it was a try. There then followed a bit of pushing and pulling on the line, the two teams ostensibly presenting their best case to the referee, whose whistle had already blown.

As for the diverse post-match reports that left Fleet Street and other presses, Deans' effort did not seem to appear anywhere near the headlines, or, for that matter, within the inside pages. In a broad sample of headlines appearing in the country's popular editions, as listed in the *Cambria Daily Leader*, we get a feel for the message of the day, and it was certainly not one of controversy: 'Wales for Ever' (*Daily News*); 'Magnificent win for Wales (*Yorkshire Post*); 'The fierce and furious struggle at Cardiff' (*Athletic News*); 'Wales to the Rescue' [of British rugby] (*Daily Chronicle*); and 'All hail Wales; what will they think in New Zealand?' (*Morning Leader*).

In answer to this last question, the message appearing in the *New Zealand Herald* was one of shared disappointment amongst countrymen that their men's magnificent run had ended. But there was nothing short of admiration extended towards the Welsh 'who are good men,' it stated, 'better than ours', whose efforts were congratulated 'heartily' – before looking to next time! As for the Deans incident, there was not a word: exactly the same in this respect as both London's (daily) *Times* and the *Sunday Times*. Interestingly, the former described the action as being 'the hardest imaginable'; the New Zealanders being devoid of luck, and referee, Dallas, 'unflinching' in his firm control.

When we consider the chaos prevailing at the over-full Arms Park that day, it must have been difficult, if not impossible, for reporters to catch most, let alone all, of the sporting action. Those jostled and disrupted in the jam-packed press box had the best chance, whilst others, less fortunate, were scribbling away in their note books, on aching legs, with limited view, at pitch level. Likewise, few spectators could have judged events accurately during those critical few seconds when history struck the Westgate Street end of the ground, when tired from standing or even dazed from drinking. For certain, most returned to their homes euphoric in victory, many having blissfully won a fortune from betting, others fulfilled by the occasion, most with implicit faith in Mr Dallas, and next-to-nobody caring about what could or should have been in an ideal world.

When the players came off the field and changed, the best of spirits prevailed, and three men in particular, all involved intimately in the tryline scene, had their stories to tell. In a much later radio programme[5] Rhys Gabe, the Welshman clutching tightly to the New Zealander near the line, spoke his mind, having initially admitted that Deans might have made it, as Deans vehemently claimed:

'Why did you pull me back?' [Deans] asked.

'Why did you struggle to go forward after you had been tackled outside?' [Rhys Gabe] replied. 'If you had been on the line you needn't have struggled to go further. If you hadn't reached the line why didn't you leave the ball there?'

Apparently, Deans chose not to reply, whilst the other Welshman interviewed on the radio, Teddy Morgan, try-scorer, actually saw things Deans' way. This is what he said: 'I was close by at the time. When I got to the actual spot Deans was over the line with the ball, but by the time the referee reached there, he had been pushed back.'

Christopher Tobin points out that early in the tour, New Zealand Prime Minister, Richard Seddon, contacted the *Daily Mail*, a popular newspaper, asking for some positive

---

5   Described in David Smith and Gareth Williams', *Fields of Praise* (University of Wales Press, 1980).

coverage of his country's footballers. This was a clever move and besides planting an ally inside the camp whose words would travel far, all good publicity would sit well in the greater political context of colonial emigration. With J. Buttery being the reporter appointed to shadow the men, and doing a good job, his articles gained increasing credence as the tour's published successes were piled high. It is therefore hardly surprising that Deans was invited by this same newspaper to make his feelings known about what transpired beneath that grey mist. This resulted in the following facsimile being sent to the *Daily Mail* – a paper that also praised Wales' performance – on the day following the match:

> Grounded [the] ball 6 inches over [the] line . . . Some of [the] Welsh players admit [to a] try. Hunter and Glasgow can confirm [I] was pulled back by Welshmen before [the] referee arrived. Deans.

When this statement hit the sports pages, referee, John Dallas, knowing his judgement was in question, felt the need to offer a response. Announcing his amazement when studying newspaper reports back in Edinburgh, he wasted no time in making his position clear. Deans' placement of the ball was '6 to 12 inches short,' he stated,[6] although admitting that when he arrived at the scene, the leather was beyond the try line. 'No try was scored by Deans,' he concluded.

And here begins 'The Story of the No Score', which would become one of rugby's most talked about incidents and whose contributors multiplied as the years passed by.

---

6   David Smith and Gareth Williams, *Fields of Praise* (University of Wales Press, 1980).

Daggers are Drawn as a
Refereeing Rumpus Threatens the Tour

Across the country on December 17th 1905 there was a greater
sense of Sunday morning calm than usual, as a nation took
stock of an early Christmas offering that brought deep inner
contentment and warmth of glow. In the packed churches
and chapels there was rejoicing as though the season's crops
had just been gathered in, a gift that called for dedicated
thanksgiving. Rugby fever had spread everywhere now,
even into the pulpits, where mention of Wales' triumph was
slipped into the sermons of the day.

Not far away from the hallowed turf where history had
been made, the Bishop of Llandaff was addressing the Cardiff
Young Men's Christian Lads' Union at the Park Hall. He
praised the nature of rugby football which kept participants
in good shape, but he was also aware that the Welsh victory
had led to some hefty gambling gains. Now he was trying
to keep feet firmly on the ground, highlighting the off-
field pitfalls to his parishioners: 'in particular the danger of
betting, which was an insinuating practice, which got hold of
[people] almost without their knowing it.'[7]

Meanwhile, the New Zealand players emerged from the
satisfying sleep of tired men and straight into the conscious
nightmare that they had fallen at the final hurdle. Although
four matches remained, this had been the last international,
and failure would be viewed with great disappointment in
their homeland despite their undeniable status as national
heroes continuing. The All Blacks were also ambassadors and

---

7   *Western Mail*, December 18th 1905.

WALES AND THE ALL BLACKS

Prime Minister Richard Seddon's best political friends, having excelled in this manly game, whilst securing followers, fans and an excellent reputation in the course of their daily business.

So, they would dust themselves down and get back on the trail – but not before accepting an invitation from the Welsh Football Union members to Sunday lunch at the Esplanade Hotel in Penarth. They were the main guests amongst a group of fifty people who included representatives of the other home unions. The party, as reported in the *Western Mail*, was transported 'in two four-in-hands from the Queen's Hotel, Cardiff, to Penarth,' and, following the meal, the New Zealanders were taken to Sully on their way home.

The next morning a small number of the touring party were signing photo-postcards in the Queen's Hotel to raise money for the War Memorial fund. The recent Boer conflict had been experienced firsthand by certain players from the previous day's game, such as Gallaher and Abbott, although the latter was not selected to play. Afterwards, the team members packed their bags for a major rugby engagement at St Helen's, in Swansea, against the best fifteen Glamorgan county could find. As they made their way towards Cardiff railway station for the 3.55 p.m. locomotive, they were prepared for an eventful few days that included getting out and doing a spot of sightseeing. The team's proposed travels included a visit to the Gower coast and also to Craig-y-Nos castle, a stunning landmark set high in the Swansea valley and the home of opera singer Adelina Patti. A drive around Swansea Docks and a trip to a local tinplate works had also been arranged.[8]

On jaunts such as these, the men were alert to the presence of northern 'League' scouts looking to offer attractive deals.

---

8   *The Herald of Wales*, December 16th 1905.

Big, strong men of proven footballing ability were in great demand in rugby league territory – the other side of the fence – and, as it so happened, neither Bill 'Massa' Johnston nor Charlie Seeling were to sail home with their colleagues at the end of the tour without having secured a rugby league future. They had both been spotted, although it was to be later in their careers when they actually played in the north of England.

This was a fruitful time for sports journalists and the *Cambria Daily Leader* of Tuesday December 19th accounted for every movement of the team from the time they were waved goodbye at Cardiff until they were received in Swansea, having been cheered by onlookers at the smaller station stops along the way. The reporter suggested that stepping into Swansea's station yard brought scenes reminiscent of soldiers returning from fighting overseas three years earlier, with Alexandra Road, just across from the station entrance, coloured with rows of onlookers as far as the eye could see. It was here that the party boarded a specially arranged 'electric car' taking them the short distance to the Tenby Hotel in 128–131 Walters Road (today's Walter Road). The writer could not conceal his admiration for this group of men, one of whom, not named, told him, 'We're having a good time, you know,' when asked if he was anxious to return home. The newspaper reporter had worked out for himself that these men were strong personalities. He appreciated just how happy they were as individuals, besides being: 'always in the pink of condition: truly a remarkable body of men'.

Their billing as sporting idols was undisputed and their appeal to adoring women also perfectly evident. Beyond their looks and stature, these men possessed a mixture of tenacity, and, dare we say, ruthlessness, at least in getting their rugby business done, which, when mixed with an easy charm is, so it is said, a potent mix, making them potentially the answer to many a woman's prayer. Rugby's physicality and sense of command had been a crowd-puller ever since ball games similar to rugby began and it is understandable if its attraction to females was, and is, alluring. During these rather different early years of the twentieth century, the game offered everybody the opportunity of dressing formally, or, at least, smartly, for rugby matches, and, hence, the perfect excuse for females to dress up in eye-catching fashion. This point is mentioned in the *Western Mail* two days after the Welsh clash of December 18th, when referring to the 'pretty picture [of] hundreds of ladies' who sat in the stand 'in multi-coloured garments' looking at their most beautiful best.

From all accounts, the New Zealanders had received many direct and unexpected invitations on their travels, including marriage proposals. In Ireland, where their welcome was almost as warm as in Wales, Christopher Tobin in *The Original All Blacks 1905–1906* explains that women found a means of discreetly slipping a letter to a member of the squad intended for the player who had interested them. Amusingly, he reports that if a player was asked to hand such a note from an attractive lady to his colleague, who had usually been identified by his shirt number, the player receiving the note did his damnedest to persuade her that *he* was the one she was looking for! The 'Swansea Belles' according to Billy Wallace were just as keen and, no doubt, many were present on this same afternoon when the All Blacks were welcomed to Swansea.

Before pulling away from the station, everybody wanted to shake the New Zealanders by the hand as compliments poured forth. Soon there was communal singing before a mighty cheer sent them on their way. Then one of the players, believed to have been George Gillett, a forward, peered down from the top tier, calling out 'Sing us *Sosban Fach*!' in his best

Welsh accent! They were endearing themselves to everybody and, not far away, there was another fine welcome awaiting them at the hotel where, after dropping luggage in their rooms, they mingled with the locals in the ground floor areas. That night most of the touring party attended a concert given by St Paul's Choir, performed at the Albert Hall, whilst others strolled to the Empire Theatre – although team members not involved with the forthcoming Glamorgan game were, perhaps, able to meet some of their admirers.

Just when the relationship between the Welsh and New Zealand rugby unions was at an all-time high, a big rumpus blew up concerning the referee appointed for this next match that was only days away. Mr Dixon, tour manager, objected to having no part in choosing the official, although Mr Games of Abercarn, a good referee, thoroughly well known in Wales, had been appointed. This was no petty squabble either; here was rugby rivalry in a most raw state.

The row broke out on the Monday after the Wales match and, having been reported on Tuesday December 19th it was satisfactorily resolved two days later. But this had been a crazy spell during which time neither the Welsh committee, who had met at the Queen's Hotel, nor Mr Dixon, tour manager, was prepared to back down. At best, this amounted to pretty serious rugby politics, jeopardising not only the next fixture but also the remaining matches in Wales. Understandably, Mr Dixon – who was not critical of the ability of Mr Games, but of the selection process – took advice from his governing body in New Zealand, and it is due to delicate footwork on his part that he managed to tiptoe through an explosive minefield.

In the *Cambria Daily Leader* on December 21st 1905, Mr Dixon was described descending the Tenby Hotel stairway to make a statement explaining that for games of such high profile, there should be a process of agreement between the two sides on the choice of referee. 'Here there has been no attempt on the part of the Glamorgan committee to come to a mutual arrangement,' he stated, 'and that is what we object to.' Explaining that the issue had only just been resolved, the New Zealand manager added that rather than to upset the local people so late in the day, he was prepared to honour the fixture but 'still protesting against the method of appointment.' Of course, the newspapers were having a whale of a time reporting this rift; the *Western Mail* of December 19th sniped 'that [for] the Colonials, who will receive 75% of the gross receipts of the County match, [to] squabble about the referee does not fit in with the best ideas of sportsmanship[!]'

During the course of these pretty hectic few days, this refereeing issue had, in fact, landed on the desk of New Zealand Prime Minister, Mr Seddon, who is said to have responded to Mr Dixon's cable with the curt message, 'Meet them! Beat Them.'[9] And that is exactly what they were to do, claiming the match by three clear tries, 9–0, in front of a large, appreciative crowd. It was another of those occasions to savour at St Helen's where the Swansea band kept everyone entertained beforehand, although there was disappointment that key men had withdrawn from the home team following, what appears at least partially to have been, another disagreement between the two unions.

Mr Dixon had been fuming because nine internationals had, apparently, been selected for the Glamorgan team. Precisely how this fitted in with the pre-tour arrangements is not known – but with Cardiff, Newport and Swansea all due to play the All Blacks within a week, the clubs, when

9   Christopher Tobin, *The Original All Blacks 1905–1906* (Hodder Moa Beckett, 2005).

focussing on their own immediate interests, appear to have withdrawn players, although exactly how much this might have been helped along, tactfully, by the Welsh Union also remains to be understood.

From all accounts this was not a strong Glamorgan team and two unnamed 'backs' were drafted into the side, having arrived as ordinary spectators, and placed straight into a tough encounter that saw one local player knocked out cold by the weight of a tackle near the try line. With the preparation of all important rugby matches beginning weeks in advance, and fine tuning starting days before the clash – each step down to the meal beforehand directly affecting performance – this was unacceptable for the team, spectators and certainly the two players called into the firing line.

As regards the visitors, the consensus of opinion was that New Zealand had slowed down significantly from the heady days of earlier weeks when they were dishing out drubbings like there was no tomorrow. In truth there was every reason to believe that their bodies and minds were tiring and unavoidably flagging. Yet, all this kerfuffle had been a red rag to these young bulls; and this, together with pride, responsibility and footballing ability, had won the day.

In the *Western Mail* of Friday December 22nd, the writer stated that the home team should have scored a few tries, before touching upon the New Zealanders' dipping form. He felt certain that if Glamorgan had fielded their strongest side, the visitors would be feeling the hurt of another setback. But the same piece offers us a new insight into the Wales match when Duncan McGregor openly stated that his countrymen were beaten by the better team. He also offered an interesting comment on the game's Bob Deans affair that was by now topical and being well discussed. He stated that 'one of our fellows got over the line,' and that his team had received messages 'from Welsh people who saw it.' He reckoned that 'when they say so it must be very nearly right.'

Besides winning, the New Zealanders, by choice, hoped to entertain, but, this day, according to *The Herald of Wales* of December 23rd, the best memory related to a determined run by one of the Glamorgan three-quarters. It followed a kick upfield by the tourists, the ball landing near their opponents' try line. Howell Jones, a centre, raced to retrieve the ball but, when attempting to kick for touch, he was caught. Doing what he could in this predicament, he linked up with a helping hand at his side. This was 'little' Willie Arnold who safely collected his pass and 'ran as if his life depended upon it across the field behind his own goal line.' With everybody gripped by this spectacle, he then hoofed the ball for all he was worth so that it 'just landed in touch,' a wonderful moment in the game.

There is little doubt that while Willie opened up his lungs, New Zealand sprinter Bunny Abbott, playing this day, was not far away, giving chase. Named 'Harold Louis Abbott,' but better known as 'Bunny' – his inclusion in the touring party came despite him having experienced little rugby. Indeed, his introduction to the game is another story, told by his friend in later life, John Sinclair of Palmerston North. John, to whom this book is dedicated, explained that Bunny, a recognised sprinter, started playing rugby at his military camp in South Africa when, seemingly, he had little choice. These are John's words:

> He was asked to take part [in a rugby game by his Army superiors] when serving in the Boer War. 'But I don't know much about the game,' he replied.
>
> 'It's not what *you know*,' barked his Commanding Officer, 'it's what *I think* that matters!'
>
> He was then given a sharp lesson. 'Now, remember this:

when they [the opposition] have the ball, they're in the wrong. Stop them, bring them down, any way, it doesn't matter how . . . As for the rest, I'll tell you at half-time!'

John explained that on the boat going over to Britain, the men used a blackboard to plan their moves, and this is how Bunny was taught to run at different angles: firstly one way, then the other. 'All of this zigzagging is good in theory,' thought Bunny, 'but how can I practise it on a narrow ship?' But eventually he had his chance on the training paddock in Newton Abbot, shortly after the team had docked. John continues:

Now, there was no stopping him. 'I just went out and started running in the open spaces,' he [the player] said. 'I ran all over the place. I thought this will do nicely for me.'

John went on to say that at least one observer couldn't make it out. 'What's that man doing down there, bouncing around like a rabbit?' he enquired. And that was how Harold became 'Bunny'.

Newport and Cardiff fall short as the Marathon Men march on

After the difficulties of the previous few days, George Dixon, the All Blacks tour manager, could look back on a job well done in ensuring the Glamorgan game was played and the tour's continuance was safeguarded, with the added consolation that Gil Evans, his first choice of referee, had been appointed to handle the last three fixtures. It had been a difficult time, not helped when seeing 'Major's' report in *The Sportsman* claiming that he and Welshmen six yards from the Bob Deans dive felt the try was good.[10] Equally disturbed about Gallaher's treatment by referee Dallas at the scrimmages, Mr Dixon had already – this surely a form of protest – expressed his willingness to the Welsh Football Union members for referees to put the ball in on his team's behalf for the remainder of the matches in Wales.[11] Events had become rather drastic but now, forty-eight hours later, on Saturday December 23rd, there was another mountain to climb at Newport. Only a few weeks earlier no one gave the local men a sporting chance of winning but, since the All Blacks had slipped against Wales and were now in the middle of a difficult run of fixtures, Newport players were within a shout of glory themselves.

The South Wales Argus describes the great excitement from the time that straw was removed from the field on the morning of the match. This ensured a good surface on a fine winter's day, which saw early spectators and 'a detachment

---

10 'George Dixon's Diaries', from Bob Howitt and Dianne Haworth, *The 1905 Originals — The remarkable story of the team that went away as the Colonials and came back as the All Blacks* (HarperCollins Publishers, 2005).
11 As above.

of sixty constables' arriving before the gates opened at around mid day. Soon the stands started to fill as spectators, snuggling beneath blankets and rugs, discussed their side's prospects. 'Of course, there was the usual talk of past Welsh, particularly Newport, victories,' said the reporter as well as key information on winning the day's battles 'by some of the know-alls' who congregate regularly around a rugby field.

At about one o'clock people were tucking into their packed lunches whilst the 'mince, and jam, pie merchants' did a fair trade. By this time the town band was playing the usual favourites, including *Farewell*, whilst everyone enjoyed the fun and good spirit of a Christmas gathering. At one stage a person innocently waved to a friend at the other side of the field, and this resulted in half the stand doing the same, handkerchiefs held aloft. Then, as sporting celebrities walked to their seats, they were given a distinctive cheer, and so also were the police officers when trying to protect the exclusive privileges of programme sellers inside the ground.

This saw one peddler announcing the sale of team photos from the recent Wales–New Zealand clash being sent on his way. 'In strident tones' he tried to prize 'elusive pennies from the pockets of the crowd,' said the reporter whilst he used all persuasive speech and powers to best effect. But, when a police constable crept up silently, 'his oration would die away into an inarticulate murmur' as he quickly put away his goods to be escorted from the scene!

Travelling to the match that morning from Cardiff, having arrived back in the Queen's Hotel the day before, the New Zealand team had declined a civic reception, preferring to meet the Lord Mayor and other dignitaries at Newport club's modern gymnasium, where they were impressed with the sporting apparatus available to local players, who, in this respect, were the envy of other clubs of the day. In like manner, following the usual after-match hospitality offered by Newport Rugby Club, the tourists were looking to leave early, in time for the curtain raiser before the evening's main performance at the town's Lyceum Theatre.

At 2.15 p.m., players from both teams were photographed, whilst the remaining New Zealanders were welcomed to their seats by the crowd. Then came the Māori chant which drew a response of three mighty cheers from the Newport players. The Welsh national anthem followed before everyone settled down to enjoy a keen contest, won by New Zealand by the narrow margin, 6–3, when scoring the only try of the match.

Playing that day was local legend Tommy Vile, who ran a soft drinks business in the town with Jim, his older brother. Tommy was a stalwart, not only for Newport and Wales but also for Welsh refereeing. He greatly respected the New Zealanders, having visited their country a year earlier as a member of the British touring team. Tommy told *The South Wales Argus* on October 2nd 1924 that what impressed him most of all about the visitors at Newport was the standard of their support play. Time and again he noticed the man being tackled popping the ball into a space knowing that his colleagues would claim it and so keep play in motion. This was an astute and pertinent observation to make and it is interesting that the All Blacks were being lauded for a skill that has ever since been integral to their game.

Tommy, who possessed one of the sharpest rugby brains, admired the tourists for their ability to keep winning at this difficult stage of the tour when injuries were limiting their performances. In particular, he paid tribute to Dave Gallaher, who he thought was a generous and good–natured fellow, despite all the criticism that had come his way. This appears within the message of his own biography, *Tommy Vile: A Giant of a Man*, and refers to the time they opposed one another in the New Zealand versus British Isles encounter in 1904. That August day in Wellington, Tommy was deeply disturbed by his opponent's manner and made it clear 'by word and action', but then this charismatic New Zealander touched him on the head and declared 'now don't worry, don't lose your temper. It will be alright.'

> 'I was letting him have it,' [continued Tommy] 'but there was something quite fatherly in his mild rebuke. However, he did not stop obstructing me.'

When I spoke to Tommy's daughter, Mary Vile, she was proud of her father, and explained that as a small boy he used to stand behind the goal posts at the Newport Athletic field (as the ground was then called), not only watching the action but running an errand for his big brother:

> Uncle Jim [Tommy's brother] used to be interested in homing pigeons and he'd persuade father, only six or seven at the time, to take a couple to the match. By half-time he'd set one free with the score – meaning that Jim was the first person outside the ground to be given details of the game.

Mary also remembers the Lyceum Theatre in Newport, mentioned earlier and visited by the Original All Blacks:

> It was a beautiful building. It looked like a Greek temple and it had a lovely stage. When my mother was 16, she and a friend were attending a performance when the curtain fell unexpectedly. Then, out came the manager. 'Ladies and Gentlemen, I have an announcement to make,' he said. 'Mafeking has been relieved. We are no longer at war. Tonight you shall all have your entrance fee refunded.'

Christmas came and went for the New Zealanders, still enjoying the Queen's Hotel in the busy seaport city of Cardiff despite thoughts being miles away with family and friends relaxing in the sun. Now another mighty challenge lay on their doorstep in the shape of Cardiff, the best club side in Wales, who were ready to do or die for victory, in front of another crowded Cardiff Arms Park. Coming so soon after losing to Wales, this was a daunting task, especially as the home team, strong as it was, could, like other clubs, invite a neighbouring player to strengthen the side. If ever lightening was to strike twice, this was as good a place as any, on this, the thirty-first match of the tour, when the All Blacks were tiring, Cardiff players were buzzing and it was a time for 'double or quits' for the gambling fraternity. If ever Gallaher had to return to the side, this was the moment, leading his men in what proved to be an extremely hard-fought match.

In the *Western Mail* of December 27th 1905, readers learnt that this was another 'international' type of experience with passengers travelling aboard excursion trains from all corners of the country. Again, the gates opened and closed early, with the Tongwynlais Silver Band keeping everyone upbeat and in buoyant holiday mood, adding to their optimistic outlook of the day's events. For the second time in less than a fortnight, Cardiff Arms Park heaved under the swollen crowds believed to be comparable, if not even heavier, than during the Welsh game: 'Such was the exigency of space,' said this newspaper, that a distinguished Labour politician had to manage with sitting 'on the floor in front of the press box.'

Here was a Welsh nation making the most of an opportunity, knowing that chances of playing New Zealand, let alone beating them, were few and far between. Everyone was geared for a positive outcome, whilst press reports and paper columns fired a Welsh nation already lost in the excitement of the occasion. It was felt that if the local men could share the forward battles, then it was 'fairly safe to prophesy that victory for Cardiff is practically certain,' said the *Western Mail*. Experts claimed that New Zealand had little left to teach Welsh rugby, because the teams were of similar ability, and this would be a motivating thought for players reading the sports pages on the morning of the match. Before the teams took to the field, the band was playing *The Colonials* but, by the time Percy Bush, Cardiff captain, led his men out, the background sound of what had now become a nation's rugby anthem, *Hen Wlad fy Nhadau*, was heard.

With fast and furious play of the highest quality, Cardiff took the lead with a converted try to be ahead, 5–0, when New Zealand forward, Jim O'Sullivan, was injured. Forced to play the last hour with fourteen men, the All Blacks still managed to strike back with a corner try, inches from the flag. This saw Bill Wallace, the tour's proven match winner, having to wait for spectators on the pitchside to shuffle aside, so that he could take his usual run-up for the kick, which he struck to perfection to level the scores.

It was after this that New Zealand attacked deep into Cardiff's territory and kicked ahead so that the ball landed over the goal line. With Percy Bush near at hand to minor it, there seemed to be no danger at all. But then the unthinkable happened, the Cardiff captain making a grave mistake to haunt him all his life, whilst breaking the hearts of his faithful fans. After hesitating, he attempted to kick the ball dead rather than touching it down, and, to every Welshman's horror, his effort amounted to a hopeless mishit, allowing New Zealander George Nicholson to dive onto the ball for the simplest of tries. The match ended with the score 10–8 in favour of the visitors, Wallace's conversion from the pitch-side seating proving to be the winning margin, and safeguarding the greatest of escapes.

A Farewell at St Helen's as the New Zealanders head for home

Within days, the New Zealanders were back in the Tenby Hotel preparing to face the All Whites of Swansea in their final match in Wales and in Great Britain. In the *Cambria Daily Leader* of December 30th, news reports whetted the appetite of rugby supporters with a brief reminder of the Natives match played against Swansea at St Helen's seventeen years earlier, in 1888. On that occasion, the victorious visitors won 5–0, scoring three tries (worth one point each), one of which was converted, to be a goal worth three points. This team, consisting mostly of players of Māori ancestry, was remembered for a series of sharp passing movements which sent their three-quarters haring down the field.

Of course, revenge would be sweet for a Swansea team which, one year earlier, had won the Anglo-Welsh League, being unbeaten in thirty-two matches and having prevented twenty-one sides from scoring a point. Although a dip in form could not be avoided, the home team was still a powerful, ambitious force. Occasions such as this suited the spacious ground of St Helen's, a rugby stronghold on the gentle sweep of Swansea bay, often lashed by Wales' westerly winds, and protected by a grandstand that had seen the game's good, bad and ugly over the years.

This day, a powerful wind blew, favouring the home team in the first half whilst assisting the All Blacks after the break. Now the New Zealanders, including Steve Casey, John Corbett, Bill Cunningham, also Gallaher, Deans, Wallace and the rest, were a spent force, hanging on for their sporting lives. They needed every scrap of good fortune that was on offer, a fact highlighted memorably in George Henry Dixon's *1905, The Triumphant Tour of the New Zealand Footballers* as it describes the months of constant rugby having turned them from 'young race horses [in]to working bullocks.'

Further evidence of this appears in Christopher Tobin's own book. The players were, in truth, ready to pack up their togs and go home. They had enjoyed the experience of a lifetime, but the tour had become a hard slog and the Welsh match had caused players to lose heart, especially as their proud record had been broken. Referring once more to the refereeing dispute, many would gladly have bowed out at that point. They were tired, weary, half-crocked and restless, with opinion being divided along allegiances either to the North or to the South Island, or so it is said.

In anticipation of this last game, members of the management committee of Swansea Cricket and Football Club had been planning ahead for months. The usual straw deliveries to protect the playing field – surely many a cartload to cover St Helen's – had been ordered well in advance, just as arrangements had been made for the first team to study the All Blacks at Cardiff earlier on tour. Meanwhile, the subject of gate money was given its rightful attention: tariffs remaining unaltered in the main, except for minor increases for admission to the Grand Stand.[12]

Without the uplifting company of a town band, there was more reason for the Tanner Bank crowd to give the New Zealanders an impromptu ditty – nothing wonderful, just a catchy little 'Ta ra ra' chorus – when welcoming them to the ground. Having travelled only half a mile from their hotel headquarters, they climbed off a brake before proceeding

---

12   Swansea Cricket and Football Club Management Committee Minutes: held at West Wales Archives, Swansea.

towards the pavilion. Minutes later they reappeared ready to play, Cunningham the mighty forward attracting attention as he stepped out wearing socks of different colours, one black, one white – demob-happy, perhaps, but as a cheerful character in the side he had been spotted with odd socks in other games. Then Gallaher, seen taking a silver-coloured belt-garment to an acquaintance beyond the field, fuelled gossip whilst supporting the belief that the All Blacks were popular with the ladies. Then, the Māori 'special' was delivered and the referee's whistle signalled the start of play.

In a match that never lived up to the highest of hopes, but which saw the diminutive Dicky Owen spectacularly up-ending an opponent twice his size, Swansea were 3–0 ahead with fifteen minutes to go. As spectators saw that an upset was on the cards, Billy Wallace, New Zealand's man for all seasons, who played his rugby into the teeth of gale-force winds in his native Wellington, recognised a hero's calling by dropping an awkward goal. Having run to a more central position from way out wide, he judged the conditions to perfection before letting fly. This gave the twenty-five thousand spectators something to remember, the ball changing course as if by remote control, before finding the pathway it was meant to take. Although benefiting from the wind, here was a genius at work, universally admired by rugby folk, especially the Welsh: a player who could alter the course of history with a dazzling run or, as in this case, an exceptional kick.

Ever since the laws of the game were formalised at Rugby School, drop goals were like cherries on the cake, rewarding attacking players who, having gained territory and posses-sion of the ball, had also mastered the execution of this skill. Of course, this served to reflect the game's purpose at the time: that of scoring from a kick achieved in the way we are accustomed to today, the ball travelling between the posts and over the cross-bar. This could have been by 'dropping a goal' in the course of active play, or 'placing a goal' (from the ground), following a touch down (try). As surprising as it may seem, when it came to a touch down it was only the actual *kick*, if successful, that initially produced a score – until tries eventually earned a one point reward from around the late 1880s before being later re-evaluated; enforcement took time! Wallace's drop goal was a treasured piece of silver in his team's earnings at St Helen's this day, rewarded by four points, one more than Swansea's try and enough to see New Zealand to safety, but only just, 4–3.

A few days before the match, certain of the touring party attended a dance at Swansea's Hotel Metropole, a city centre venue at the bottom of Wind Street, whilst during the evening before the clash selected players settled for a quiet visit to the Star Theatre. But, following the post-match pleasantries, the men were back in their hotel ready to catch the 8.55 p.m. evening train to Paddington. Scheduled to arrive at 3.30 a.m. the next morning, they had been booked into the nearby Great Western Royal Hotel for some sleep and breakfast, before leaving Victoria at 10.00 a.m. for a 'Folkestone to Boulogne' ferry crossing. Understandably, the tour itinerary had been planned well in advance, which explains an uncharacteristic entry appearing in the Swansea Cricket and Football Club (management committee) minutes: 'It was resolved not to entertain them to dinner; they had expressed a wish against being entertained.'[13]

It is such efficient planning on the part of the manager George Dixon – helped, no doubt, by his leading men – that allowed this helter-skelter tour to proceed. Due to arrive in Paris in the early hours of New Year's Eve, providing a few

---

13 Swansea Cricket and Football Club Management Committee Minutes.

hours of freedom, the team was then due to line up against the French the next day. George Dixon was indeed a busy man, although he still found time to update his diary. Looking back, he felt that the Swansea encounter fell short of expectations whilst bad weather accounted for his men playing a cautious game. Likewise, he acknowledged his side's good fortune in winning the match, before logging more favourable public reaction at most station stops along the way when his team journeyed to Paddington.

Few of the game's followers in Wales were surprised when the New Zealanders defeated the French, then a far weaker rugby nation, by thirty clear points before embarking upon a short series of low-key matches in America on their way home. This was in response to Prime Minister Seddon's best political intentions at a time when advertisements placed in overseas newspapers invited the more adventurous to consider a new life in his country. In terms of global relations, his rugby men were leading the way, in every sense envoys for a country undeniably proud of its sporting stars on and off the field, some of whom, incidentally, whilst attending an agricultural show at Islington before leaving England, had been introduced to King Edward VII.

There would be plenty of time to reflect upon their successes when the team, having returned from France, assembled in Southampton ready to board their ship for the USA. Of all fixtures played, the Welsh games had least gone to plan, five fixtures in fifteen days, each a desperately close affair, 29 points scored, 17 conceded, proving that there was precious little daylight between the teams. But now, with time to relax, the men could, at least, hope to forget about Wales – but they were out of luck!

As documented in *Fields of Praise*, at the point of stepping onto their ocean-bound liner, the All Blacks heard the sound of familiar songs, synonymous with Cardiff and other grounds in the Principality, courtesy of a group of thirty students, themselves from the Land of their Fathers, clad in red, but also representing Hartley University School, who were intent upon launching the New Zealanders on their way. Suffice to say, this had been an extraordinary tour, promoting rugby's great name – but regardless of the All Blacks' winning statement, here were the Welsh, at it again, sneaking in at the close to have the last word!

By now, families of the players looking forward to their return home would have read in the *New Zealand Herald* of January 3rd 1906 an interesting article stating that the British could justifiably be proud that their forefathers who settled in New Zealand had maintained high standards of 'physical stamina' and 'organisation', virtues that had given England a proud name. This was, of course, a direct compliment to New Zealand's latest sporting heroes whose continued globe-trotting and winning ways was to earn them the finest public welcome upon their return to Auckland. Furthermore, in a résumé of the rugby expedition appearing in the *1905 The Triumphant Tour of the New Zealand Footballers*, a recommendation was made that regular matches involving the 'Colony and the Motherhood' continue to be staged 'with increasing popularity and stimulus to good old rugby.'

Three months later, in early March 1906, thousands of excited fans – including the Prime Minister and Mayor of Auckland – met the team upon arrival at the city harbour. *The New Zealand Herald* tells us that this was a day that work in the city came to a halt, as shops were shut and celebrations overtook all else. These mighty men had certainly made their mark, as had George Dixon, their manager who received 'a silver hot water kettle' as a thank-you from the team members, conveyed by officials of the New Zealand Rugby Union.

Many more kind words were spoken but, in this passionate rugby country, a post-mortem of the Welsh match was top of the agenda. Here are a few of the words of Billy Stead, team vice-captain, but who missed playing in the international in Cardiff. They were released initially in the *Southland Times* on March 23rd 1906, before being published in 2005 in the form of his personal tour diary, *Billy's Trip Home*. The words have been taken from a speech at the 'Welcome Smoke Concert' honouring Billy's return to Invercargill at the foot of South Island. Understandably he had a lot to say about Wales, emphasising how 'it was almost impossible to express' the passion of Welshmen for rugby, whilst not forgetting his team's wonderful reception in Cardiff.

As regards the famous match, he stated that Dave Gallaher's men had charged all over the field 'but all their efforts were unavailing'. And, in response to a question from the floor about the one issue that is still talked about, the Deans 'try', he mentions that when talking after the match to Gwyn Nicholls, the Welsh captain, who he claims was a sporting character, Nicholls said 'that morally the game was a draw, as [the] try was a perfectly fair one.'

Stead, who was pictured in the team photograph and who is known to have run touch, felt that the above words, coupled with Bob Deans' own assertions, best demonstrated to his rugby audience that the score was legitimate – although, as the passage of time has proved, the great sporting rivalry will not allow this matter to be laid to rest.

PART II

CLIFF PORTER'S 'INVINCIBLES' OF 1924

Welcoming Long-lost Friends after Nineteen Years

As the crowds left St Helen's on that late December day in 1905, they did so in the hope and expectation of seeing the New Zealanders returning within a few years. The tour's success had raised the profile of a game whose popularity was soaring, whilst gate receipts, essential to cover the tour costs, had far exceeded expectations. But more importantly, rugby was seen as uniting sport-minded nations across the world, providing common ground, something to share, and plenty to aspire to in the way of attaining better standards and rising expectations. It was, perhaps, time to consider how the game had developed in Wales and in the land of the silver fern.

Long before rugby arrived at Lampeter College in the mid-1800s, games between teams of many men passing a ball, or such object, by hand were popular within the Principality as they also were in other countries. Cnapan, for instance, played in seventeenth century Pembrokeshire, was one such sport enjoyed by local villagers as both participants and spectators – proving that recreation of a hurly-burly nature had a place in the hearts and minds of Welsh people. It was later in 1875 that the formation of the South Wales Football Club (and later Union) cemented the country's rugby foothold, before Wales participated in its first full rugby international, against England, in February 1881.

This early sighting of the red shirt and three Prince of Wales feathers, the words 'Ich Dien' [I serve] emblazoned thereon, saw a colossal 82–0 thumping based on today's scoring, and was shortly followed by the formation of the Welsh Football Union – today's Welsh Rugby Union – after a meeting held at the Castle Hotel, Neath, in 1881. This boosted the game within South Wales, leading to clubs being established in many towns and large villages, before a gradual migration north in later years.

In a similar way, rugby's arrival in New Zealand was equally cohesive and entirely natural. The concept of men competing for an inflated bladder or some other make-do ball on the open fields dates back long before the game was officially introduced in 1870. This was when Charles Monro, the son of Sir David Monro, New Zealand's Speaker at the House of Representatives, ventured home to Nelson, New Zealand, after three years of study at Christ's College, Finchley, in London, to influence players from Nelson to try their luck at the handling game.

The resulting fixture staged at the Botanical Reserve, in Nelson, kick-started the arrival of rugby which, suiting its country inhabitants well, was adopted and later regulated by the New Zealand Rugby Union's formation in 1892. By this time the adventurous New Zealand Native team of 1888 had returned from its marathon 107 match tour of its homeland, Australia and the British Isles, with just 26 players in a re-markable 14 months! Today, such a workload is unimaginable but these hardy warriors survived it, kitted out in black shirts and with a large silver fern image on their jersey. This plant is linked to Māori proverbs, signifying that when a fern perishes it is replaced by another, just as 'when one warrior dies another arises.' When, at the Annual General Meeting of the New Zealand Rugby Union, a resolution was passed and accepted that the 'representative colour be a black jersey with silver fern leaf and a black cap with silver monogram'[14], amongst other accoutrements, the die had been cast.

With the game's popularity spreading like wild fire, clubs were formed up and down the two main islands. This was exciting news, and, just as hardworking miners lined up alongside steelmen, farmers and physically strong men of Wales – not forgetting smaller characters of strength and iron will such as Dicky Owen – so also were descendants of New Zealand's early settlers from Polynesia (later termed 'the Māori') scrumming down alongside Pākehā (in general terms the country's non-Māori residents) in their mutual enjoyment of the game. Keeping pace with modest progress in other walks of life, when times were harsh and money scarce, rugby was cutting its own pathway and it was making ground.

Coming together to play under the guidance and control of two captains, the number of players in each team was often boosted by casual observers, everyone making light of the limitations of the day, often having to clear the fields of sharp objects beforehand so as to make it safe. Alan Turley's *Rugby: the Pioneer Years* is full of such detail, adding that rugby venues lacked even the basic requirements of our modern era, meaning that participants went home mud-splattered in their kit – unless fortunate enough to have a quick wash behind the undergrowth with water from a well.

By the turn of the century Wales, now a well-established rugby nation, had long since bagged its first Triple Crown in 1893, just as New Zealand had been engaged in battle with Australia in this time. Throughout, events on the field led to an accepted social fellowship after the game had ended. Newport, Swansea and Cardiff clubs bear testimony to this,

---

14   Bob Howitt and Dianne Haworth, *All Black Magic: 100 Years of New Zealand Test Rugby* (Harper-Sports, 2003).

having returned home victorious from leading fixtures across South Wales around the 1880s to street celebrations and music from local bands, an expression of happiness and sense of occasion not dissimilar to what we see today.

Had world events not been so cataclysmic one can only guess at the way rugby would have developed. The Great War to all intent and purposes kicked the game into touch as rugby clubs up and down New Zealand and Wales cancelled fixtures and encouraged men to enlist. As war slogans initiated a new way of life, rugby grounds were adapted to the day's needs. Aberavon R.F.C.'s website notes how in response to the 'Save Food' campaign the club divided its field into allotments, and its young footballers were encouraged to respond to the request of Lord Kitchener, Secretary of State for War, to help Britain in its fight against enemy forces.

Likewise, the green turf at Cardiff Arms Park and Auckland's Eden Park staged wartime fundraising and recruitment events, as players of the world strode onto wartime battlefields. It is interesting to read in *Eden Park: A History* that during the midpoint of the war the *Poverty Bay Herald* of July 5th 1916 informed readers that almost all rugby players of repute were engaged in war activities. Doubtless, the same applied in Wales – and amongst these soldiers were players involved in the epic encounter of 1905 who were later to die in the fighting, as poignantly recalled in *Last Post: Rugby's Wartime Roll Call*.

Although Eric Harper was merely supporting his colleagues at the Arms Park on that famous 1905 December day, he scored two tries in the following match in France. He was a barrister from Christchurch and died in service in Palestine. Charles Pritchard was another, a mighty forward for Wales, who hurled his body at opposing packs, just as he showed bravery and spirit for his country. But as a captain in the South Wales Borderers, he also met his end in 1916. Then there was Dave Gallaher, the All Black captain; he was killed by gunshot wounds near Gravenstafel Spur, Flanders.

Dave Gallaher's story is compelling. Having fought in the Boer War, where he climbed the ranks, he again volunteered to serve his country, our country, in the Great War. Now almost 43 and soon to be a company sergeant major, his wont was to soldier on. As a legend in his adopted homeland as well as at his birth place Ramelton, in County Donegal, Gallaher is respected for injecting military discipline and bravery into his All Black colleagues. As a club and international player, and also as a national selector, his influence was significant, as was his legacy lasting. Indeed, Gallaher was ahead of his time, expressing surprise within 'The Captain's Retrospect' in *1905, The Triumphant Tour of the New Zealand Footballers* that most forwards he opposed on this tour had no inclination to grab hold of the ball and run upfield, so as to instigate a passing movement.

It was in the aftermath of the Great War in 1919 that the New Zealand Army, with service personnel stationed all around Britain, provided top-class rugby opposition up and down the country, whilst their senior XV competed for, and won, the King's Cup. Being young and raring to go, they reignited rugby's great light, challenging a dozen and more Welsh teams and losing only to one of these. Their varied fixtures thrilled crowds in most corners of the country, dropping into the valleys north of Bridgend to claim Ogmore Vale's ground record in front of five thousand local spectators, as well as drawing, 0–0, with high-flying Pill Harriers watched by a crowd of twice this size. Then the team met its only loss, to Monmouth County, by a single point, 4–3.

The match that took place against Wales in April, 1919, was a close affair, the visitors winning 6–3. If it was seen as a setback for the Welsh, it certainly got the national team back together, dusting down the famous red shirt for future use. Although the three feathers had been lowered, Welshmen had enjoyed tackling future All Blacks in the army team, this being the perfect preparation for Home Nations matches looming around the corner.

When five years later captain Cliff Porter's New Zealand 'Invincibles' walked the gangway to board *RMS Remuera* in June 1924 at King's Wharf, Wellington, they carried the hopes of a nation determined to advance New Zealand's rugby status just as their predecessors, the Originals, had done nineteen years earlier. But, above all else, they planned to silence a Welsh nation that had spoilt the magnificent run of these men. With them on board they carried the team's mascot, a stuffed Kiwi inside a wooden presentation box, which was openly offered to the first side to topple the All Blacks. It was a friendly gesture, a gift meant for a good rugby home – although everyone in New Zealand hoped and prayed that it did not end up in Wales!

As coincidence would have it, Cliff Porter's side opened its own Welsh chapter at St Helen's, Swansea, the scene of Dave Gallaher's departing 'Originals'. Since that earlier event, the term 'All Blacks' had been widely used in New Zealand, and across the world, meaning that Cliff Porter's side was flying the flag of an accepted brand. They were well prepared, too, primed for action, having learnt valuable lessons from Gallaher's legacy, George Dixon, Billy Stead, Billy Wallace and other members of the Originals team. There would, for instance, be no refereeing issues this time, for Mr Dean, manager, had written in advance to the Welsh Football Union to liaise on the subject and knew about the men who were likely to control his team's matches in Wales. They were building on past successes, channelling information and policy into its national team, nurturing a growing legacy for the future – a policy that has remained to this day.

There is little doubt that Dave Gallaher was at the forefront of Cliff Porter's mind as the All Blacks pulled into Swansea in the early afternoon of the match, patently aware of the boots he was to fill. But there were no weaknesses in Cliff Porter's armour either: a strong, sturdy man in his playing gear, just as he was smart, diplomatic and engaging in his blazer. Ahead of this fixture, his team had played four, won four, without having conceded a point. Only a few days earlier they had silenced a huge Gloucester crowd, boosted by city workers who had been granted time off to see the match. Such was the pull of the All Blacks and it was no different this day in Swansea.

From early morning, the East Dock Station was geared for an invasion of people as excursions arrived from Birmingham, Bristol and Aberystwyth. There were others, including a locomotive from Neyland in Pembrokeshire, whose rugby followers had travelled to cheer on local boy, Tommy Evans, in the Swansea side. Likewise, across the Loughor Bridge, neighbourly rivals Llanelli could not resist a peep at the All Blacks ahead of their own big fixture in the coming weeks. In the *South Wales Daily Post* of September 27th 1924, it is stated that 'practically every charabanc and taxi in Llanelli' had been booked to deliver rugby spectators 'from the tinplate town', with a dozen 'motor coaches' making the journey from distant parts such as Mountain Ash.

When Mark Nicholls, a utility back for the All Blacks, arrived at Swansea, he was amused to note the reaction of factory employees to his team as they headed towards the ground. His words, appearing in the 'Bay of Plenty versus British Lions' programme of 1971, mention his colleagues walking one after another through a mass of people, to 'exclamations of delight' from locals because of their smaller than expected stature. But this 'changed to consternation' when they realised that the backs had led the way, soon to be followed by the mighty men of the pack!

As the local Llansamlet band led the singing this day, few expected a Swansea victory against athletes of greater speed, power and skill. They were correct, Cliff Porter's men charging through some desperate tackling to run up a 39–3 score. Afterwards the Mayor of Swansea hosted the teams at the Hotel Metropole, where he was quoted by the *South Wales Daily Post* of September 29th 1924 as saying he 'never saw a finer body of footballers on any ground.' He felt that the game was being advanced to the highest of standards in the Colonies by men whose 'dexterity' and sharp, decisive nature was so apparent. He added that it seemed that their homeland 'was conducive to breeding men of that sort.'

Cliff Porter acknowledged the crowd's sportsmanship, the vast assembly of around forty thousand having enjoyed the fine football throughout, before he praised the quality of the St Helen's field. The bigger venues suited his team, and he was thankful that for the first time on tour the weather had been fine and the surface firm. He also spoke kindly of the referee for his handling of the game.

It was left to Stan Dean, tour manager, to toast the well-being of the Swansea side that, in his opinion, had played more adventurous rugby than the combined efforts of the four teams earlier met in the West Country. More importantly, he appreciated the 'good feeling' that defined the day, stating 'Such a spirit as that shown would lead to closer relations, and the betterment of the Empire.' Furthermore, Mr Dean complimented the spectators for being so utterly sporting. Then, following the Welsh National Anthem, the All Blacks left for Newport on the nine o'clock evening train.

Down to Earth at Ebbw Vale Colliery and a Fine Sporting Gesture

The New Zealanders looked a fine group of men as they lined up in their shirts and ties, jackets and hats, before taking their pit lamps down the Prince of Wales Colliery, Ebbw Vale. Enjoying themselves ahead of a mid-week match with Newport, the *Western Mail* of September 30th 1924 describes their visit to the local steelworks, where they were shown around the blast furnaces and coke ovens, before being treated to a good Welsh canteen lunch. In the company of the Mayor of Newport, they travelled by road along the Risca, Cross Keys and Abercarn stretch, before passing through Bryn-mawr, Abergavenny, Usk and Caerleon on the return journey that same Monday.

Two days later, Wednesday, the men were on a sightseeing tour of Monmouthshire, conducted by Councillor Geo Boots, whose friends and associates provided cars. The *South Wales Argus* of October 2nd described the visit: the party touring through Caerwent, Chepstow and Monmouth, before returning via Usk. Having been impressed with the Roman relics, including the remains of a Roman amphitheatre, the All Blacks walked around Tintern Abbey. Then, they went on to Monmouth School, dating back to 1614, where Mr Boots informed his visitors that it was here that R. B. Griffiths, the player who scored Newport's points against the 1905 Originals, was educated. When it was time to leave, the excited school pupils directed loud cheers at the New Zealanders as a mark of their full appreciation.

Now ready for the Thursday match with Newport, the All Blacks players were eager to consolidate their good form.

Newport's Rodney Parade was chock-a-block with excited spectators, smartly dressed with coats and hats, filling every available seat down to the roped enclosure on the pitchside, where cigarette and pipe lovers puffed away, breathing clouds of smoke into the air. Emerging through a small gap in the tightly packed enclosure, Cliff Porter led his men onto the field with the same easy walk of Dave Gallaher. He was preparing for an onslaught from the home team which duly arrived, its severity taking the All Blacks by surprise.

With their pack of powerful forwards known for dribbling the ball at their feet, and with a line of skilful backs, Newport fancied their chances. They had manoeuvres of their own, taking the lead twice and clinging to a slender advantage as the game entered its final stages. But Cliff Porter was not the All Blacks captain in name only: comfortable in varying tactics so that Newport's defence became bombarded with high and awkward kicks for his forwards to chase. This brought possession of the ball near Newport's line, and a converted try, enough to win the match 13–10 in the nick of time. This was hard luck for Newport who, many believed, deserved to win. Mr S. F. Wilson, 'a delegate of the Imperial Rugby Conference,' as the *Western Mail* of October 3rd 1924 describes him, was one of these, stating in the after-match supper at Newport Town Hall that, regardless of the result, on the balance of play the home team should have triumphed.

As keen a contest as the players made this match, in the eyes of sportsmen the All Blacks had gained great credit for playing down an incident that occurred in the second half, resulting in their centre three-quarter Bert Cooke, a natural sprinter, being injured in a late charge having just kicked ahead. This was an ugly, careless incident and Cooke, who returned to the field although still a little shaky, did so to everyone's wide acclaim. But what is most noteworthy is the fine sporting gesture on the part of Newport spectators who called aloud for the transgressor, their own player, Tom Jones, to be dismissed. In the national press this challenge was severely frowned upon, whilst the sporting gesture was given the praise it fully deserved.

George Nēpia, full back, was the new and rising star on this tour, and, although being a hard tackler himself, he was shocked at the severity of the challenge. George, just twenty at the time, had the distinction of playing in every one of the tour matches and admits that this game so nearly slipped from the All Blacks' grasp. In *Rugby Every Time, George Nēpia's Own Story*, George describes his love for the game which began at an early age when he played truant at school so that he could watch local Māori teams in action. For this, he had his comeuppance, time and again, although it did not stop George, a tough young contender who surprised the rugby world when selected for this tour.

In his book and in his own words, George explains to readers that he acquired skills to help improve his game whilst attending a Māori Agricultural College at Hawke's Bay in the North Island. He writes of his meeting with a sports coach from America who could throw the ball in torpedo fashion, and this impressed George so much that he became determined to kick a rugby ball in like manner. After endless practice over two years, he had mastered the skill, adding to his other competencies, so that his career moved onwards at an alarming rate.

George goes on to explain that in a Māori trial match between the North and South Islands, he was asked to switch position from second-five-eighths (centre) to full back. At first, this disturbed him, believing his chance of selection for this 1924 tour might be ruined – but how wrong he was. Well ahead of the full squad being named, he was one of sixteen 'certainties' to be chosen, despite there being further trial matches to play. He never forgot the scene as he sat among forty or more players in a Wellington hotel reception, all hoping for good news, most too nervous to eat. This is when Stan Dean, tour manager, walked in, a powerful figure whose presence caused the room to fill with tension. Then, George heard his name called out, meaning he was one of the fortunate ones to have booked his place on the boat: stunning news for one so young.

The late John Sinclair, mentioned earlier detailing the story of Bunny Abbott's more familiar name, also knew George. John remembers how extraordinary praise was lavished upon him:

> In most people's eyes, he was far from first choice for the tour. He was a Māori boy, who hadn't played that much. But he could kick the ball over the moon with either foot and they took him.
>
> 'Sit down George,' they said to him on the boat going over – George not knowing fully what to do, full back being rather new to him. Techniques were taught, and he learnt quickly.[On arrival in England] he started well and met with a lot of praise.
>
> 'If you like what you've just seen,' George thought to himself, 'well you haven't seen anything yet!'

People in the British Isles travelled far to see such talent. He boosted the gates, spectators wanting to see *him* first of all, the All Blacks second. 'He also had a phenomenal tackle,' said John. 'Again, he was taught. George was told to launch himself forward at a speed greater than that of the man approaching with the ball!' It was hardly surprising that spectators heard his tackles from the stands! 'No one was expecting them,' said John. 'George hit hard. But everyone remembers his spiral kicks; his trademark was to punt the ball over the stand.'

George Nēpia felt the full force and passion of Welsh rugby at Newport that afternoon, just as his opponents felt the thud of his heavy tackles. On one occasion this almost got him into trouble: not with Newport players, but with two spectators in the packed terraces who sought retribution. Again, in his book the young full back described the moment that their eyes glared menacingly on him as they stepped from the crowd onto the field of play, heading in his direction.

But their bravado was short-lived, better judgment causing them to backtrack to where they belonged. In the way rugby men look after each other and having sensed that trouble lay ahead, two teammates were ensuring that their young colleague was safe: the mighty Maurice Brownlie and 'Bull' Irvine running to his aid. Thankful, and not surprised to see his potential assailants jumping back over the fence, George was simply relieved to get back to the game.

From Cardiff City Hall to
Tenby's South Beach

Cardiff in 1924 was a bustling city on the receiving end of a steady stream of coal trucks that wound their way by rail from all over the South Wales coalfields. Despite trade having dipped, and the uncertainty of export prices being a concern, here was a city getting busier and bigger by the day. And so it was into the precincts and high streets of this world that rugby supporters spilt in great numbers on Saturdays, aboard electric trams, trolley buses or in the cheeky little cars of the day. Match days made the streets come alive and, with the home team riding high and challenging the mighty All Blacks, Cardiff Arms Park was the place to go.

Having now notched up nineteen straight wins in the course of performing a clean sweep of the elite teams in British rugby, just as their predecessors had done in 1905, opponents were lying in wait, determined to get their hands on the Kiwi mascot that accompanied the touring side. In scenes reminiscent of nineteen years earlier, a huge crowd of rugby enthusiasts met the All Blacks at Cardiff Station, led by an official reception party that included Gwyn Nicholls, the victorious Welsh captain of that day. Once again the streets were lined for their journey through St Mary Street, Queen Street and towards Park Place, before passing near King Edward VII Avenue that was bursting with students.

It was as if the years had been rolled back, a feeling of déjà vu descending upon the Welsh city. At a reception in Cardiff City Hall the Lord Mayor of Cardiff was soon reminding his visitors of the challenge awaiting them. He had done his homework as well, recalling the details of Wales' victory in

1905, as well as earlier matches against the Native touring team of 1888. He spoke of Cardiff's game in particular, when Mr W. T. Morgan, the present-day club president, who was standing by his side, played in a tough forward contest in the mud, scoring a try and helping Cardiff to victory.

The next speaker, Sir Thomas Hughes, did his best to persuade the New Zealanders to support the Cardiff Boys Club by playing a fundraising match on New Year's Day. At a time when charitable deeds considerably helped the world go round, this gentleman's request was understandable, although unrealistic in terms of the tour's excessive demands. Mr Dean, the manager, was quick to point out that he had been inundated with such invitations, and this latest would be considered with the rest.

On the day of the match, Saturday November 22nd, spectators rose early to secure a place on one of the three open terraces. First to arrive was a gentleman who appeared at the 'pay box' at 9.30 a.m., where he was pictured by the *Western Mail* at the head of a queue of men along the narrow walkway leading into the stadium's wider width, all wearing winter coats and hats. Many of these enthusiasts were soon to file into the front enclosures at the pitchside, behind the ropes, hoping to get as near to the action as possible. But glory for Cardiff this day slipped away: the men in black, who, having earlier been photographed in a large group standing alongside their opponents, as was usual at the time, pulled away at the close to win 16–8.

Later, at the Grand Hotel, Mr Dean thanked everyone in Cardiff for their hospitality. His team had enjoyed their stay and valued the friendships made, and he was pleased to leave Cardiff Arms Park victorious and without having to play there again on tour because New Zealanders were wary of the place! Mr Dean's men had been well entertained in the city, although he felt that 'too much of a good thing' was not ideal. They had come to carry the rugby message, and he recognised that prestigious sporting occasions as this spoke volumes for the game. Mr Dean added that in his business dealings, he preferred employing a man who participated in 'the grand game of rugby', because it gave him breadth of view and made him 'a better man.'

Meanwhile, Mr Morgan, the try-scoring Cardiff president, praised the amateur game: expressing his delight in the past purchase of Cardiff Arms Park for rugby's gain, and spoke of the charity work carried out by his club. He referred to matches played during the war when soldiers on 'home service' took part, everybody giving generously, resulting in the sum of £2,000 being handed over to the Prisoners of War Fund.

Later that evening as some of the touring party watched *Six Cylinder Love*, a silent film comedy, at the Playhouse, many radio listeners tuned in to hear talented All Blacks singing in a Welsh concert. The programme was advertised in the *Western Mail* and promised to be a rather different event, the first of its kind. The New Zealanders were scheduled to follow instrumental pieces of music provided by William Murdoch, pianist, theirs being an 'impromptu' performance with a Māori feel to some of the songs, including a haka. Then, according to the press release, Cliff Porter, the captain, was expected to address listeners 'on ships, shoes, sealing wax and rugger.'

On Sunday afternoon, the entire party went for a drive through the Vale of Glamorgan, in motor cars and cabs. Admiring the beautiful countryside, they called at Cowbridge for tea, before visiting Barry Golf Club, where, after meeting the club captain, it is understood that a quick round of golf took place. This outing was followed the next day by a visit to

Cardiff Castle, courtesy of Lord Bute, although some players preferred to tour the capital's main attractions in vehicles provided by a local tramway proprietor. But, at midday, most met at the Cardiff Coal Exchange, where coal proprietors, businessmen, and shipping merchants struck bargains in the course of everyday commerce.

As deals on November the 25th were briefly suspended, local dockworkers requested the full-blown Māori chant, but, as the guests were missing a few leading performers, the All Blacks, as the *Western Mail* reported, improvised with a few thunderous 'Hurrahs'. The tourists were then praised for their tour record by speakers standing on the balcony of the Coal Exchange, with Mr Dean responding in typical diplomatic fashion. His men were sad to be moving on, but were next heading to a peaceful retreat to prepare for Saturday's international against Wales. It seemed that the Welsh off-field tour was taking its toll in kindness and welcome, and this was noticeably greater than anywhere else.

Mr Dean and his men were soon pulling out of Cardiff station, heading one hundred miles west to Tenby on the South Pembrokeshire coast. The delights of the famous resort had been chosen to recharge the All Blacks' batteries ahead of the crunch match at St Helen's, Swansea. Nineteen years had been a long time to wait and these men carried on their shoulders their nation's hunger for victory. If ever there was unfinished business to attend to, here it was. This All Blacks outfit was shaping for the battle of a lifetime, but if they thought Tenby was all peace and quiet, they were in for a big surprise.

Over the years, this fashionable and charming small town had become recognised as a most stunning venue for anyone in search of a splendid seafront stage. Just as important to international footballers was Tenby's proud rugby history and the respect for its club as a strong team in this rural corner of Wales.

The All Blacks would have sensed a slower pace of life as their train travelled through the smaller railway stations before arriving in Tenby in the dark early evening. In the weeks running up to their arrival, members of Tenby United Rugby Club had joined forces with the mayor and town council to form a working party, ensuring that their guests enjoyed the break. The locals who shared the special thrill of hosting rugby's biggest names had considered every possible detail, and as the All Blacks pulled into town, cars were waiting to take them to meet the crowds at the Royal Assembly Rooms.

The Tenby Observer of November 28th and December 5th documents this momentous stay. At the first reception in the Picture House – an occasion that was said to be 'unparalleled in the annals of the town' and full of excited local people – the All Blacks were greeted with music by the town band. Then – having at first been taken into a separate room to meet the mayor and leading members of the town – the party stepped onto a raised stage in front of the full audience. Next came a prolonged period of cheering, as never before witnessed at this venue, followed by an orchestral performance of See the Conquering Hero Comes, prompting everyone to sing.

Councillor Thomas Hall, the mayor, then spoke of the 'honour' of having these sportsmen in their midst. He wished the All Blacks well with their rugby preparations and with the social side of their stay, hoping that they take away happy memories of the town. Tenby's inhabitants 'had the greatest interests in their movements' as 'kinsmen from beyond the seas.' In response, Mr Dean stated his men had immediately settled into their new surroundings, where they hoped to make lasting friends. Before deciding on Tenby, many attractive proposals had been recommended, but 'glowing reports' of the town had tipped the scales in its favour. Then, Mr Dean had a 'comical' story to share: explaining that on the journey that day, he spoke to a young lad at one of the station stops who in his innocence uncovered a misapprehension that would, surely, be shared with others way beyond his years. Mr Dean asked the boy what he had been hoping for and the response was 'All Black!' Next, the manager enquired if he was 'disappointed', to which the reply was, 'Yes!' Mr Dean was not pleased to let anyone down, but begged to make known that the term 'All Blacks' referred to their playing outfit and not to 'themselves'.

The evening came to a conclusion when everyone sang 'For they are jolly good fellows', followed by *God Save the King*. It had been a long day and the men wanted to book into the Royal Gate House Hotel and take rest. But as for Messrs Porter and Dean, the All Blacks captain and manager, they were due to meet the mayor and his organising committee to plan social events for the stay. Everyone wanted the company of these men, but they would not lose sight of their goal, the hard work starting early next morning with training at the town's rugby field in Heywood Lane, although it is understood to have been a different venue from today's ground.

As reported in *The Pembrokeshire Herald* of November 26th 1924, later that following morning the men were driven to Milton, a few miles from Pembroke, to attend a 'meet'. Walking around in the countryside made a pleasant change, but there was an amusing twist to the tale in that when following the horses and hounds, there was not a fox to be seen! Mr Dean was thoroughly amused by this experience, which he commented on at the grand dinner in the Picture House that same evening. Tenby's notables, including local ministers and rugby club members, attended this formal function which reflected the standards of the era. There was a resident orchestra playing and a generous spread of food, and the New Zealanders were met with overwhelming applause as they walked into the room, where a reporter for *The Tenby Observer* was taking notes.

After dinner, the mayor proposed a toast to the King, followed by a short performance by the orchestra whose varied programme, and presence between each course of the menu, added to the evening's entertainment. Then Mr T. P. Hughes, a well-known businessman, toasted the Queen, the Queen Mother, the Prince of Wales and the royal family. He appreciated their involvement in the sporting events of the country, especially the Prince of Wales, a man with similar ideals as the King in preserving the nation's good name in the eyes of the world. Indeed, 'nobody worked harder', he remarked to 'loud cheers', there being few countries with British interests that he had not frequented, including the distant homeland of this evening's important guests.

Messages and apologies for absences were read out aloud by His Worship, the mayor, before proposing a toast to the guests, who had emulated their predecessors whilst making history of their own. The All Blacks were informed that Tenby had in the past helped prepare winning horses for the Grand National, and many successful jockeys had been raised in the area, as had other sportsmen, including Ernie Finch, the dashing Welsh wing three-quarter, selected to play against them on Saturday. As regards the All Blacks' outstanding run of twenty straight wins, the mayor mentioned that if this was bettered by beating Wales, Tenby would 'share in the joy of such a victory.'

Loud applause accompanied this gentleman's return to his seat, at which point the orchestra stepped in to play another spirited rendition. Then, Mr Dean rose to respond, most grateful to all, hoping that the side deserving victory on Saturday emerged the winner. Should this be his men, Tenby inhabitants would certainly be a part of the triumph because 'they had, in a certain sense, adopted them' (cheers and laughter). Without doubt, Tenby would be remembered as a rugby base that served this current team.

Mr Dean stated that earlier that morning, as he peered out of a hotel window onto the harbour, the scene reminded him of a canvas painting that he had viewed back home in a Wellington exhibition. Then, referring to New Zealand being a far away land, he amused his audience by stating that a certain Lord Mayor they had earlier met, greeted them as visitors from Newfoundland! Mr Dean said this person's following of the game was not keen, 'although his intentions might have been well meant.'

Adding a few words about the Great War, Mr Dean stated that it had enhanced the relationship between Australia and New Zealand, drawing the two nations nearer to their 'Mother Country.' In fighting alongside members of the Empire, New Zealand had demonstrated loyalty, especially as 'ten per cent' of its population had gone into battle. Of the current team, eleven players 'had served their King and Country.' As regards the remainder, they were too young: 'Some of them were still boys.'

Next, referring to their visit to Milton, he offered his gratitude to Mr Seymour Allen, 'the Master of Hounds', whilst being thoroughly amused at the way events turned out! Then, concluding his address, he stated that upon his return to New Zealand he would arrange for an official team photograph, duly framed, to be sent to the council chambers for hanging on the wall. On behalf of his men, he thanked the local people for such an enjoyable stay.

A toast from Cliff Porter, the All Blacks captain, was then made to 'Tenby United [Rugby] Football Club', thanking members for their support and also the use of their field, before he called upon his men to line up for two of their famous 'war-cries'. Each was of the 'weirdest description', and rather 'unintelligible,' said the newspaper reporter who had hardly seen such a performance in Tenby before. Next, Captain Hugh Allen, chairman of the county rugby movement, responded, being somewhat relieved that his playing days were over having just witnessed this spectacle. He felt the All Blacks 'had done one of the finest things possible' in arriving at Tenby to prepare for what might be the most important contest of their rugby lives.

Mr Sandercock, another dignitary, spoke touching words, acknowledging that whilst Tenby's guests were not British citizens, 'their forbears had been', and they were seen 'as flesh of their flesh and bone of their bone.' He had not forgotten how men of the Colony had arrived to help the country 'when the enemy was at the gate . . . From the bottom of his heart he would say, 'God bless you every one.'

Throughout these formal speeches, there was plenty of clapping and cheering and laughing by those present, making it a night to remember. Then concluding events: Miss Maggie Davies sang *Land of My Fathers* – but probably the original Welsh version – before everyone joined in with the singing of *God Save the King* and *Auld Lang Syne*.

All Blacks onslaught ruffles Welsh feathers

Mr Dean had been touched by genius when taking his men to Tenby. They left the seaside resort invigorated and ready to face the Welsh team, also prepared to put right the result of nineteen years ago. They had drawn benefits from a varied social programme, including a tour of Tenby and a visit to Pembrokeshire's nearby castles and dockyards. Following the official dinner on Tuesday, members of the party were involved with the local dance group at the De Valence Gardens, whilst a whist drive and social was arranged the next evening, again at the Picture House where, according to *The Tenby Observer*, dancing 'with the greatest of zest' continued well after midnight. As the All Blacks headed for Swansea on Friday November 28th, they were primed for rugby action, lungs full of fresh sea air and ready to do business. And, in customary manner, they left Tenby railway station with loud cheers ringing in their ears, fog alerts adding to the din.[15]

Justifiably, manager Stan Dean was quietly confident of victory. Beyond a thorough preparation, statistics – published in the *South Wales Daily Post* on November 28th – favoured the New Zealanders, whose pack averaged 13 stones 9 pounds, half a stone heavier than each of the seven Welsh forwards on duty. New Zealand's backs also had blistering pace and would take some stopping on a wide-open field like St Helen's. In the official tour diary, kept at the New Zealand Rugby Museum, Palmerston North, Mr Dean describes the Wednesday before the match as 'wet,' the field as 'slippery' and the team as '[skilful] when playing soccer.' Later that

---

15   *The Pembrokeshire Herald*, December 3rd 1924.

day there was a visit to Tenby School to speak to the pupils: good news for the children, but who would have envied the teachers trying to hold the scholars' attention when the All Blacks were due to arrive!

On the Thursday, Cliff Porter, captain, called at Pembroke East End School and presented a shield to members of the school rugby team, honouring an outstanding three-year unbeaten record. This was a meeting of the 'Invincibles', the two teams sharing a winning run, in the company of 'His Worship the Mayor' and Messrs Rowlands and Lowless, the chairman of the local education authority and the town clerk respectively. Pembrokeshire Records Office provides the details, stating that 'Mr Dean and Mr Porter [who arrived at 3.40 p.m.] were afterwards presented with photos of the school team – which they suggested should be placed in the headquarters of the New Zealand Rugby Union [as well as] in principal schools in New Zealand.'

The two gentlemen were also provided with 'a copy of the *Pembrokeshire Telegraph* [dated] October 30th containing a report of East End's three year unbeaten record'. Had Mr Dean found time to read this, it would account for his diary entries being decidedly brief, although still informative. Here are some of his jottings, with hints of calmness emerging between the lines as the big day approached:

Friday 28th November — [Weather] Fine. 7.15 a.m. walked to beach and scrum practice. Left for Swansea at 2.30 p.m. Met by Mayor and rugby officials and escorted to Hotel Metropole. Bed early, in anticipation of match v. Wales in morrow. A large mail cheered up the Boys.

Saturday 29th — Showery. Thousands of people [are] flocking into city. Team confident and anxious [to] avenge 1905 defeat.

By comparison, the Welsh run-up to the match was very different. Unlike in 1905, Wales was no longer the main force of British rugby. Indeed, the team was not performing well on the big stage. The depressed economic outlook did not help this situation, nor the exodus of leading players to rugby league in the north of England. A year or two earlier, players of the calibre of Edgar Morgan moved from Llanelli to Hull; and Frankie Dafen Evans, a Welsh Union international, transferred to Swinton, where he secured a cap for Great Britain. The outcome of the 1923 Home Nations Championship had also been conclusive enough, losing to England, Scotland and Ireland with the only victory secured by way of a slender margin against France. The following season saw virtually an exact repeat of results, hardly the form to carry into a match against the All Blacks.

However, no one dared to underestimate the *hwyl* of the Welsh, who would, perhaps, have the flair to conjure up a big surprise. Fifty thousand Welshmen would also play a part, having poured into the city by every available means, singing, cheering and hoping to lift their men to great heights. In the previous few weeks, the two trial matches had gone well. If Wales could follow Newport's recent form, a shock could be on the cards. Optimists felt that on balance the match was there for Wales to take. The weather, too, would have its say: rain would slow down the men in black, while Friday's dry spell and sunshine would return a quick-draining St Helen's to its best. And if the ground was dry, the All Blacks with their running game would have the advantage.

Shortly before 2.30 p.m. on match day, Major Brunton, from Northumberland, privileged to referee his first international and soon having to handle an eleventh-hour rejection of two match balls by Welsh captain, Jack Wetter, walked down the long, narrow corridor leading to the team's two dressing rooms, and invited the players onto the field. He, just like everyone else in the bowels of the grandstand, had heard the crowd high above, responding to the band with *Aberystwyth* and *Cwm Rhondda*, but now the moment of truth was at hand – the long-awaited return fixture – and, as noise levels hit an unforgettable pitch, far away in New Zealand a nation could not sleep due to the excitement.

Prime Minister, William Massey, had already sent his good wishes, as had so many fellow countrymen, while the likes of Billy Wallace, the hero and highest scorer of points in 1905, was apparently pacing around too excited to sleep. Little would stop this man following the progress of his countrymen on and off the field. From letters, telegrams and newspapers he knew of their recent visit to Swansea Docks before taking tea with W. J. Winfield Esq. (understood to be a relative of 'Bert' Winfield, a member of the victorious 1905 team). But now, as New Zealand performed their haka, recently rehearsed in Tenby's Picture House, a Welshman, Dai Hiddlestone, anxious to do something in response, took a punt at a version of his own. But, despite it being full of good intention, the idea lacked respect and understanding for this proud Māori ritual, and fell flat on its face.

With St Helen's a blaze of hustle and bustle, colour and noise, this Mumbles Road ground had never seen so much life. As spectators backed onto Bryn Road, the *Western Mail* reports that a wall fell down during the afternoon, as did a small railing near the main stand – but thankfully no one was hurt. Journalists and reporters who had been invited beforehand to refreshments at Patti Pavilion by the Mayor of Swansea were now in their seats, notepads and pencils at the ready and scribbling away. And, as the foolhardy men perched high upon a nearby telegraph pole held on for their lives, everyone waited for the first kick of the day.

It was to be a good start for the men in red, making forays into the All Black half and looking threatening. But those redoubtable men in black, with the uncanny ability to turn an opponent's most trifling mistake into an advantage, were soon ahead, having kicked a three-point penalty on the ten-minute mark. Now, inching in front, they were next storming for the line, crossing on four occasions, despite close attention and keen tackling from the Welsh.

It had been some battle, fast, furious and full of incident, yet the New Zealanders held the upper hand, coasting to victory at the close when their win became assured. In a match that saw boisterous play and thunderous forward charges, the referee had to stop the action at one point to 'warn players' about their behaviour. 'Feet could be seen flying about when the ball was nowhere near,' said the *Western Mail*, which was half expected in a local club derby, although 'a most deplorable thing in an international match.'

That afternoon, Cliff Porter, New Zealand's regular captain, had failed to make the starting line having lost his place to an in-form colleague – although there is a line of thought that he may have been rested for the following difficult match at Llanelli, only days after the Test. In the dinner at the Hotel Metropole, the man-mountain, Jock Richardson, who had led the side, was, according to a report in the *South Wales Daily Post* on December 1st, pleasantly surprised at the condition of St Helen's after so much wet weather. Manager Stan Dean spoke of his joy at returning to Swansea and clinching the result he had worked for – hoping also that there would be no more mention of 1905!

Whilst giving his address, Mr Dean responded to a current affairs issue that had just been raised by Mr H. S. Lyne. This was, no doubt, the great Horace Sampson Lyne, a well-respected sportsman, long-term President of the Welsh Union and member of the International Rugby Board, who, when earlier proposing a toast to the health of the New Zealanders had 'alluded' to the rather prickly subject about the All Blacks '[giving respect to] the Scottish football clubs'. The fact that no matches were scheduled to be played by the tourists north of England this time round had not escaped rugby minds, and, as can be expected, all sorts of rumours were flying about. Memories of the less than cordial meeting of the two teams in 1905 were opening up a hornet's nest and this is why Mr Lyne wanted to play down any unwanted speculation, as reported in the *Western Mail* of December 1st 1924.

Stating that the one point the Scottish Union wanted to make was that the New Zealanders had been asked to the country by the English Union instead of the International Rugby Board, Mr Lyne suggested that people were jumping to the wrong conclusions because there was no rift between the two rugby powers. Mr Dean emphatically endorsed this statement; there was no disagreement with his Scottish friends and neither did he object to being allocated their country's referees. However, he felt that his team could only entertain the Scots in future matches if it was arranged 'under the regularly constituted authority.'

Following a toast to Major Brunton, the referee responded by saying that he would not have dreamt of missing the contest and he commiserated with the unlucky Jack Wetter, Welsh captain, on his injury which forced him to go straight home. Major Brunton was returning to rugby-conscious England, where players of his national team fancied their chances in the Twickenham Test against the All Blacks early in January. *The Times* of London would be covering the build-up to the match against the so-far 'Invincibles' who had, according to the reporter, obtained 'their hearts desire' at St Helen's in beating the Welsh.

It had been a good day for New Zealand and to make matters almost perfect for them Teddy Morgan, the one Welshman from the 1905 team who believed that Deans had scored, wrote a much-publicised statement confirming this opinion on a post-match dinner menu. Although Bob Deans had died a few years after the 1905 match, this revelation was to reignite interest in the disputed try in his homeland and Cliff Porter would make sure of this upon his return.

In Swansea's rich rugby history this international had been a major event and, as the beer slipped down in the packed public bars, many could look forward to further viewings of the match at the town's Albert Hall Cinema starting on the following Tuesday. An advertisement in the *South Wales Daily Post* stated that a film recording was being shown throughout the week and this would have been the closest some enthusiasts got to seeing the match. They would have heard of the great collision that took place as George Nēpia dived for the ball at the Welsh forwards' feet when they pressed for a score, so as to retrieve the ball for New Zealand and run upfield, injuring poor old Jack Wetter in the process, and effectively ending his afternoon.

No one could doubt the strength of this New Zealand juggernaut. Having defeated all the Welsh teams to date, responsibility for its derailment would now fall three days hence upon the steelmen of Llanelli. With more than a stuffed Kiwi waiting to be claimed, a town rallied to support its heroes, whilst the All Blacks set aside the day's victory to focus on this last match in Wales.

A 'Stradey Special' earns
Glowing Tributes at the Thomas Arms

Llanelli needed no greater inspiration to succeed against the All Blacks than to recall Harry Bowen's fifty-yard drop goal in 1888, which sent the Māori team home defeated. Stradey Park, a red-hot bed of rugby, fuelled in this more rural setting by unbridled passion of a particular variety was – and is – able, occasionally, to topple the largest of sporting giants. These industrious men in scarlet, with the ability to pull the game out of the fire and possessed of silky running skills had, in 1908, also turned the Wallabies from 'Down Under' upside down. In truth, even this rampaging New Zealand outfit – bigger, better and with great pedigree – entered Stradey's gates at their peril, such was the home team's uncanny ability to punch above its weight.

In Llanelli, meaningful rugby days such as this, the first of many battles with the All Blacks, are blessed with at least half a day's holiday so that school children and their teachers and as many of the town's workers as possible are free to watch the game. There was to be little sheet metal rolled in the famous tinplates either, as men of the puddling and pickling processes set aside their tools to enjoy the occasion. They took their place amongst a twenty-thousand strong crowd, boosted by the erection of temporary stands that snuggled behind the goal posts – where, possibly for the first time ever, a little saucepan ('Sosban Fach' being the name given to Llanelli R.F.C.) had been secured on top of one of the posts on the eastern side of the ground.

Long before kick-off, as the *Llanelli Mercury* of December 4th 1924 points out, there was not a spare seat to be found, nor a place to stand. Even the club's 'promenade' was full, as was a solitary tree in amongst the terracing, half-strangled by a dozen hangers-on. This day was to be a lively stage for the Llanelli Silver Band whose members played a succession of Welsh songs, not least, the club's favourite, 'Sosban Fach'. As crowds filtered through the narrow neighbouring streets to the ground, many having travelled long distances by train and coach, spectators sensed the opportunity presented by Stradey's open green rugby field.

Welcomed by the mayor at Llanelli Town Hall, Cliff Porter's All Blacks had now captivated Welsh rugby with strong physical dominance and efficient support play. Their workmanlike manner was a joy to watch, such as when attacking Llanelli's try line early on they forced the home side to minor the ball on two occasions. In the game's far earlier days, this event was seen as the opposite of a try, a last resort for a team under pressure, even a surrender of a kind and, so it is understood unofficially, an act that determined winners when matches were drawn.

In a contest that saw try-scoring opportunities going astray by a Llanelli side quickly forcing the pace, one cannot but commiserate when noting that a free kick successfully placed between the uprights by local hero Albert Jenkins was disallowed because the ball was 'touched in flight', therefore 'deflected', and would not count.

Although lighter by far, Llanelli's forwards played valiantly, pushing, pressing and tackling with gusto throughout. Not to be outdone, so did the backs, with Ernie Finch, mentioned in an earlier game, making his mark by scorching down the touchline and beating the player who others could not beat. This fullback was the one and only George Nēpia, whose comprehensive style of defence came close to tipping opponents onto the terraces – literally, by way of his muscular frame and the influence of watching hard, physical Māori sides in his youth. But on this occasion, George was beaten by a flash of inspiration from a winger who would be talked about for years. Spectator Wilfred L. L. Davies never forgot the episode. Recalling the action years later in the Llanelli versus New Zealand match programme of October 31st 1972, he described Nēpia as shaping for the tackle just a fraction too early, allowing Finch to race clear and score, an incident that has been a topic of much discussion over the years.

What George Nēpia probably did not realise is that Ernie Finch had been practising his skills all week, courtesy of an understanding headmaster and a supportive educational authority responsible for the school where he taught in Pembrokeshire. This happened to be the East End Boys' School, Pembroke, visited by Cliff Porter, All Blacks captain, alongside Mr Dean, manager (and Bert Cooke, centre three-quarter), when presenting a shield to its rugby team two days before the Welsh clash.

Referring again to the school log book, an entry written in bold red ink refers to Mr Finch being away for the whole week leading up to both the Welsh and Llanelli matches against the tourists, which, of course, followed one after another within days. Having been granted generous leave, it is little wonder that Ernie was in the form of his life and although he missed his school's big visit, the shield reflected well upon his teaching of the young scholars who were dominant in local rugby between the years 1922 and 1924.

When Master Finch returned to school his mixed thoughts about two difficult matches accompanied him, both hard fought and physical. But 'rugby,' wrote the *Western Mail* at the time, 'is essentially for the strong and the brave,' before adding conclusively that, 'No faint-hearted man ever became a great rugby player.' But however brave hearted Llanelli had been they lost 8-3. Not surprisingly, the tributes flowed at the Thomas Arms, where the mayor spoke of Llanelli's game with a New Zealand Army team five years earlier in 1919. The fixture had brought happiness to the crowd and gains to the club, financially and otherwise; and the mayor was pleased that Captain Clarke, in charge of the visiting team, was awarded life membership of the club that day.[16]

Stan Dean, who had spent all afternoon functioning as a touch judge feet and inches from the excitable crowd, pointed out that Captain Clarke was his personal friend. Then, he thanked the people of Wales and members of the Welsh Football Union for their continued kindnesses and hospitality. When Mr Dean sat down, he made way for the President of Llanelli R. F. C. to speak for his men: 'The Scarlets are the finest lot of boys you could hope to meet, as sportsmen, as gentlemen, and, what is more, as working men,'[17] he said. Then, addressing his visitors, he hoped that they would accept his message in the right spirit when suggesting his men deserved at least a draw on the day. More compliments rained down on the home team from Cliff Porter, the All Blacks captain, who, feeling that the game had been enjoyable for all, thanked Llanelli for providing a tougher battle than Wales had done days earlier.

Here was rugby friendship, warm and genuine, at its best, but the day was not yet finished. Later that night, the All Black flying three-quarter, Bert Cooke (who visited Pembroke school), was treated to a reception in his honour at Llanelli Liberal Club. Twenty-five years had passed since his parents had left their native town for New Zealand. Now, life's unpredictable course had brought him 'home', and, in

---

16   *Western Mail*, December 2nd 1924.
17   *Llanelli Mercury*, December 4th 1924.

being presented with a cigarette case of silver, duly engraved, the three-quarter, whose thrilling running had injected such life into the match earlier that day, was left with another recollection of his visit to Llanelli.

Young Bert Cooke was with the team leaving Swansea station the following day for Northampton to play a match against East Midlands. Beyond some good times and great fellowship shared, there may have been a few broken hearts among the many women seen chatting to the players before they boarded the train.[18] These were chivalrous characters, not least Brian McCleary, the reserve hooker who had played against Llanelli. Brian, also a well-known and successful boxer, was making his own headlines this same week in the *Herald of Wales*, on account of a sea rescue he made months earlier in his native South Island. 'All Blacks Bravery' is the headline, followed by 'Plunge into Boiling Sea to rescue a Woman'; and the article provides an account of Brian's arrival at the scene of stormy waves where a woman was struggling for her life. In a flash, he was in the water, swimming to her rescue before bringing her safely to shore.

Once again the efficiency and simplicity of the All Blacks' system had proved overpowering and Wales would miss these men who, after a few more difficult matches, would be on their way to Nine Elms Cemetery in Poperinge to lay a wreath on Dave Gallaher's grave. Then it would be time to sail to Canada for more rugby, before another hero's welcome awaited on the other side of the world.

---

18   *South Wales Daily Post,* December 3rd 1924.

All Roads lead to Abertillery Park as Battles Resume

In November 1926, two years after Llanelli's battle with the All Blacks, the West Wales club was again riding high, this time beating the Māori tourists 3–0. They and Pontypool (winning 6–5) were the only two victors from a pack of leading Welsh clubs who had faced the touring side. During those difficult years of economic depression, rugby, like all other aspects of life, was feeling the pinch. There would be no All Blacks visits in the immediate future – and for most teams, the primary aim was to keep their heads above water. Unfortunately, some failed.

But all was not doom and gloom. In 1930 the British Isles representative team sailed to New Zealand with a Welsh contingent that included Ivor Jones, a fast and determined wing forward who could run like a three-quarter. His presence and influence was so significant that he was nicknamed 'King Ivor' by Kiwi admirers and is remembered for snatching victory in the dying minutes of the Test at Carisbrook, Dunedin. With only minutes remaining and the score locked at 3–3, the match was destined for a draw. But then 'Ivor intercepted a pass' and sprinted fifty yards before George Nēpia, the New Zealand full back, moved in to make his challenge. It is then that Ivor looked for support: 'I gave the ball out to Jack Morley', he said, who sped into the distance to score. Ivor's team won 6–3. Years later he confessed, 'It was my greatest moment in rugby.'[19]

Rugby in these years was moving forward in many ways. The All Black tour of South Africa in 1928 saw the Springboks and the New Zealanders confront each four times. Then, in 1931, Lord Bledisloe the fourth Governor General of New Zealand, made available the Bledisloe Cup, a trophy to be contested annually by the All Blacks and the Australian national rugby team. Similarly, the game progressed in Wales, and ground improvements at Cardiff Arms Park saw, in January 1934, the building of a large stand as interest in the Home Nations championship continued to increase.

Of course, representing his country was the ultimate honour for a player and came with pride and honesty, typified by the words of Scottish full back, James Kerr, as he described a chase for the ball that had been driven downfield over the try line at Twickenham in the mid-1930s.[20] Mr Kerr and an Englishman dived to put downward pressure onto the ball but it catapulted away causing the Welsh referee, chasing upfield, to ask the Scottish defender if it was a try. 'Yes,' replied Mr Kerr, whose own side conceded the score and the match, 9–8, and lost every fixture that season!

In trial matches for places in the All Blacks touring party to visit Britain in 1935 no fewer than two hundred players battled for places. Their prize was a ticket aboard the RMS *Rangitiki*, setting sail from Wellington in July of that year. The manager, Vincent Meredith, supported by captain Jack Manchester, a towering figure, keen and competitive, led the tourists. Aged 27, over 6 feet tall, almost 14 stones, Jack was a popular figure who played for the Christchurch Club and

19   Esdale Maclean of the *Llanelli Star*, 'Llanelli versus New Zealand' programme, October 31st 1972.
20   Robin McConnell, *Inside the All Blacks* (HarperCollins, 1998).

Canterbury Province – and had, in the words of Scotland's Bill McLaren, 'hands like great buckets.'[21]

As is customary in New Zealand, Jack Manchester was shown the ropes by earlier tour captain, Cliff Porter, so as to take on board words of advice and experience before setting sail. He got to know what to expect and who to look out for along the way, especially in Wales, the scene of one big shock by now and more than a few narrow escapes. Surprisingly, one name to emerge was a highly respected Welsh referee – not an opponent – who had entered the record books for sending the first ever player from the field of international play. This was Albert Freethy of Neath, who had dismissed Cyril Brownlie of New Zealand for allegedly kicking an opponent when playing against England at Twickenham in the Invincibles' last international of their British tour in early January 1925.

Throughout his native land, Cyril, a gentle giant, was known to be the quietest in the side. 'If Cyril deserved to be sent off,' said John Sinclair of Palmerston North, 'then the rest of the pack should have gone to jail!' As they neared the end of the tour Cyril had not yet scored a try and felt mildly left out, prompting his colleagues to conjure up something for him in a later match. This is when an attacking movement switched direction in search of the big-striding second-row forward, catching some opponents completely unaware, as well as Mr Freethy, the referee that day who obstructed Cyril when, ball in hand, he was about to score. Afterwards, Cyril could not stop himself: 'Hey ref . . . I'd have my try if you hadn't been in the way . . . you silly bugger.'[22]

Of course, many a comment like this, and a lot worse, will

---

21   Bill McLaren, *The Voice of Rugby: My Autobiography* (Bantam Books, 2004).
22   Tony Williams, *100 Great Moments in New Zealand Rugby* (David Ling Publishers Ltd., 1999).

fly past a referee's ear, and despite reports of players having incurred lengthy bans for speaking out of turn to referees in far earlier days, it is extremely unlikely that an experienced man such as Mr Freethy batted an eyelid about the remark. However, the fact remains that, not long afterwards, Mr Freethy, who had a difficult job to do at Twickenham, sent Cyril on the lonely walk back to the changing room with an hour left to play for allegedly kicking an opponent. With such a happening being unheard of at the time, Jack Manchester, leading the latest All Black tourists to Britain, had to take note, for he would most certainly be crossing paths with Mr Freethy in future matches.

This sending-off incident shocked the rugby world and its impact was also felt in Wales. *The Times* of January 5th 1925 stated that it was 'an unprecedented indignity' for such a sporting contest, especially as the future King of England had been watching. This had caused New Zealand, the nation, to be embarrassed and the *New Zealand Herald* wanted to confirm forthwith that relations with the English had not been affected and that lessons had been learnt. Jack Manchester, likely to face potential problems of his own in the course of the forthcoming tour, had to understand the weight of responsibility resting on his shoulders – as well as realise how saddened Stan Dean, the Invincibles' manager, and Cyril Brownlie had felt about the incident. This was despite the fact that not one of the English team could recall being kicked, and the All Blacks winning with fourteen men – whilst the story of His Royal Highness in the stand enquiring if Cyril might return for the second half is likely to have brought a little light relief to those afflicted most!

Such events advanced the game and would not be forgotten, and, equally, they were adding to the New Zealanders' determination to keep returning to the British homeland –

and especially to Wales – to lay down more challenges for the home union. As for Jack Manchester and his men, all that mattered to them was proving to the New Zealand Rugby Union that in being fit to travel they satisfied requirements by having 'six stiff shirts, and boots and £40 in [a] personal bank balance.'[23] This was the directive given to an unnamed member of the touring party, as clear an indication as any of the strict standards and disciplines that were being adopted by the rugby hierarchy in New Zealand to build the All Blacks name. Once under way these young sportsmen were to receive a daily tour subsidy of three shillings in the form of exchangeable coupons, in addition to playing kit, trousers and one or two extras. Deck training on board ship would be the next priority, and the men would benefit from an improvised 'scrimmage' machine, thrown together by the ships' crew at sea, as we are led to understand.

The valleys town of Abertillery was the site for the first of their tour matches in Wales on Wednesday September 25th, after beating Devon and Cornwall, Midland Counties and a combined Yorkshire and Cumberland side. Everyone in the community had waited far too long for the arrival of these sporting greats and the little train station that catered for the heavy industrial output of this beautiful location was full of passionate rugby folk making their way towards the ground, Abertillery Park. This wonderful, picturesque playing area would be a splendid setting for the game, recognised as being the rugby highlight of many a recent year.

The South Wales Gazette of September 27th 1935 provides details from the moment dozens of news reporters took their places in the freshly painted grandstand ahead of kick-off, whilst photographers busied themselves at various vantage

---

23   Robin McConnell, *Inside the All Blacks* (HarperCollins, 1998).

points around the ground. Prior to kick-off, the Six Bells band was directing the singing into powerful accord, as volunteers took every opportunity to sell mascots, raise money for local hospitals and promote other worthy concerns. Soon the players were leaving the pavilion to a loud 'roar' as captain, Jack Manchester, recuperating after an injury, ran up and down the field, flag in hand as touch judge.

This day's hosts were a combined team representing the best players that Abertillery and nearby Cross Keys rugby clubs could find, but the combination did not win the day. Despite strenuous efforts by the home side to quell their opponents' attacking flow, the New Zealanders were able to score seven tries in a 31–6 victory, one of the most comfortable outings up to then of any All Blacks side to have played in Wales. Later, as the two teams were entertained at a dinner dance, many of the twenty thousand crowd were enjoying a drink and anticipating the special matches that lay ahead, none more important than the international at Cardiff. And when those with thick heads awoke the next morning, they knew that it had to be the All Blacks who were back in Wales.

The All Whites topple the All Blacks at Swansea

Three days after their easy win at Abertillery, New Zealand would face a more serious challenge at St Helen's, Swansea. It was one that proved to be historic – for on September 28th 1935, Swansea beat the mighty All Blacks, the first ever club side to do so. All worries about the good form of their visitors prior to the contest were thrown overboard as a high-class Swansea performance based on meticulous preparation and clinical attacking, as well as a youthful half-back pairing, shook the rugby world.

Established in 1872, Swansea Rugby Club was a founder member of the Welsh Union at its formation in Neath in 1881, just a month after Wales' first rugby international against England at Blackheath. This was in the days when teams changed in a nearby hostelry (which, being a recognised provider of alcohol caused religious minds to frown upon the game) and when referees wore clothes more suitable for harvest thanksgiving than 'scrimmages' on wintry days.

Although this afternoon's match referee had not travelled far – Mr F. G. Phillips lived in Pontardulais – the administration of fair play had come an enormous way from those early days. It is appropriate to recognise that New Zealand, Australia, South Africa and the Home Nations made great efforts in this respect before rules were codified within the framework of an International Rugby Board.

In many ways the earliest encounters resembled the break-time games seen on school yards, where two leaders divided the numbers, with late arrivals joining a side. The two captains, or their appointed deputies, called the shots, until along came umpires, usually two per match, moving up and down the field, a flag in hand, as general arbitrators if the two captains could not agree. By the mid-1880s referees, with ever-improving knowledge of the laws and the game's intentions, stood strong worldwide and had sole responsibility for matters of play. These men, assisted by another on each touch line, relied on their own voice for command – until William Atack, whilst refereeing in his native New Zealand in 1884, reached inside his pocket to find a revolutionary piece of rugby equipment: a dog whistle! Playing to the whistle had commenced.

With his own variety in hand, Mr Phillips, distinguished in a dark blazer, watched Jack Manchester lead his men onto the field in almost stately procession, before both teams lined up facing each other, parallel and only yards apart. But there were no intimidating stares on this occasion, just nervous glances and concentration as the national anthems were sung ahead of a fast and physical encounter that occasionally saw punches thrown. Swansea's agile and lightweight pack battled valiantly, ensuring that plentiful ball was made available for their talented backs.

This day saw the arrival on the big stage of Haydn Tanner and Willie T. H. Davies, scrum half and outside half respectively, still in school and having been granted leave of absence to play. Their refreshing enterprise and youthful endeavour brought immense impact on the game which, had it been soccer, was a *Roy of the Rovers* performance out of a Christmas annual. In the *Western Mail* one of Willie's outstanding bursts is described when, having collected the ball, he made all sorts of body movements to wrong-foot the All Blacks' defence, before passing to Welsh centre, Claude Davey, who galloped thirty yards for the line. As David Farmer recalls in his *The Life and Times of Swansea R.F.C.*, spectators on the open terrace felt that 'even the train station buffers' stood little chance of halting Davey on the burst.

The match ended 11–3, a total of three tries to one, despite the All Blacks unleashing high punts, difficult to deal with, to test Swansea's strong defence. This was the return to action from injury that Jack Manchester least expected and certainly would have dreaded if, beforehand, someone had predicted such a performance from a club side. New Zealand rugby writer Terry McLean, whose own brother Hugh was playing this day, notes in a column he wrote in an earlier New Zealand team match programme that Jack Manchester was heard relaying a desperate message to his men at a late scrum to the order of, 'Guys, we can't be losing like this . . . come on!'[24] And, in quick response Artie Lambourn, a straight-talking prop, is remembered for telling him it was too late: the writing was already on the scoreboard!

This result sent shock waves not only throughout the national sporting press but also throughout New Zealand. The successors to Cliff Porter's proud 'Invincibles' had been beaten by a club side! This news took some digesting, especially when considering the magnitude of Swansea's 39–3 defeat in 1924. But, although this had been a setback for a country used to winning, they gave full praise to the Welsh, a rugby population that never sits still, one that lifts itself back up, no matter how many times it is knocked down. *The New Zealand Herald* saw this as being the first big challenge presented to its team in a total of five tour matches played. Acknowledging both the determination of the Swansea forwards, and the sharp movements of the backs, this writer must have wished for a different outcome at the close of play.

Victory warmed the cockles of every local heart from Penclawdd to Port Tennant whilst licensees, granted extended opening hours for this special rugby occasion, served

24   'West Wales versus New Zealand', October 25th 1978: Swansea Archives.

the happy, singing supporters into the night. Meanwhile, as *The Herald of Wales* reports, the mayor and a host of dignitaries entertained the New Zealand party to a musical accompaniment at the Hotel Metropole.

Stepping forward to propose a toast to the All Blacks, the mayor praised his native town, Morriston, for raising many of the current Swansea players. Then Jack Manchester rose to his feet. Responding to more compliments than usual as his team had lost, he praised the home side's young half back pairing of Haydn Tanner and Willie Davies, and also Dai Parker who had played well in New Zealand with the most recent British team. The All Blacks captain was as magnanimous in defeat as he was humble in victory and would not forget Mr Phillips, the referee, proposing a toast to his health.

It was in the aftermath of this defeat that Jack Manchester made one of his most celebrated comments in Wales: 'Tell them we were beaten,' he said to a match reporter understood to be from his homeland, 'but, please, not by a pair of schoolboys.' We can only wonder if these impromptu words found their way into the *Canterbury Rugby Weekly*, a publication Jack knew well and which, sourcing rugby news in his home province at the time, could have made another fine story. Known to be a great character, it now remained to be seen if Jack could raise his troops for the even bigger challenges that lay ahead.

On a night Swansea never forgot, Mr Meredith, the tour manager, feeling the loneliness of defeat, took his turn to speak amongst an eloquent cast. But the simple message of Edgar Long, Swansea captain, eclipsed all else this day. Edgar, demonstrating heartfelt respect for his club and for all that it had achieved that afternoon, wished the tourists well in their future tour matches. He wanted them to win every one – so that his side could earn even greater acclaim!

Jack's men bounce back as Welsh teams tumble

When the New Zealand party left Swansea on that late September day, they returned to England, and later Scotland, for the next round of matches. Just as they had been invited to London's Savoy Hotel at the start of the tour, courtesy of the British Sports Association, they continued to be wined and dined by influential people of good reputation and with sporting interests. They were a respected team of players who played and practised hard yet enjoyed themselves when time allowed. In victory and in defeat, they were proving popular, but they relished returning to Wales, into the nitty-gritty of a do-or-die culture of rugby where they wanted to redeem themselves in the eyes of the sporting world.

Three weeks later, towards the end of October, that opportunity came when they were to play Llanelli, Cardiff and Newport in quick succession. And, as one would expect, the Welsh had also been counting the days. All three sides had proud records against the All Blacks who knew that this leg of the tour was an intimidating task. The elite of Welsh rugby, whose players were mainly local boys, were of similar footballing ability to Swansea. Taking their own potential into consideration alongside the victorious men of St Helen's, each man knew that there was all to play for against the touring side, sensing that the chance of a win had never been better. The enforced wait due to the All Blacks playing elsewhere had already given Welsh clubs more time to prepare, whilst newspaper coverage had sharpened belief that more victories lay ahead. Now, whenever colliers, clerks, clergy – or anybody – found a few spare minutes in their busy days, the return of the men in black was uppermost in thought and speech.

The *Llanelli Mercury* of October 24th 1935 states that as early as 9.30 a.m. on match day a keen group of spectators from Ystalyfera, in the nearby Swansea Valley, had arrived to bag the best available seats at Stradey Park. By mid-afternoon every nearby tree looking onto the field had been colonised by ticketless fans, whilst the more adventurous had climbed on to the cricket pavilion and even on to the roof of the Stradey grandstand – until anxious officials and spectators sitting below and fearing the worst, insisted they came back down. Llanelli on match day, 'Scarlet Fever' as they say, was running away with itself – but, in truth, no different from Rugby Park in Hamilton or Carisbrook in Dunedin, where excitement gets the better of spectators and a carnival atmosphere prevails.

'King Ivor' (Jones) was still involved in first-class rugby and proud to renew battles with old adversaries, this time on home ground. However, giving all was not enough and it was Jack Manchester's men who triumphed, capitalising on Llanelli mistakes and taking the points in a thrilling and hard-fought game that was deservedly won 16–8.

Later that night, as members of Llanelli and District Supporters Club enjoyed their own Colonial Ball, the players and officials were entertained by the president of the Llanelli club. 'Any luck that was going, came our way today,' said Jack Manchester, referring to the spilt ball that they had latched on to, before going on to acknowledge the home team's 'greats', as was customary when he rose to speak, Ivor Jones amongst them. 'King' Ivor responded with praise for his old Kiwi pals, recognising 'the cleverness with which they took advantage of Llanelli's mistakes.'

There then followed a surprise when Dr Rocyn Jones, responding to compliments paid to the Welsh Football Union, stated he had just received an enquiry from the Press Association about undesirable on-field events that day. This, he said, was all too difficult to comprehend because the game had been a fair and thrilling one – the few punches thrown being not worthy of mention and, at least, half expected! Dr Jones also referred to newspaper comments suggesting the tourists, when compared to earlier All Black sides, were below par: a suggestion he was quick to refute in the strongest of terms. Indeed, Dr Jones was determined to defend his visitors on all accounts, stressing how greatly British rugby had improved in recent years. Such a defence in the face of media speculation highlights changing times and a keen worldwide interest in this sport whose players had by now become fair game for newspaper attention.

With formalities drawing to a close, the local jeweller, Mr W. J. Thomas, presented the All Black captain with a 'silver saucepan', this, in addition to miniature models earlier given to his teammates – besides a few removed from the clubhouse wall in the day's excitement and probably filled with beer! Here was a town enjoying the social aspect of its favourite game: the action-packed eighty minutes being no more than a prelude to shared times and lasting memories. And in this home of West Wales rugby – where action photographs and memorabilia adorned the walls and local brews lifted the spirits – the All Blacks mixed freely, giving the townsfolk plenty to talk about in the weeks and years to come. But Cardiff was waiting for Jack's men.

Cardiff had never forgotten the day in 1905 when Percy Bush failed to minor the ball, allowing the Original All Blacks to scrape to victory by a narrow 10–8 margin. Now, only weeks before the bell sounded for round three of this epic fixture, Percy was back in familiar surroundings for a reunion at the Grand Hotel with the old boys of his playing era. Over the past twenty-five years Percy, who thrilled New Zealand crowds in 1904 with sharp attacking flair for the

British team, had lived in France, which provided him with another rugby challenge at the end of his career. This is where he was to return, but not before catching up on past events, reliving old matches and drinking to absent friends, with the added bonus of a bottle of champagne to take home from past Welsh captain Gwyn Nicholls.

These former players were relishing seeing the present team locking horns with the All Blacks. Cardiff, still a busy port and bustling city, had also a soccer team, the Bluebirds, who had famously won the FA Cup final at Wembley eight years earlier. It was not unusual to see fifty thousand fans packed into Ninian Park on Saturdays – yet without interfering with the healthy rugby following of its neighbours, who, for this match, would fill Cardiff Arms Park. As the day drew nearer, the All Blacks tour manager, Mr Meredith, often seen performing public engagements, had been speaking to school pupils in the area about the lifestyle of his countrymen in New Zealand.

Mr Meredith was excited and concerned about visiting Cardiff Arms Park, a ground full of memories and history, as well as being a cathedral for match-day singing that can upset even the strongest of visitors. Rugby came to this famous setting shortly after the Cardiff club formed in 1876, and its distinguished name was derived from the 'Cardiff Arms', an old public house nearby. The beautiful green fields of earlier times had been made available to the townspeople by the Third Marquess of Bute, and the rugby ground was later to stage Wales' first home international match against Ireland in 1884. The playing field, however, was near to the River Taff and was prone to flooding, as was seen four years later when Cardiff beat the touring (Māori) Natives in atrocious mud and rain when the pitch resembled a quagmire. But during those distant days the players could, at least, enjoy the comforts of the nearby Angel Hotel that, until 1904, provided changing facilities for teams before a new pavilion was built.[25]

Long before Cardiff Rugby Club was formed, the First *Rules* of the game, as written by senior scholars of Rugby School in 1845, were established, which, in their thoroughness, made provision for such eventualities as the ball hitting nearby trees! The revised rules of 1862 went into more details clarifying the game's principal objective: that of scoring goals[26] by kicking the ball between two uprights, eighteen feet tall, and over a connecting crossbar, ten feet from the playing surface. What is most interesting is that the thrill of crossing the line for a 'touchdown' (later known as a try) was only a means of earning points from the resulting kick, as mentioned earlier.

We might expect the try's worth to be increased by the kick; not so. The act of scoring a 'touchdown' merely allowed the opportunity of points to be earned from the resulting kick (today's aptly described 'conversion'), whilst other forms of gaining points came from the 'drop goal', which was struck in open play, just as we see today and from 'fair catches'. As for other rulings, the ball could be delivered back to a teammate, but never forward, and knock-ons were taboo, as was offside. Players were allowed to stop opponents in possession of the ball severely, although 'strangling' and 'throttling' had, thankfully, been removed from the game! The scholars of Rugby School, who played their favourite sport in smart uniforms and caps, had done its followers proud.

In the same year that the Rugby Football Union was formed in 1871, the older 'Rules' gave way to the revised 'Laws' as written by legal men with the input also of various

---

25   David Parry-Jones, *Taff's Acre* (Willow Books, Collins, 1984).
26   http://www.rugbyfootballhistory.com: 'The Laws of Football as played at Rugby School, August 28th 1845' (Copyright Nigel Trueman, 2002) and 1862 Rugby School Rules (Copyright N.C. Trueman 2006).

schools and other resources. Of course, both Wales and New Zealand adapted to these same standards whilst a steady stream of proposed law changes came forward over the ensuing years, some accepted, others rejected, as is the case today. By 1887, by which time the International Rugby Board had been formed, a try was soon to earn its keep: worth a miserly one point!

So far so good; the game had opened up into an entertaining sport. Such was the nature of play at Cardiff Arms Park on Saturday October 26th 1935, when New Zealand and Cardiff engaged in a running, try-scoring game where the ball handling was a pleasure to see. This was the day that Jack Manchester's men slipped into top gear with a glorious display of rugby that earned great praise in a 20–5 victory.

As reported in the *Western Mail* on the following Monday, the post-match party saw Mr Meredith describing Cardiff 'as a coal-producing seaport' catering for many related industries. Yet, undeterred by this, the city had grown in terms of 'civic design' and 'historic' appeal with a 'romantic' feel according to Mr Meredith. He believed Cardiff would soon be flourishing when the upturn in the economy arrived. As for Mr Goldsworthy, the referee, he had been first reserve for Cardiff's team when they played the tourists in 1924 and he was complimented for his handling of the game. Meanwhile, Tommy Stone, Cardiff's captain, a player who had progressed through the club ranks since boyhood, described the occasion as 'the great day of his life.' Tommy, an attacking full back, felt the honour of leading his men. 'It had been a pleasure to lose to such a great team,' he said.

On the following Sunday, as part of the celebrations leading to Remembrance Day, the All Blacks party visited the Earl Haig Memorial Institute in Whitchurch where their presence amongst former soldiers and British Legion members had added meaning because of their own countrymen's service in past wars. The next day, Monday, would see them facing up to mighty Newport, a bogey team for the All Blacks in many ways. Only six points separated them in two close matches over the last thirty years.

Those who had been privileged to attend that 1924 match would remember George Nēpia calling the shots. Eleven years on, incredibly, he was still within a shout of making the tour, having been recalled for the trial matches, and many of his closest fans were shocked at his exclusion. But in these more recent years his form was slipping slightly, causing the great player to accept the opportunity of playing and earning money by signing for Streatham and Mitcham, a rugby league side in London. His across-the-world relocation demonstrates how connected the two distant nations had become and how easy it was to transcend the 'union' and 'league' codes.

Although the *South Wales Argus*, as usual, had provided a generous sporting spread attracting people to the game, the continuous rain had made the field sodden and had, undoubtedly, affected the numbers and the spirit of the spectators. However, the rising cost of tour-match tickets had not helped matters either, a subject that was topical in the national papers. The *Western Mail and South Wales Daily News* of November 1st 1935 ran a report explaining why prices had risen, suggesting that, contrary to popular opinion, these high prices were not the fault of the clubs but the result of decisions made by the International Rugby Board in its fuller autonomy, whilst only a portion of receipts was set aside for Newport as hosts.

In a close contest with a wet ball, Rodney Parade saw the All Blacks claiming victory 17–5, one try apiece cushioned by two drop goals (still worth four points each) and another kick, direct from a mark (worth three). It has to be said that both still appeared to be easy pickings when compared with the fuller efforts required when scoring a try: a realisation that was corrected by the game's regulators in subsequent years.

At the after-match reception four senior players who had played for Newport during the mid-1870s were guests. These gentlemen could remember the country's early internationals at Rodney Parade, when fans made rugby pilgrimages to this ground, known for its distinct atmosphere, before Cardiff Arms Park took over the honours. These octogenarians had also caught the tail end of the South Wales Football Union, which led to the formation of the *Welsh* Football Union – an era when action-packed cup contests and derbies came with bravado and brawling, frustrations and free-for-alls, everyone embroiled in the afternoon's battles, players, spectators, all.

But times had changed: the game was now more structured and expectations, both professionally and personally, were higher and more focused. As Jack Manchester and his winning team went on to Newport Corporation Baths for a special dance organised by both the 'Athletic' and 'Supporters' clubs, one can only guess at what those four elderly gents thought of the new world. Perhaps it was too good to be true.

The Day the All Blacks went to Aberdare

It came as a surprise but in December 1935 Aberdare was given the honour of hosting a midweek match between the best of the local rugby teams in the Mid-District of Glamorgan and the touring All Blacks. Many towns had hoped to secure this event, but the combined forces of a hardworking community and a supportive Welsh Rugby Union won the day for Aberdare. This was the biggest day in this small cultured town's strong rugby history.

Thirty years had passed since former 'old boy' and strongman Dai Jones raised Aberdare's profile when playing in the famous 1905 international against the New Zealand Originals. Now, working to facilitate Aberdare's own major rugby event, an organising committee, ably helped by well-intentioned locals, tore into the multitude of tasks required to make it happen. The nearby colliery, for instance, assisted with improving the playing surface, attending to the pitch embankments and enhancing the grandstand, whilst all and sundry decorated the town and promoted the game. In many respects, it was like preparing for a royal visit – councillors and shop proprietors at their imaginative best, everyone raising the appearance of the town.

Local newspapers, such as the *Aberdare Leader* and the *Aberdare and Merthyr Express*, cleverly slotted match publicity between local stories. In bite-sized bulletins, readers learnt about New Zealand's history and a little personal background of the tourists, be they office clerks, travelling salesmen, farmers, meat traders, forestry workers, or engineers. Of course, many New Zealand rugby players had and have direct family links with Wales, and, although no direct examples had been provided by the local press, this was a general point mentioned by a special correspondent in the *The Aberdare Leader*, who also keenly felt the sense of occasion:

> A rugby game you say! Why all this fuss . . . [well] it is of symbolic importance. Our children after years of absence have come home. Is it not the prerogative of every child to have the warmest of welcomes in his own home? He expects it; he demands it. Aberdare will see that he gets it.

These were stimulating words but this really was a day to celebrate in the town and, in providing a snapshot of early life in New Zealand in the 1800s, this same gentleman provided a succinct précis, describing the arrival of Polynesians in wide canoes and the later arrival of Europeans (the Welsh among them) bringing horses, crops, plantations, and a new way of life. After much fighting, the integration of the two sets of people eventually brought great relief, ensuring everyone lived alongside each other peacefully – helped by the diplomatic work and humanity of Governor [Sir George] Grey.

On that Thursday, December 12th 1935, the All Blacks were an hour late arriving in Aberdare having, perhaps, lost their way travelling from their hotel in Porthcawl, hardly the easiest of journeys. As one would expect, this caused initial concern, especially as daylight hours were short, but the welcome at the Black Lion Hotel and later on the rugby field, following music from a Pontypridd ensemble who took the place of the Aberaman Silver Band, was sincere.

In a good atmosphere some six thousand people witnessed a well-contested match at the Ynys Stadium, although attendance figures and resulting revenue were far lower than had been hoped for – but these were difficult days and money was short. Those fortunate enough to be present witnessed a feast of tries as the All Blacks pulled away to win 31–10.

Eric Tindill, a drop goal scorer, played in the 'first five-eighth' position (outside half), a description that hasn't altered since Fred Childs of Merivale club, Christchurch, decided that if two men played between the half and three-quarter positions (half back and centre three-quarter), they had to be the 1st and 2nd five-eighths (half as a fraction being 4/8, three-quarters 6/8, in between 5/8). Likewise, All Black Jimmy Duncan had innovatory views on this subject.

At the post-match reception in Aberdare's Boot Hotel, Major Williams, chairman of the organising committee which was coordinating events, led the way as reported in the *Aberdare Leader* of December 21st 1935. He proposed a toast to the King before 'God Save the King' was sung by about one hundred people. Then Councillor Tom Meredith JP welcomed the visitors as 'members of the same vast commonwealth' – before his namesake, Mr Meredith, tour manager, rose to speak, accompanied by a loud chorus, 'For he's a Jolly Good Fellow'. Mr Meredith was enjoying the day, having been impressed that rugby was part of the 'blood' of so many upstanding men of the district. He noted also how obvious it was that rugby united men of any social group.

John Eaton 'Jack' Manchester, New Zealand captain, could not agree more, the big, engaging character with a low hair-line and prominent ears stepping up to speak to a rising crescendo of 'Why was he born so beautiful, why was he born at all' – to which he stood in defiant appreciation, beaming 'all over his face'. Then, thanking the referee, the All Blacks skipper added that his men 'had heard about [the day's match official] Mr Freethy, before coming to Wales' (because of Cyril Brownlie's sending-off in 1925). This brought knowing laughter, well intended, of course, before the captain praised Mr Freethy. 'It was,' he said, 'a pleasure to play under him' – Jack Manchester being too wise a counsellor to elaborate on his earlier comment!

By the time he sat down, complete with a souvenir 'white rugger cup,' Jack, too, was a 'Jolly good fellow,' in this, the most relaxed of gatherings when compared with receptions of earlier tours. In turn everyone was thanked for their contributions, from the management of Powell Duffryn Colliery to members of Aberaman R.F.C., the latter being providers of the rugby posts and temporary seats. The day had been an overwhelming victory for community rugby, catering for an All Blacks team on peak form and which had in the past month beaten both Scotland and Ireland. At different stages of the event soloists, tenors and other artists sang alongside the local pianist before the real party began, at a public dance in the Central Hall where Jack's sporting celebrities had been invited as the town's most honoured popular guests.

On Monday December 16th Mr Meredith, the tour manager, left his headquarters in Porthcawl to address three hundred scholars at Aberdare Boys County School where he received a tumultuous welcome. His speech, inspiring and well practised by now, and reported by the *Aberdare Leader*, praised the land, people and lifestyle of New Zealand before he spoke of the character-building effects of rugby, which taught young men quick thinking and the ability 'to take knocks, give knocks and then shut up about it.'

After gripping everyone's full attention, Mr Meredith received a three-minute ovation from his enthusiastic audience and a formal word of appreciation from the school rugby captain, Noel John. Noel drew applause of his own when referring to the 'excellent rugby' played by the All Blacks at Aberdare, which had motivated his team to beat Cathays High School 36–0 only two days earlier!

A warm-up at Aberavon and a one point win for Wales

In the early afternoon of Saturday December 14th 1935, exactly two days after the Aberdare match, thousands of rugby followers stood shoulder to shoulder in warm winter-length coats, flat caps, hats and scarves waiting to enter the turnstiles of the Talbot Athletic Ground in Port Talbot. On a cold day they had arrived with hopes of seeing the best of a combined Neath and Aberavon team upsetting the New Zealanders in full flight.

Such was the good feeling that Dai Hiddlestone, the popular local referee on duty, was presented at half-time with a bouquet of flowers, an unexpected gift from an unidentified admirer in the crowd. He had been a dedicated club player over many years and a seasoned international, playing with great tenacity for Wales against the All Blacks in Swansea in 1924 when his faux haka response caused a stir if not the greater appreciation he had hoped for. Mr Hiddlestone had presided over a brisk first period, the All Blacks nudging in front despite dogged determination from the home team. In the second half the lead was stretched as a nastiness crept into the game, but all were friends after the eighty minutes, the All Blacks victors 13–3, by three clear tries.

That night in Aberavon, seasonal celebrations had come early for the big crowd but not for the day's players who were to be involved in the Wales–New Zealand clash in Cardiff exactly one week later. This forthcoming match was going to be the rugby highlight of the season and, like their opponents, the Welsh were also confident of victory and with every good reason. Unlike in 1924, Wales this time had the pick of strong players, many of whom had already performed well for their clubs against the tourists. Despite the Welsh conceding weight in the pack (the All Blacks forwards were now averaging around 14 stones), the final Welsh trial had given good reason for confidence and it was believed that the crowd and the singing at the Arms Park would make a difference. At the final workout, staged at Cardiff High School's ground before the all-important body of Welsh selectors, the players were well prepared as long as injuries or other setbacks did not arise.

In the New Zealand camp, Jack Manchester and his men could take comfort from a run of impressive wins in Scotland, the first return to the country since the frosty welcome of 1905. Winning divisional matches at Glasgow and Hawick on the way to playing Scotland in Edinburgh was the best way to put right whatever wrongs had in previous years occurred. The test match played on a beautiful crisp day in Murrayfield saw everything going well for the All Blacks, who won the contest 18–8. Then, travelling to Aberdeen for a match with the North of Scotland, they were met on the station platform by officials excited by their arrival and schoolboys anxious to fill the little pages of their autograph books.

Interestingly, this All Blacks match in soccer-loving Aberdeen had been made possible with the help of Sheriff John Dewar Dallas, who thirty years earlier had refereed the first Wales–New Zealand match in Cardiff. Just as respected men of the game had staked a claim for the Mid-Districts match in Aberdare, here in Aberdeen Sheriff Dallas had spoken up for his town and district in like manner. In a later edition of the *Aberdeen Press and Journal*, August 1st 1942, Sheriff Dallas was recognised for promoting rugby in this north-eastern part of Scotland, which 'owed much to his interest and encouragement.' In his prime he had been an athletic man with skills in tennis, boxing and other sports, and, as a rugby player, Sheriff Dallas had been capped by Scotland and later became a well-respected international referee. Now he was a Scottish representative on the international stage. He knew this match in Aberdeen was the rugby highlight of many a recent year because the All Blacks, seemingly unbeatable once again, were playing magnificently.

Having followed his father into the legal profession, the young John Dallas was invited to the Scottish Bar in 1905 (the year of the famous Welsh test match), before seeing active service in the Great War in German and Portuguese East Africa. A few years after the ending of hostilities, he entered into the 'Sheriffdom of Aberdeen, Banff and Kincardine', being universally respected 'in the administration of justice.' Now in his late fifties, this family man was still immersed in the game, making him well known, and this is why he seemed fully acquainted with the New Zealanders when they stepped from their train carriages in Aberdeen that day.

Pittodrie, the football ground, was dressed for rugby: moss having been laid around the perimeter 'to prevent players being injured' and rugby markings overruling the football lines that gave the stadium its fame.[27] The match took place on a fine, cold day, the North of Scotland holding firm in the scrums, drawing 6–6 at half-time and ultimately outscoring their opponents by two tries to one, although losing the game 12–6. It is known that Sheriff Dallas spent time with the tourists who, staying at the Caledonian Hotel, visited the local fish market, played golf at Balgownie and visited the Tivoli Theatre, although one unnamed All Black, an admirer of George Arliss, according to the *Aberdeen Press and Journal* of November 27th, chose to view *Cardinal Richelieu* at the

---

27   *Evening Express* of November 27th and 28th 1935.

picture house. Sheriff Dallas would have been one of the attendees attired in formal dinner suits at the evening reception held at the town's Douglas Hotel. Doubtless, he felt the pride of making these important visitors feel welcome and wished them well for their forthcoming battle with Wales, which he would read about and might even have attended.

Before returning to Wales, Jack's men had an important date with the Irish and, like most teams visiting Lansdowne Road, his side felt the physical bombardment of opponents whose collective force resembled a team of twenty or more Irishmen. Such was the fervour during a second half of wind and rain that it was as if they were playing into a green shirted blizzard, although, remarkably, they held on to win 17–9.

The big question on everyone's mind was, 'Could the All Blacks claim their third test victory in a row?' Indeed, this was the serious yet pleasant consideration of Jack Manchester now that his team had hit good form. When two months earlier his party visited Lord and Lady Bledisloe at Lydney, Gloucestershire, the sting of the Swansea setback was severely felt. As Jack Manchester strolled through Bledisloe's Gloucestershire estate on a shooting expedition, how could he not be concerned about the forthcoming games and the form of his team? Yet, two months later, with precious few matches left to play, his side was on track for a Grand Slam.

And in Cardiff the excitement mounted as road closures were announced in the local papers days before the game and people were asked to note rearranged timetables for electric trams and other public services. The increased capacity at Cardiff Arms Park, now approaching fifty thousand, was attracting more people into the city on match day and this, coupled with increasing modern transport, was capable of causing major disorder. Shopkeepers and traders, alert to opportunities that they would seize with open arms, had planned accordingly: just as the National Museum of Wales, a popular city centre attraction, was staying open until 8 p.m. so that visitors could call on their way home.

With the public wanting to know more about the 1905 encounter, members of the victorious team were invited to talk about their historic victory on a radio programme broadcast from Cardiff in the run-up to the game. Chairing the small panel was 'Old Stager', a critic for the *Western Mail and South Wales News*, but now given the pleasant task of lining up questions for the men to answer into a recording mouthpiece. As expected, conversation soon centred around Bob Deans' 'no score'.

Rhys Gabe was still adamant that Deans had failed to cross the line – and who would expect anything different? However, there was a major surprise, for Gwyn Nicholls – captain of the Welsh side in 1905 and said by Billy Stead (at his welcome home party in Invercargill) to have told him that he believed Deans had scored – was now saying that Deans should 'have been penalised for not playing the ball'.[28] Had Stead misunderstood Nicholls all those years ago, one wonders, or had the Welsh captain reconsidered the facts and come up with a different interpretation of events? Although Teddy Morgan's stance had not altered – he still believed the 'try' was good – the story seemed to be assuming greater proportions with the passing of the years.

Days later, on the eve of the match, the 1905 team was back together again enjoying a reunion at the Park Hotel. Each player could take delight in reliving Teddy's winning try after Dicky Owen wrong-footed the New Zealand backline and switched direction with a long pass that went to Pritchard, then on to Gabe before ending up with Morgan.

---

28   *Western Mail and South Wales News*, December 21st 1935.

And they would remember nullifying the quick heel of the New Zealand two-man front row, a terrific achievement that knocked the All Blacks right out of their rhythm, whilst hoping for a repeat performance in the new-look scrums of this modern day.

By now, all British teams were packing down to a compulsory three-man front row, despite the traditional two-man version still being employed to an extent in New Zealand. But this new directive was causing problems with the feeding of the ball into the scrums. The unnecessary delays were frustrating front row forwards who remained bound in stooped positions longer than was comfortable whilst allowing bad feelings to creep into the game and also boredom for those viewing. The recent Cardiff match had, in part, been affected by this and, with rugby's hierarchy looking to put the matter right, it is again interesting to note, as reported in the *Aberdare Leader* only two weeks earlier, that New Zealand's suggestion was to see *referees* putting the ball in.

The official who had charge of this third Wales–All Blacks game was Cyril Gadney. With him was Morgan Moses who, having served as a Welsh referee for years, was invited out of retirement to be a touch judge. This was a 'thank you' and a huge honour from the Welsh Rugby Union, whilst the away team members took it upon themselves to appoint someone to mind the opposite touchline. When these three officials stepped onto the field, frost-hard in places and still bearing loose strands of straw, they were deafened by the crowd's roar. And what followed is remembered as a wonderful occasion that caused the *Western Mail and South Wales News* to state that no writer could describe 'the glories and thrills' of this most amazing rugby match, considered generally to have been one of the best of all time.

Spearheading Welsh charges into All Black territory were Claude Davey of Swansea and Cliff Jones and Wilfred Wooller from Cambridge University. The game offered unrelenting forward battles and scintillating play with tries, goals and uncanny bad bounces that kept everyone on tenterhooks. In a ding-dong battle, Wales won by a single point, and by the time everyone returned to the crowded streets and pubs and city transport was back to normal, Jack Manchester and his men were feeling the hurt of the close defeat at the after-match event. Applauding the Welsh on their victory, the great man told *The Herald of Wales* that he had not enjoyed such an enthralling contest whereby 'the fortunes fluctuated so often.'

Of the many tributes that poured in, D. R. Gent of *The Sunday Times* had never known such a second half for excitement; Walter Rees, of the Welsh Football Union, told the *Western Mail and South Wales News* that he was just too content to make any further comment. S. S. Dean, tour manager of the 1924 Invincibles but now chairman of the New Zealand Rugby Union, sent good wishes to his old friends in Wales. In Mr Dean's homeland, the *New Zealand Herald* led with the gracious words, 'Better Team Won', describing great jubilation at the final whistle when women ran onto the field to kiss their winning heroes. Meanwhile, Mr Meredith, the All Blacks tour manager, did not disagree. He complimented the Welsh players and he had been uplifted by the crowd in full musical voice. He recognised how well the team flew the flag of its passionate countrymen.

For this gentleman and his touring party, it was now time to leave Wales, but without realising just how distant the next visit would be. They had beaten Scotland and Ireland, and, having come close at Cardiff, had England left to play. But, as for the Welsh, all that mattered at this moment was the leader board. It simply read: Wales 2, New Zealand 1.

PART IV

BOB STUART'S TOURISTS OF 1953

World War II and a Rugby Round-up

For the first time in their rugby history, England beat the All Blacks at Twickenham in January 1936. This achievement had taken them over thirty years and the result, 13–0, meant that Jack Manchester and his men had to settle for a far less favourable international record than earlier hoped for and expected. This meant that Wales could again feel proud of its rugby men, although in the remaining years of the 1930s, the team would experience mixed results: winning the Home Nations tournament in 1936 before subsequently languishing lower down the table. Far away in New Zealand rugby men were building upon experiences gained during past voyages to the homeland, whilst revelling in the regular challenges provided annually by Australian and South African teams.

However, by 1939 Europe, and, before long, the world, was at war and although rugby affairs were put on hold, the link between New Zealand and the United Kingdom remained strong. It was a connection that saw rugby men from these distant nations standing shoulder to shoulder in combat against the enemy. That, however, did not stop rugby emerging as a regular topic of conversation and often slipping into everyday life when least expected. For example, take 'our Mary', the daughter of Newport's Tommy Vile, who, during the war, worked as a Wren in a hospital in today's Sri Lanka.

'One evening,' [she told the author] 'I was sitting quietly in my office and became conscious of a shadow outside.'

'Yes, sir,' I called out, seeing the large figure of a man near the doorway, 'can I help you?'

'They tell me your name is Vile,' was the reply.

'That's correct, sir.'

'Is your father's name Tommy?' he asked.

'Yes, it is.'

'Well, do you know what that *bugger* did to me – he disallowed my try!'

Mary explained that the naval officer was referring to an international match that her father had refereed. The gentleman, as she recalled was English:

> I can still see him standing in the doorway. In later years, my father told me a little more about the incident. He had warned the fellow because he had been going off-side a couple of times. Then he did it again. My father was stooped down low for the scrum, but glanced momentarily between his legs and caught him in the act.

Mary remembers that both her parents had struck up lasting friendships with New Zealanders, many of whom called to see them in Newport when supporting their countrymen on later tours. They enjoyed keeping in touch, often sending photographs to one another and, had the Vile family been able to, they would have journeyed abroad. Mary continues:

> My father wore two wrist watches and carried a stopwatch for injury time. He wore cream-coloured flannel shorts. We had a copper tub to wash the clothes. One day his shorts went through the mangle with his stopwatch. The next thing was who was going to tell father what had happened:
> 'When he comes home let's be careful what we say to

him,' we said, one to another. We expected him to be like a
bear with a sore head, we were prepared for him to explode
– but he simply went out and bought another.

One of Mary's favourite players was international sprinter
Ken Jones – 'Oh, my word, that man could shift,' she recalls
– who at that stage was a young and promising Blaenavon
player with the rare potential for puncturing holes in rugby
defences. Mary was soon to be captivated by his scorching
pace when he played for Newport, starting in 1946 – although
he arrived a fraction too late to claim a place in the side to play
against the New Zealand Army servicemen of 1945/46. These
were a talented group of Kiwis who were still stationed in the
United Kingdom following the war and who were more than
a match for most top teams. They toured Britain, entertaining
large crowds with thrilling, running rugby, many honing
their skills for future years in the black shirt with a silver fern.

Such was their daring, dashing brand of play that they
brought much distraction to a country rebuilding its battered
homeland. They reignited the national game, playing eight
matches in Wales, winning six, drawing with Newport, whilst
falling to Monmouthshire, 15–0, on a bitterly cold day at
Pontypool Park. But they seized glory by walloping Wales in
Cardiff, 11–3, in front of a much reduced crowd, given that
the north stand and western section had been hit by bombs.[29]

One of the up-and-coming players of the army side
was prop forward Johnny Simpson who, after the fifteen-
a-side game had ended for the season, played some sevens
tournaments. Bob Luxford, in his *Johnny Simpson Iron Man*,
refers to the time that Johnny, who led a New Zealand side
to victory in the National Sevens competition at Llanelli,
was playing for his countrymen in the Middlesex Sevens at

---

29   John Billot, *All Blacks in Wales* (Ron Jones Publications, 1972).

Twickenham. He was never to forget the 'porcelain baths and back scrubbers' of London's grand old stadium where he lined up against Cardiff on the way to the final. This is when Wales' own Dai Davies played with a strip of plaster outside his boot covering an injured toe, yet still managing to outpace the New Zealanders to cross the line for the winning try.

There was a craving for rugby's full return and when the Home Nations Championship resumed in 1947, Welshmen were raring to go. None of the earlier passion for the game had been lost; to the contrary, the enforced absence had intensified feelings, rugby's return being with a vengeance. It is likely that the hardship of war experiences heightened the physicality and pace of the game whilst the impending British Isles tour to New Zealand in 1950 was enough to ensure the Welsh were peaking around this time, guaranteeing a strong national presence on the tour.

New Zealand were equally as eager: their post-war excursions into Australia and later South Africa, where they played strong teams, had given them a sharper edge. These were exciting times, featured at length in the national newspapers and well covered in *The New Zealand Sportsman*, a popular magazine serving most sports but devoured by rugby lovers. Against the British Isles, the All Blacks got down to business quickly, wrapping up the series in the first three tests with a draw and two narrow victories. But then, in the fourth Test, came something special to delight the supporters at Eden Park on a glorious late-winter's afternoon. Everyone was in for a treat, a feast of fine action, but the best score and one that has not been forgotten, belonged to the long-legged Welshman who 'could shift'!

Graham Walton, an Auckland historian whose contributions to *Eden Park: a History* are central to the book's popularity, explained to me that as a child he watched the match with his father. They, too, as did thousands of others, had jumped onto a tram, before crossing over a 'rickety old railway bridge' on their way to the ground. As Graham stood in an empty stand peering across at the wonderful expanse of today's Eden Park, he remembered watching Ken Jones, the Welsh flyer and Olympic sprinter:

> It was about 4.30 in the afternoon and he was chased by Peter Henderson and Roy Roper, the two New Zealand speedsters. We were all shielding our eyes as he broke an attempted tackle before doing an amazing swallow dive under the posts. That was some chase and it left an indelible and abiding memory on me.

The move had started well inside the Lions' half, as these popular tourists would run the ball from everywhere, with other Welshmen, Bleddyn Williams amongst them, also involved. When Ken received the ball he had about fifty yards to go. The excitement intensified, for Peter Henderson was another international sprinter. It was a scene from a racetrack, a scorching run and everyone held their breath. In the *New Zealand Herald*, Terry McLean, in his most eloquent way, described people from all walks of life celebrating a truly amazing score.

New Zealand went on to win this Test in a close and dramatic finish. Now the international flame was alight and all thoughts raced ahead to the next clash of rugby's sporting giants. This would see Robert Charles 'Bob' Stuart, of the Fleet Air Arm, assuming captaincy of the touring party of 1953. But, having ridden the choppy waters in the course of his naval duties, there was to be no sea voyage this time for him. For the first time in the illustrious history of the All Blacks, they were taking to the air and a different 'touch down' would get the show under way.

Wyn's old Wolseley and Bob's bumpy ride

In early October 1953 the All Blacks fastened their seat belts and prepared to leave early summer warmth for the nip of British autumn. Having enjoyed a celebratory lunch at Wellington Town Hall in the company of past captains Cliff Porter and Jack Manchester, they were taken through the streets accompanied by local pipe bands and well-wishers high in hope and expectation for this latest series of matches. As if embarking upon the fourth tour of the British Isles was not important enough, the All Blacks' choice of transport was attracting further interest. Although jet aeroplanes of the day were becoming ever more sophisticated, this was still a long and daunting journey, with stops in Sydney and Darwin before the party proceeded to Singapore. It was there that a training session and an overnight stay kept the team fresh before being dined by members of the Malayan Rugby Union. The party then continued to London via Karachi and Zurich.

Unlike their predecessors, whose midriffs may have expanded a little whilst at sea, these men were in peak form, prepared to take on the world. After skipping through the English counties, where they won all their early matches, they were met on arrival in Wales by a crowd of Cardiff players, including Bleddyn Williams, the 'Prince of Welsh Centres'. After a lunch provided by the Rotary Club, Bob Stuart was asked to speak, and he was in fine form. *The New Zealand Herald* of November 18th 1953 describes him quoting a Welshman from an earlier fixture, caught in a huddle of bodies near the bottom of a ruck. 'Wait until you so-and-sos get to Cardiff,' the player had snorted, causing amusement at the time and now another chorus of laughter.

Among those present were Rhys Gabe, Wilfred Wooller, Bleddyn Williams and Dr Jack Matthews, all of whom could picture the scene: a player caught in the most unenviable position but, restricted as he was, he was courageous enough to instigate a little outburst of his own, a personal objection of a verbal kind. The likes of Kevin Skinner (also a boxer) and Tiny White, both hard men of New Zealand rugby would know that there was no stopping a Welshman from having his say, even when the poor fellow was getting booted about! It is this type of story that rugby players relate to well, having been in the same position themselves, probably, more times than they would care to recall!

Suitably replete having enjoyed good food and wine, this had been a fine start. Later the tourists went for a stroll across Cardiff Arms Park, and saw the piece of turf – reported as being between '15 and 18 yards from the left-hand upright' – where Bob Deans dived for the try line in 1905. This is, of course, yet another description of the spot, for it is understood from the *Western Mail* years earlier to have been nearer the corner flag – whilst Billy Wallace, playing that day, later stated in *The New Zealand Herald* of November 19th 1953 that all the excitement had occurred 'eight yards' from the posts! Was it a case of the accuracy of old memories fading with the passing years, or simply the drowsiness of that extra lunchtime glass of wine? For certain, playing on the same turf would have to wait – the men of Llanelli stood next in line.

Days ahead of their arrival at Stradey Park for the first match in Wales, every one of the eighteen thousand or more match tickets had been claimed. At midday the men in black pulled into Llanelli for a civic reception and then a rotary lunch, attended by Sir Donald Cameron, previously mayor of Dunedin. Rugby was certainly connecting the world now, just as the Welsh band was coordinating mixed voices at pitchside

into a powerful community choir. Most people had arrived
early, intent upon making the most of the day, except Wyn
Evans, scrum half, and Gethin Hughes, second-row forward,
for the Llanelli team.

By now, Gethin was an apprentice surveyor in the
Gwendraeth Valley group of collieries. Like so many of the
local boys, Gethin worked hard whilst giving all he had left to
rugby. On match days it was usual for Wyn, who owned a car,
to pick up Gethin on his way to Stradey and, for away matches,
they drove into the town and parked at Llanelli Railway
Station. In those days they caught a steam train, having
received a little bag of sandwiches from a committeeman to
eat on the way. When they returned, sometimes a day later
from fixtures in England, the car was always safe and sound.
But on this important occasion, Wyn had been held up, as
Gethin recalls:

> Wyn had an old Wolseley. It was a real old banger of a car,
> and he was a bit late that day. I was hoping to get to Stradey
> early, so as to get a feel of the atmosphere, but when we
> arrived it was time to get changed.
>
> 'Ble buest ti, Wyn?' [Where have you been, Wyn?] I asked
> in our usual Welsh. 'Pa amser yw hyn?' [What's this time?].
> Mae gêm bwysig 'da ni heddi!' [We've got an important
> game today!]

Gethin explained that on the morning concerned, Wyn had
genuinely been delayed; something had cropped up and his
late departure could not be avoided. So Wyn's ever-reliable
took its place in the heavy flow of traffic heading for the match
– surely a player's worst nightmare. 'Was I glad to see the
old changing room!' exclaimed Gethin. Gethin remembers
it being a small area with wooden panels that smelt of
wintergreen ointment with a large community bath but just

the one shower. 'We had some muddy days at Stradey,' said Gethin, 'and if you ever happened to be the last in, you'd be lucky to get out clean from there.'

Gethin described the tingling feeling he had deep down inside when he ran onto the field. Besides their clinical black outfit there was a distinct confidence about the New Zealanders. In the line-out, he and Rhys (R. H.) Williams jumped against Tiny White and Nelson Dalzell, two big men, both immensely strong, but it was to Peter Jones, another line-out specialist, that Gethin spoke at length after the game. 'He was a young man, new to the All Blacks' set-up but soon to make a big name for himself in the jersey,' said Gethin. Peter Jones was to remain an All Black for many years.

Ray Williams, a schoolteacher, was playing centre three-quarter this day. Ray taught many a rugby genius, including Barry John, Gareth Davies and Robert Morgan, all great Welsh internationals, and can remember sitting in the changing room before the game, thinking, 'Thank goodness I'm playing for Llanelli today and not New Zealand.' Ray could hear the singing in the old wooden stand above him, a chorus of voices, a powerful sound. 'There was plenty of *hwyl* and we could feel the vibrations,' explained Ray, who recalls:

> We took the match seriously and, beforehand, we had committee members and other respected rugby men talking us through our plans. We thought we were in with a shout of winning, but, on the day, New Zealand had a strong pack of forwards and a special movement which we should have stopped. It resulted in a couple of scores and this was the difference.

In the evening, Ray remembers the two teams being treated to a meal by Llanelli Rugby Club. The New Zealanders were fine men and good company; they mixed well with the Welsh.

'We had speeches and I remember bottles of locally brewed Buckleys best bitter were laid out on the tables for everyone,' said Ray. 'In those days we went to the Ritz Ball Room after matches and this is where we ended up that night.'

During the match, Ray, a strong runner, was kept busy trying to keep the score down, the match finishing 17–3, this being four tries to one. The All Black forwards were highly effective, big men, always in command, but also labelled as being over-robust by some sections of the crowd. Indeed, this suggestion endorsed comments made in earlier tour matches that some aspects of their play, such as rucking, were severe. Peter Evans, the blond Llanelli captain, would hear of no such thing; *The New Zealand Herald* of November 20th quotes him as saying, 'It was a hard game, as clean as a whistle', but others, including match reporters, felt differently. 'Cut out the rough stuff,' was one comment, 'We could dish it out, too,' was another: hard-hitting words from domestic reports that were relayed to All Black supporters in the *New Zealand Herald* days later. Clearly, such accusations were adding another dimension to these matches, which, keen enough already, had now become compulsive viewing.

Of course, the adverse press comments were nothing new. Dave Gallaher's players attracted public scrutiny in 1905 just as Stan Dean's team did in 1924. Mr Dean stated that his side had often been reminded of its weaknesses and vulnerability and were told that they would get beaten. It was little different for Jack Manchester's men years later. Eric Tindill, who played on that later tour, can remember some 'brutally frank' comments from a few writers who 'ripped into' his team[30] – despite Eric being greatly enthused by the welcome his men received on their travels and personally shielded by the praise

---

30   *New Zealand Herald*, November 19th 1953.

he received for his drop goals. Clearly, changing attitudes and tolerances were producing different lines of reporting – so it was 'Look out All Blacks' from now on, whether at Stradey Park, St Helen's or elsewhere!

The dance that Ray mentioned at the Ritz Ballroom following the Llanelli game, was one of the social highlights of the tour. Situated in the middle of the town and only a walk from the rugby ground, the Ritz was, around this time, a popular dance venue. On a Saturday night it was the place to go, an ideal meeting spot where young people congregated from miles around. Of course, it was an honour if the All Blacks walked through its front doors: so, as can be imagined, this was another night to remember, ending all too soon when the All Blacks returned to the Seabank Hotel, Porthcawl.

Preparing for the following Saturday's match at a jam-packed, all-singing Cardiff Arms Park was another daunting prospect, fuelled, of course, by these latest media comments concerning over-fiery play. Cardiff, now one of the leading teams in Britain, possessed forwards who drove forever onwards whilst being complemented by a lethal back division. Captained by Bleddyn Williams and supported by the likes of Cliff Morgan and Rex Willis, the Cardiff players were themselves potential world-beaters.

Quickly into the action, the home side scored a try after six minutes, near the goal posts, still bare, unprotected and dangerous during these years. The conversion was a formality, soon followed by a penalty to the visitors and another try to the home side, taking the score to 8–3. Now, with one hour remaining, the Cardiff players defended for their place in history as the All Blacks battered their way towards the line, determined to strike back. But they were denied; Cardiff hung on for victory, an amazing achievement which meant that the Arms Park had again proved to be the downfall of the New Zealand national team. At full-time, the crowd erupted. 'We will be back and we will fight every inch of the journey,' said Mr J. N. Millard, the New Zealand tour manager, to the *Western Mail* and indeed they would. But, in the meantime, floods of praise from all corners of the world descended upon Bleddyn Williams' triumphant men, such was the shared joy of the occasion. A feel of this exuberance can be seen in Bleddyn Williams' papers at the Glamorgan Archives, Cardiff.

After performing in front of an increased fifty-six thousand crowd at the Arms Park, the All Blacks would entertain another forty thousand people at St Helen's a few weeks later, a ground the New Zealanders knew better than most ever since David Gallaher's Originals performed there on two occasions in 1905. Of course, time had moved on, but nothing had altered the habit of a lifetime as far as the 'All Whites' were concerned, in undergoing thorough preparation for every match.

In hoping to emulate the famous victory of 1935, the committee had been working diligently and, as this was the biggest social spectacle of the year, members of the local supporter's club were also alert to making the most of the occasion. Together, they were arranging a raffle, with a treasured souvenir being available for the winner. In a short minute from the management committee of the Swansea Cricket and Football Club held at the Pavilion, Bryn Road, in Swansea on September 4th 1953, a motion was carried to help the supporters club to obtain a rugby ball (this being the prize) signed by the All Blacks, whose captain was to draw the winning ticket on the day.

Apart from a fierce onslaught by the All Blacks, and equally tenacious tackling by Swansea, the game fell short of expected standards on a day when tour captain, Bob Stuart, was rested. Nevertheless, Swansea secured a historic result, drawing 6–6 after the tourists had seemingly kicked away far too much possession of the ball when making ground for their big forwards to exploit. It was a case of two hard-earned tries for New Zealand cancelled out by two long-range penalties for the home side. These were struck by John Faull, a young centre three-quarter in his first season with the club, who impressed teammate Horace Phillips when he heard 'a distinct singing sound as the boot struck the leather.'[31] Horace was standing only yards away as John's first attempt was sent fifty or more yards sweetly between the two uprights.

Horace, a fast wing three-quarter, would have enjoyed the celebrations that evening – just as John Faull did, following a similar dream entry onto the big stage as experienced by Messrs Tanner and Davies eighteen years earlier. But, as for the All Blacks, scheduled that week to attend a concert in their honour at the Grand Pavilion, Porthcawl, no manner of social events would correct the frustration of this poor result. They had been expected to win and to win it well. A disappointing draw was another setback for Mr Millard and Bob Stuart and a major concern as they prepared to face the Welsh at the Arms Park in a week's time.

---

31   Swansea Rugby Club History, www.swansearfc.co.uk, accessed March 31st 2013.

What a win for Wales as Ticket Touts lose out

As the All Blacks slipped quietly into a week of training and practice at Porthcawl, two pieces of news raised their spirits. Firstly, the team's official flag, missing from the pavilion of Swansea Rugby Club since the previous match, had been found. It would, after all, be flying the team colours from Cardiff Arms Park in the next match, just as it had done at rugby venues earlier visited on tour. Secondly, Bob Stuart, captain, was declared fit and would lead the side. His presence would lift the men as was proven when he took charge of the week's most demanding training run before explaining, behind closed doors, what was needed to beat the Welsh.

For this match, media attention was sky-high. Over many years, live radio commentaries had been described as the next best thing to standing on the terraces, as gifted commentators painted a picture for their audience. One such master with a microphone in hand was Winston McCarthy, a man from Wellington but well known in Wales. He had played both rugby union and league before injury ended his career, and had become the voice of rugby in his native land.

It is said that the eloquence of his commentary when describing Jim Sherratt's seventy-yard dash in the Wales versus New Zealand Army game of 1946 prompted excited New Zealanders to run outside beckoning neighbours to tune in, despite this being in the middle of the night! Winston, who was fast on the way to becoming a national legend – and his career is celebrated today at the New Zealand Sports Hall of Fame in Dunedin – used to invite his audiences to judge for themselves whether or not a goal was successful. 'Lissaaaannnnn!' [Listen!],' he called out loudly, before confirming the crowd's reaction by adding 'It's a Gooaaaallll!' Apparently, those sitting in tight circles around crackling radios and straining for his every word were so mesmerised by his rich outpourings that they hardly dared to breathe.

As the day of the match drew nearer, Winston, now engaged with All Black commentaries the world over, was preparing to view the action from his usual bird's-eye seat in the grandstand. The *New Zealand Herald* of December 16th 1953 stated that his words would be transmitted live from 2.15 a.m. on Sunday (there being, of course, a twelve-hour time difference between the two countries) and further snippets would be repeated throughout the morning for those less inclined to have their sleep disrupted. Meanwhile, Wales' *Western Mail* was responding to increasing instances of booing on the terraces by urging spectators to behave better, particularly when visitors were taking kicks at goal.

Of course, television coverage was an even greater break-through, although up until now match recordings had been shown as edited highlights well after the actual event. This allowed viewers to see the best action in their homes, without affecting the day's crowd attendances. However, this epic Wales–New Zealand encounter was to be broadcasted live, attracting a flow of opinion from across the country. What could be better for home birds not wanting or able to go to the live event? Likewise, who could doubt the concern of traditionalists worried about the long term-effect on the game? Those opposing changes felt that floodgates might open to more television sporting coverage at the expense of crowd attendances – and what then for the future of sport? Giving strength to this argument was the fact that for the first time since Wales and New Zealand scrummed down together, a glut of spare match tickets was available.

Understandably, the *Western Mail* wanted to shed light on

the matter: confirming that, yes, many unused tickets were handed back to policemen before this latest Wales–New Zealand match and that those feeling the blow most were ticket touts, some unable to give away their usually precious assets in this darkest of black market days. But, this aside, interest in the crunch fixture was, as usual, unquestionable, supporting a recent suggestion from the New Zealand Rugby Union in Wellington that the Welsh should travel across the world to continue this amazing rugby story. In many ways it was surprising that this had not happened before and Cardiff's victory had prompted Christchurch Round Table members to send a message of congratulations to their brethren in a city that was gaining prestige and soon to become the capital of Wales.

In the match programme, Rhys Gabe, Welsh centre three-quarter, gave his account of the big day in 1905. He explained the New Zealanders' shock from the moment their 'scrimmage' formation was challenged early in the match. This was done by standing two players either side of Wales' two-man front row, so that one of them could conveniently 'jump in' as a third member. In a three-versus-two situation – especially when the third man was joining at the most advantageous side – the Welsh secured the loose head every time. This was regardless of who put in the ball, a ploy that was allowed and won invaluable scrum ball on the day.

Rhys mentioned that the move providing the winning score was suggested in a training session on the Thursday before the game, when it was practised repeatedly. Then, describing the Deans tryline incident, he stated that the Welsh defence was so 'nearly pierced'. However, Rhys remained convinced throughout his life that Deans' effort was, most certainly, not a score. He said:

When I brought down Deans, I thought the ball was on the line and he had scored. But when I found him struggling to go forward I naturally pulled him back. I knew then that he had not reached the line.

Forty-eight years later Cardiff's victorious captain, Bleddyn Williams, was leading his team onto the field. Bleddyn's job had been to prime his forwards for the daunting task of denying New Zealand's big and robust pack the ball. But a performance of grit and determination, as epitomised by Gareth Griffiths returning to the field following a shoulder dislocation, meant the score was tied at 8–8 with just minutes to go. It needed a tiebreaker, and it came in the form of a cross kick.

Having seized possession of the ball near the left touchline, playing towards the river end, Clem Thomas checked his balance before hoofing the leather towards the open flank where two sprinters faced each other. It could go either way: for an unkind bounce could win or lose the game. This time the rugby gods favoured Ken Jones, as they ghosted the ball into his lap for him to scorch over the New Zealand line and plant the ball firmly on the grass. As for Ron Jarden, the All Black winger with similar hopes of scoring at the opposite end, this amounted to a double dose of hard luck.

No one could have envisaged such drama and neither could Bleddyn Williams have dreamt about a second victory over the All Blacks within a few weeks. John Gwilliam, who, approaching the end of his own remarkable international career, was one of Wales' heroic forwards, admitted all these years later to feeling sorry for the All Black winger: 'It was bad luck for New Zealand,' said John, who remembers Ron Jarden 'lying on the ground waving his arms in despair'.

Playing that day was local favourite Cliff Morgan, and in his *Beyond the Fields of Play* he relates that this victory sparked an annual reunion between the players of both Cardiff and New Zealand. Convened at 9 p.m. in some central social venue in Cardiff where the men could enjoy a meal, the two captains later relayed their best wishes down the telephone line as the New Zealanders likewise sat down to breakfast.

Cliff, who had expected to receive a pass at the point when Clem Thomas kicked the ball across field, also mentioned that Ivor Jones, one of Wales' former forwards, but on duty this day as a touch judge – appearing in a 'blazer, grey trousers tucked into his socks, flag in hand' – was proud to reveal that he had played a part in the try. In loaded words he said, 'It was I who instructed Clem to kick across the field'!

The likes of 'King' Ivor were big allies to the former teams: old heads or father figures on the periphery of play, giving a few quiet words of encouragement when the side needed it most. This day Ivor did not disappoint in front of a crowd that included Sir Frederick Doidge, a High Commissioner for New Zealand, and Lady Doidge, as well as Lord Moran, Sir Winston Churchill's personal physician. As fate would have it, the *Western Mail* reports that on this day of Lord Moran's attendance, the great man, miles away, needed medical attention, having burnt his left hand when inadvertently placing his cigar near a box of matches. It is by strange coincidence that Allan Elsom, New Zealand's wing three-quarter against Wales, also had a cigarette burn in the after-match reception, a rare achievement for a fit young man who did not smoke! But, this did not stop him moving on with the team as they aimed to recover winning ways, in amongst the picture-postcard scenery of Abertillery, hitherto a happy hunting ground for the All Blacks.

Bob Scott's bumper goals and
Winston McCarthy's sacks of Coal

It was a new-look New Zealand side that was called to duty on a windy day in a Welsh valley. As rugby fans walked the narrow channels down to the playing field of Abertillery Park, police cars and motorbikes patrolled the crowd with another useful invention: the radio-telephone, an essential aid to communication that, having arrived at sporting arenas, was destined to stay. Inside the ground, the band of the 2nd Monmouthshire Regiment led the singing, all hoping for a feast of running rugby and high scores. They were not disappointed, although all five touch-downs, came from the visitors, whilst the usual forward charges added to the spectacle.

The sight of large men rushing downfield in tight little huddles with the ball at their feet had been part of the game throughout the years. Commonly known as dribbling, this was a controlled attack on an opponent's defence, calling for basic footballing skills from the forwards and being rather difficult to stop, especially in the mud and rain. Indeed, it took a brave man to dive into the studs of five or more pairs of leather boots to steal the ball, especially when such footwear belonged to the mighty All Blacks. Yet this day, the combined valley clubs were playing the tourists at their own game, and doing rather well.

In the heartland of valley rugby, this was another big occasion, one that Roy Lewis, a stalwart for the 'Steelmen' of Ebbw Vale, would not miss. In later years Roy was to prepare programme articles and newspaper reports for the club, whilst all aspects of the game interested him. Only days earlier as a spectator in Cardiff in 1953 Roy had witnessed Wales' latest win, making him proud of his own family's Triple Crown of All Black victories: uncle Elgar *witnessing* the match in 1905, father Wilfred witnessing the same in 1935 before Roy's day arrived eighteen years later, making it three in a row for the Lewises at the home of Welsh rugby.

'We used to run special trains to the internationals,' Roy explained to me recently when reflecting upon the good old days, 'and as soon as we jumped on board at Ebbw Vale and found a compartment, the rugby talk was rich.' Roy was opposite the try line where Ken Jones scored late on, alongside the old South Stand in the so-called 'Cowshed.' 'That is where it used to happen,' he smiled. 'Wales scored at the death and the place went wild. This is when someone behind me jumped high in excitement, landing on my back: and he, a policeman!'

Before this latest All Black match in Abertillery in 1953, Roy would see the home team players around town. 'Good luck on Wednesday,' he said to them, 'see you up in the park.' Roy remembers travelling the half-hour journey over the mountain in a Jones bus, crawling up the hills but feeling many a pothole along the way. 'We were all packed in like sardines,' said Roy, 'half of us smoking, and the conductor having problems trying to take the money, but we thought it was wonderful. There weren't many cars around in those days and the bus was the only way some of us could get to Abertillery, and it never let us down.

Roy knew that this game on Wednesday December 23rd 1953, two days before Christmas, was the career highlight for local men of Abertillery and Ebbw Vale tackling a leading world team on their own ground. 'It was just terrific,' he said, whilst musing over the problems of choosing one team to face Bob Stuart's tourists from two neighbouring clubs.

Communal rivalry was a never-ending challenge in a country that had been afflicted throughout the years by selection issues of an 'East versus West' variety. This had brought disagreements, squabbles and resentment – albeit hardly different from the division caused by the Cook Strait which separates North Island and South Island in New Zealand, and which had split rugby issues from the days of Dave Gallaher and the Originals, and even earlier still. Roy continues:

> There was terrific rivalry, but it was healthy for the game. In the valleys we were packed full of strong clubs – and every one of us was a selector, for club and country! We had our favourites; we knew who should and shouldn't be playing.

Roy remembers that Abertillery Park looked a welcoming scene for the All Blacks game. He stood on the open terrace, cut into the bottom of the mountain, looking across the field at the grandstand and an expectant crowd. 'The All Blacks are always special visitors and there was the usual hype about this game', he said, before adding, 'And they were beatable in those days; most Welsh sides felt they were in with a chance.' But, at the close of play, the win was emphatic, Roy seeing a scoreboard that read 22–3 for the visitors, an enjoyable run-out that saw the All Blacks back to winning ways.

As Welshmen took comfort from their earlier Test victory and looked forward to a busy Home Nations campaign, thoughts turned to the traditional friendly matches being played over this same festive season, popular fixtures involving visitors from beyond the borders, when it was not unusual to see a player or two swapping teams for the day's action. Cardiff hero Jack Matthews would be no exception, running out against his own club, Cardiff, in a match with London Wasps, an action so typical of the good sportsmanship prevailing at the time. Meanwhile, the New Zealanders were heading into England and then crossing the Irish Sea before they would return to Wales.

Another founder member of the Welsh Rugby Union was Pontypool Rugby Club, which despite struggling to keep going in the difficult late nineteenth century was reformed and rejuvenated at the start of the next century to great effect. Pontypool town had experienced two unforgettable fixtures with New Zealand sides to date, the club team beat the Māori visitors 6–5 in 1927 and a Monmouthshire team defeating the New Zealand Army, 15–0 in 1946. A proper showdown with the All Blacks was long overdue and was now to take place on January 16th 1954, with a little help from friends and neighbours, Cross Keys.

For this, their final flurry in Wales of the 1953/54 tour, the All Blacks stayed in the Queen's Hotel, Newport, a fine Victorian structure built in the 1860s less than a decade before internationals kicked off for two halves (of about 50 minutes each) with twenty players on each side, and two referees (but known as umpires), one from each participating country. After travelling from Ireland on the ferry and then by train from Fishguard to Newport, the New Zealanders were met on the platform of the local train station by members of Newport Rugby Club, this being more convenient for all concerned. It was evident that the two sets of players were keen to see each other, especially Ken Jones, captain of Newport, and Ron Jarden, a close friend and rival sprinter. Accompanying them was the New Zealand radio commentator Winston McCarthy, now sporting a warm winter hat. The *Western Mail* of December 24th 1953 told its readers that Christmas had been kind to Winston, who had, by entering various raffles, won a turkey and half a ton of Welsh coal, much of which had ended up on the home fires of Rex Willis, Cardiff's scrum half, saving Winston the need to cart it around with him on tour.

The match between the two valley giants and the All Blacks took place at Pontypool Park on the day England defeated Wales at Twickenham. In front of a crowd of twenty thousand, Allan Elsom, the tall, slim All Black winger, ran freely for two tries although denied a third by teammate – and touch judge – Jim Fitzgerald. But it was the redoubtable Bob Scott at full back who stole the show, a player who kicked barefooted goals in practice and was now converting drop goals with great aplomb. His speciality was to seize upon desperate defensive clearances around the half-way line, before returning the ball smack bang between the posts. This day was no different.

By the mid-1950s, Newport had long ago said goodbye to the most industrious days, when coal and iron were carried by canal to its docks. But the playing fields made available to the local people by Lord Tredegar,[32] with the town corporation's blessing, were now serving up rugby football of the finest quality for its loyal band of spectators. Enjoying support from a rich hinterland of feeder clubs, Newport was riding high, overjoyed to be renewing battles with the All Blacks. Perhaps victory would come at the fourth time of asking.

Mike Dams, Newport's club historian today, is a lifetime spectator of the 'Black and Ambers', whose memorable 9–3 victory against the South African Springboks, way back in 1912, reminded everyone at the time that Newport was a club capable of challenging and beating the best teams. Local support would be strong and the All Blacks recognised the keenness of the contest awaiting them at Rodney Parade. Mike has many recollections of visits from major touring

---

32   A Brief history of Rodney Parade, Newport: Cricket Archives, web site as at March 31st 2013.

sides, when members and followers of rival 'valley' clubs – who all wanted to beat the Newport 'townies' – descended upon the old ground:

> Every now and again the rivalry was forgotten! Many came to Rodney Parade hoping to witness a historic win, especially when you only got to see major touring sides every few years. In the old days, the bus station was in Dock Street and we would see crowds walking over the one and only town bridge, crossing the River Usk on the way to the ground. Inside Rodney Parade we had the usual bit of banter between spectators at the Corporation Road side – known as the 'Corpa Road' or 'Bob Bank' – which was slightly cheaper to enter, and those who stood in the so-called 'posh' enclosure beneath the Hazell Stand.

For this particular match on January 21st 1954, Mike recalls Newport taking a gamble by playing talented outside half, Roy Burnett, whilst still recovering from a leg injury. Roy was from a local rugby family which felt sadness and loss in 1950 when Roy's brother, Doug, a talented centre for Abercarn, was among many passengers who died tragically when the plane returning spectators from the Ireland–Wales match failed as it landed in Llandow, Glamorgan. Now, on this most important day of his rugby career, Roy had hoped that he would comfortably last the match, but he struggled from the early stages, as Mike again explains:

> Roy had a strained Achilles tendon and was severely handicapped from the beginning. Try as he did, he couldn't get his line going as everyone had hoped. Then we lost Malcolm Quartley from the back-row with a cut head. Now a man down and against a juggernaut pack, our men were up against it.

Mike remembers that the Newport forwards rose magnificently to the occasion, inspired by Leighton Jenkins, a young student then but later a Newport legend and Welsh international. 'The game could have gone either way,' added Mike. 'It finished one try apiece, and with better kicking we'd have won.' This 11–6 victory was, however, a welcome result for All Black captain Bob Stuart; he could not have been more content. 'We have never run into such enthusiastic autograph hunters,' he said, his team happily obliging all who produced signature books or programmes for signing in their keenness. He then praised the 'give-and-take spirit' of the match, before his manager, Mr Millard, gave a signed photograph of the All Blacks to local captain, Ken Jones.[33]

Fifty miles west along the old trunk road, Neath, a vibrant rugby town, was waiting for its own chance against the All Blacks. Many years had passed since the New Zealand Army team triumphed at the Gnoll in 1919, as did their later compatriots in 1945: both close encounters against determined local men. Now a combined Neath–Aberavon side, captained and coached by the legendary Rees Stephens, was the next in a line of difficult opponents for the All Blacks to overcome. The home players had prepared well and, following a training run, and in accordance with accepted practice, arrangements were made for the half-back combination from the two clubs to develop a working relationship beforehand in a full match for Neath.

At 11.30 a.m. on match day, the All Blacks were given a civic reception by the mayors of both towns in the Gwyn Hall, Neath. Then the tourists were taken to the famous Castle Hotel – mentioned earlier for its part in the game's history – for a lunch hosted by Neath Rotary Club before making

33 *Western Mail and South Wales News*, January 22nd, 1954.

their way to the muddy playing field of the Gnoll. Outside the ground, programmes were sold with a warm message for the New Zealanders from the rector of Neath, T. A. Roberts, who had served alongside their countrymen in Gallipoli some forty years earlier. Remembering many of the 'greats' who had visited Wales over the years, the minister opened his heart to the men in black, on account of past rugby and world events. 'We welcome you sincerely, gladly, almost madly,' he said. 'May you be worthy of your great traditions'. He added that he hoped that the game would live up to its high sporting expectation – sentiments surely seconded by all.

Early in the game Bob Scott pounced on a defensive clearance to strike a 45-yard drop goal. During a contest that saw Neath prop Courtney Meredith thundering across the line for a try, New Zealand triumphed 11–5, two tries to one before being officially welcomed to a formal reception in the newly built clubhouse alongside the Gnoll field. Later, a dinner was held at the Castle Hotel, before the evening ended with a dance arranged by members of Neath Rugby Supporters' Club.

When, one month later, New Zealand returned to Cardiff to play the Barbarians, a crowd of fifty-four thousand was present to bid their visitors goodbye. In a match remembered for running rugby, the home side scored a converted try to go in front – before the visitors struck back, crossing the line for four special tries of their own. This afternoon's entertainment would not have been complete without a long-range drop goal from Bob Scott, which duly arrived from the half-way line. At the end of play, the scoreboard read 19–5 and this is when the stadium witnessed touching scenes as recorded by J. B. G. Thomas of the *Western Mail*. In honour of the New Zealanders, the band played *Now is the Hour*, a favourite song amongst Māori people and this day sung by the capacity crowd. On the field the players, next singing *Auld Lang Syne*, linked arms in a big circle and moved inwards – rather like a pub scene at the countdown to a New Year – and in the midst of this party mood, there were chants from the terraces of 'We want Scott' (the drop goal expert), who was soon hoisted onto willing shoulders, as was his captain, Bob Stuart.

It was a fitting end to a memorable tour, readily acknowledged by All Black team manager Norman Millard in the after-match reception. 'Tell the people of Wales that we are very proud to have won at Cardiff Arms Park,' he said tactfully, before his party left to play in France, Canada and America on the way home. But what he didn't say is probably what he really meant: 'Look out Wales when we next return!'

The Woes of a Newport win as Welshmen Sing their side to Victory

The defeats suffered in Wales had stung the All Blacks and by the time Bob Stuart's team had returned to their homeland strategies were already being devised as to how they would beat the Welsh at the Arms Park next time round. Tactics, perhaps, that would soon be tested on Ronnie Dawson's 1959 British Lions.

At this time, men such as Bryn Meredith, Malcolm Thomas, Haydn Morgan, Roddy Evans and Rhys Williams were at the top of their game and anxious to lay down Welsh markers on New Zealand soil. Packing their bags for a four months' tour with the elite of British rugby was the highlight of their sporting lives. These were exciting and challenging days for the Welsh tourists, and every man wished to fly the flag of his home town and rugby team. One such man was Rhys (R. H.) Williams, the 6 foot 4 inches second row forward whose Royal Air Force discipline and determination was to make him one of Wales' greatest ever forwards. This would put the little village of Cwmllynfell on the world map, whilst adding to Llanelli Rugby Club's rich stock.

Rhys' widow, Megan, met her husband in the town's Ritz Ballroom after a home match in Llanelli when Rhys was twenty-four. By then Rhys had been playing for the club for some five seasons during which time Megan is aware that the team occasionally changed at The Salutation, where a bus would be on hand to take the players to and from the ground. In the late 1950s, Megan remembers watching Rhys as he drove into Stradey car park to be greeted by faithful fans, before 'peeling himself' out of his little Austin A35. Megan viewed this spectacle whilst sitting in the stand, always amused to see Rhys, such a big man, getting out of such a small car. Megan realised from a young age just how big rugby was in Rhys' life, and how she came to accept that they had to be apart longer than they both wished:

> When Rhys was based at RAF St Athan [in the Vale of Glamorgan], I only saw him on Wednesdays, and on Saturday evenings if he happened to be playing at home. Time was precious and when we went into town for a meal, Llanelli supporters kept coming up to him: 'Beth ddigwyddodd dydd Sadwrn, Rhys?' [What happened last Saturday, Rhys?] they asked. 'Beth am y gêm nesaf yn Abertawe? [What about the next game in Swansea?] . . . I couldn't believe it at the time; I felt the town owned him!

Megan told me that when Rhys had to stay away overnight, he packed a holdall with his belongings, whilst carrying all rugby kit in a little boot bag, along with his other 'bits and pieces' – a far cry from the volumes of sporting gear and accessories that are carried around by our internationals of today. 'I have a picture of him boarding a train with these in his arms,' Megan told me. 'Sitting in the carriage with a broad smile is Ray Williams, another Llanelli favourite, while Carwyn James, nearby, kept a close eye on everyone.'

Megan explained that for the tour to Australia and New Zealand, the British Lions had a training camp in Eastbourne before they flew out. 'I was given a concise itinerary so that

I could track Rhys' movements,' said Megan. Rhys, just like all top-class internationals, loved travelling around New Zealand. 'And, for my part,' added Megan, 'I made sure that letters were waiting for him as he went on his way.'

Rhys distinguished himself in the eyes of the New Zealand public on this demanding tour in 1959, but nonetheless the All Blacks won the series by three tests to one. As a result of the hard matches and pulsating action, and especially as the Lions won the last Test 9–6, prospects for a fifth All Blacks tour to Britain in 1963 could not have been more exciting. Captained by the quietly determined and proven Wilson Whineray, the team arrived in Britain in October intent upon making their mark early on, which they did with two comfortable wins in England. But, when they arrived in Wales for the next fixture, fifteen well-prepared men in black-and-amber jerseys had rather different plans of their own.

Although Newport had by now beaten the Australian Wallabies in 1957, adding to their remarkable Springboks triumph of 1912, most people felt that toppling the All Blacks was a little too much to hope for. As for the New Zealand public, who knew of the Welsh ability to cause a surprise, they were reluctant to underestimate the Welsh. In the newspapers, reporters were going one step further, acknowledging a mysterious force that had, so far, plagued All Black teams over the years. Better expressed as the Welsh *hwyl*, Terry McLean, writing for the *New Zealand Herald* on October 30th 1963, described this as being 'a mystic spiritual force' driving Welshmen onwards when representing their country. Then, outlining its effects in a past match in Cardiff, when the capacity crowd started to sing, he stated that every member of the Wales team was 'stirred to a skill and performance beyond all understanding.'

And so it was in Newport on Wednesday October 30th

1963: the home team rose to new levels of sporting achievement by winning by a solitary score to nil. Little did the All Blacks imagine such scenes of Welsh happiness when, before the match, they settled for a peaceful lunch in the Westgate Hotel. But that drop goal by John (Dick) Uzzell on a wet and miserable afternoon caused painful memories for rugby followers in New Zealand. Mike Dams, Newport's rugby historian, was there, having watched rugby at Rodney Parade since he was a young boy. He recalls:

> When I arrived for this match at my usual time, the ground was so full that I had to move further downfield. But, by sheer luck, I was more or less level with Dick (John) Uzzell when he lined up his famous kick. I remember thinking 'Why are you dropping for goal? We could have scored a try,' but we were all happy with the outcome. John scored only a handful of 'drops' in his career for Newport, but this one really counted. There is a painting in the clubhouse of the ball soaring high between the posts – but in truth it struggled over; it was definitely not one of his better efforts.

A try-saving tackle can be every bit as valuable as making a score. History has already recorded the name of John Uzzell as one of rugby's great sporting achievers, yet it was the fortitude of another young man who raced across the field to bundle Bill Davis, the All Black winger, into touch, yards from the corner flag, that, without doubt, saved the day for Newport at the final whistle. The tackler was Alan Thomas, young, with boyish, handsome looks and blond hair, but already battled-hardened as a wing forward and someone who knew how to survive in the top-class game. Originally from Beckenham in Kent, Alan was, on the strength of his performance for Newport, to win his first Welsh cap against the All Blacks only weeks later. In a conversation, Alan recalls the words of his manager at Penallta Colliery, near Ystrad Mynach: 'Don't come into work, Alan. It's a big match.' Was there ever such an understatement?

Alan explained that about two years earlier he had represented Pontypool and Cross Keys against South Africa. They were a big, physical team and he bounced off one of the forwards in a tackle. Now, as he faced the New Zealand haka, he vowed there would be no such repeat of that incident. Alan remembers the noise being enormous throughout, a chorus of *Bread of Heaven* echoing loudly around the ground near the end. Beating the All Blacks was the greatest moment in his sporting life, a fantastic achievement – 'especially as they had the likes of Colin Meads and Earle Kirton in their side,' added Alan, 'and a back-row of Kelvin Tremain, Brian Lochore and Waka Nathan.' Later, the players were taken to the top floor veranda of the clubhouse, where Alan had not been before. 'All I can say is that I'd never witnessed scenes like it,' he said, 'there were people everywhere, all happy, shouting, cheering us, thrilled about our win.' Alan continues:

> That night, there was a dance in the club. The jive was a big thing then and the All Blacks were having a good go – when a few of their forwards took me into a corner: 'Al [Alan], we play the back-row differently to you; tell us about it.' Of course, having had a drink or two, I explained the way we did things – then it dawned on me later that Wales still had to play them in a few weeks' time!

Just as Alan had lived the rugby dream from a young age, so also had his namesake, Malcolm Thomas, who, having earlier represented Wales at schoolboy age, had by now emigrated to New Zealand where, continuing his rugby career, he worked as a teacher. Malcolm, whose own grandson, Aled de Malmanche, became an All Black in 2009, can remember stirring early the next morning, anxious to know how the Newport match had gone. 'I got up for the six o'clock morning news,' said Malcolm, 'knowing I'd hear the result and I'll never forget the way it was delivered. The newsreader could hardly say the words; it was too painful, as if announcing a recent bereavement, funereal: "The result of the All Blacks match in Wales is . . . Newport 3 . . . New Zealand . . . nil."'

Half a century later Mike Dams is extremely proud of Newport's achievement and, if anything, he is disappointed that his side for some reason has not received greater credit from the media over the years. The fact remains that Wilson Whineray's side lost to ten uncapped players with the remainder sharing no more than twenty-four caps between them. This was to be the only loss the All Blacks suffered on that tour. That day the home team was inspired and could have hit double figures, Glynn Davidge being absolutely fearless. He put his body on the line and took a pounding from the New Zealand pack for his work on the floor. 'He was magnificent,' said Mike, 'always the last man up.'

'But could he have been killing the ball?' I asked. 'Was he preventing its release?'

'Well, he was certainly holding on to it as long as he could,' admitted Mike after a lot of prodding, also confirming that this had been a directive from the coaching advisor, Bryn Meredith. Mike's confessions do, at least, explain a statement made by the player himself on the fortieth anniversary of the great win. Mike explains:

> On the Saturday after the game Glynn was due to play for Newport against Ebbw Vale. In the dressing room the referee noted his cut and bruised body and insisted in no uncertain terms that if he did take to the field, he would send him straight off.

There were some battered bodies amongst the New Zealanders this day as well, one belonging to the All Blacks' captain who, in a later memoir entitled *Wilson Whineray remembers Newport* (held at Newport Rugby Football Club), shares his thoughts from the moment the players came off the field. 'I had somehow found my way through the milling masses to our room,' he said, before removing his boots and 'mud soaked jersey' and putting on 'a warm sweater.' Hearing great celebrations coming from the Newport players, he walked into their dressing room still in his rugby socks.

At that moment there was gradual silence as he admitted his side had been 'outplayed'. Indeed, speaking for his team, he said that 'in fairness Newport should have won by a further three points, [if] full back Ray Cheney's kick [had] not hit the crossbar and bounced away.' He acknowledged that his team had been defeated by 'dedicated individuals' who were 'wonderfully prepared', and he saw Newport's achievement as being 'a reminder of one of the great truths in sport and indeed in life, that dedication, purpose and enduring resolve usually lead on to victory.' These are magnanimous words, from one of life's 'winners' at the moment of his team's defeat.

Before crossing into Wales the All Blacks had attended a sporting luncheon at London's Savoy Hotel, as they had done in 1935, as well as a function at the Royal Pavilion, Brighton, while some players had been invited to Arundel Castle by the Duke and Duchess of Norfolk. But it was whilst travelling back to their Porthcawl headquarters, after having watched Llanelli playing Cardiff in a midweek match, that they ran into one of their most memorable welcomes. Quietly stepping into a pub called 'The Star', the men were treated to a reception that neither they nor the locals could forget.

In an article found in the *The New Zealand Herald*, October 31st 1963, headed 'All Black "Spies" have Merry

Time at Village', we read of the fun enjoyed amidst 'gales of laughter', autograph-signing, the haka and rousing singing, when a small group of the All Blacks walked through the door. Entering the little pub at around 10 p.m., their presence sparked one of the happiest evenings in the locality for many a year. It was certainly too good to be true for an elderly gentleman, bursting to make an impression: 'The 75-year old sang his song, very tunefully, too, and had to be prevented from singing some more . . .' reports the *Herald*.

The Llanelli–Cardiff game had been a floodlit fixture, a novel experience for the New Zealanders, but, by now, a regular midweek feature in Wales which gave a somewhat new complexion to Welsh rugby. However, more matches were taking their toll on the playing fields as the All Blacks soon found out at Aberavon in their next fixture.

Entering the field on an afternoon that had earlier seen thunder, lightning and lashing rain, a close to capacity crowd witnessed a mudbath as two powerful packs slogged it out in atrocious conditions. And with only minutes to go, a strong Aberavon–Neath side were holding their heavier opponents to a six-all draw, defending their line. But to the disappointment of the home players and fans, a late score settled the contest in favour of the All Blacks, 11–6. Playing at full back that day, and in outstanding form, was Neath's Grahame Hodgson, who still feels the sadness of the final score. Grahame was asked for his thoughts as he left the field:

> I was not in this world. I was emotionally disturbed about the last try and I had also taken a heavy hit under a high ball. I was catching and kicking everything that day. Then, with twenty minutes to go, I was shaken so badly that I couldn't remember a lot.

But, Grahame can recall Don Clarke and Wilson Whineray escorting him off the field. Also he remembers being one of the last two to leave the shower where he stood in tears. 'I was crying like a baby,' he said, 'I was that disappointed at the time.' Grahame, who missed the reception after the match, told me that he actually enjoyed playing in such dreadful conditions:

> The funny thing is that I have always enjoyed playing in the mud. I believe that a player needs a high level of technical expertise to play well with a wet ball. When I was growing up in Ogmore Vale – where my grandfather just missed out on the New Zealand Army match of 1919 – the ball kept disappearing over the fence and into the river. By the time we got it back it was so heavy that it was like kicking a lead balloon, but this prepared me well.

Being involved in such close encounters and forever looking to improve their match performances, the All Black management was now assessing the pros and cons of staying at Porthcawl, where the Seabank Hotel was a familiar and friendly base. Although motorways had arrived in Britain, and were extending further day by day, the M4 across the southern base of Wales was still a few years away. This meant that journeys to places such as Newport were difficult drives, along packed A-roads, a state of affairs that could cause fatigue and loss of form and which was being monitored as the tour progressed.

For all its natural beauty, Abertillery is not the most accessible place when twenty thousand spectators are converging on its park. And although a number of special trains had been arranged for this next All Blacks encounter against a combined Abertillery–Ebbw Vale team, there were more road delays and traffic jams to contend with. With many fans arriving late, the match began in lacklustre fashion and, despite Haydn Morgan, Alun Pask and Denzil Williams appearing for the home team, little could prevent a forward-driven All Blacks side pressing onward to victory, 13–0.

Amongst the in-form players on this still winter's day was fullback Don Clarke, who converted kicks from all around the field. He was, perhaps, feeling more agile after his much-publicised diet 'contest'[34] with All Black assistant manager Mr McPhail. This gentleman had effectively laid down a personal challenge to help Clarke, a naturally big man, to return to his fighting weight. As it so happened, Mac Herewini, a bustling first five-eighths, was another encouraged to shed the pounds after a recent weigh-in. This young player was enjoying an interesting tour; having recently, in Brighton, met the midwife who delivered him,[35] he now looked forward to catching up with his father. Along with his Māori colleagues, he shared a deep appreciation for Welshmen's singing and, as he quite rightly told a *South Wales Argus* correspondent, they 'sing their sides to victory'.

Another happy tourist who was enjoying himself while making a huge impact on the New Zealand game was Colin Meads, a man whose playing career extended a remarkable fourteen years in the top flight. His brother, Stan, was another powerful forward on this tour. In a match only a few weeks earlier, Colin had been described by the *New Zealand Herald* as being 'absolutely splendid, full of fire and determination in everything except, perhaps, his old fondness for sneaking into the opposing side of the ruck.' This hints that he was a law unto himself – which he was – but he was also an irreplaceable workhorse in his team. Colin succeeded in doing something

---

34   *The New Zealand Herald*, October 23rd and 30th 1963.
35   *The New Zealand Herald*, October 31st 1963.

that all outstanding forwards strive to do well: expressing himself to the point of 'bossing' the opposition. And, in the rough and tumble of top-flight rugby, it is this that made him great.

Colin explained to me that the next match against Cardiff at the Arms Park was immensely important, tantamount to being another test. So many All Blacks sides had fallen at this famous ground that the present squad had truly raised themselves mentally and physically for the game. But this did not stop the unexpected happening on the day, even before a ball was kicked. The late Sir Colin Meads explained:

The thing I remember about being in Wales in 1963 was playing our first game on Cardiff Arms Park. It was against Cardiff who had beaten us in 1953, and this was a ground where the All Blacks had never beaten Wales. We used to get telegrams from home: 'Take no prisoners!' they'd say, and other comments of this sort. I always remember before the match we talked about the Welsh singing, but we'd never witnessed it. Ian Clarke was the only one of our team who had experienced it before. 'It will blow you away,' he said.

In those days we only did the haka on tour; it wasn't for matches at home and it wasn't like it is now. We had Māori players leading us and, that day, after we went onto the field and heard the singing, Waka Nathan was supposed to get us going. But Waka was crying, he was balling his eyes out; I can remember this well. Then Wilson Whineray, our captain, called over to Mac Herewini, also a Māori, 'Mackie, you'd better lead us' – but Mackie, the wee fellow, was crying worse than Waka! In the end Wilson Whineray stepped forward and it was the worst haka that we've done in our lives!

New Zealand scraped home to victory by a single point, 6–5, a penalty goal and drop kick being the winning cards to trump a converted try. The game was probably never intended to be a feast of glorious silky running skills, but nevertheless the All Blacks had succeeded in 'breaking its duck'. After the match Pat Walsh, the injured five-eighth who orchestrated Māori 'Ka Mate' cries amongst team reserves in the North Stand, shared the sad news of his father's sudden passing with his teammates. Having been informed only hours ahead of the match, the injured player bravely put the interests of his team first. 'Now, I don't want you to say a word about this, Frank,' he stressed to his manager, Frank Kilby. 'We've got to win this one today. The boys simply mustn't be disturbed.'[36] Such a consideration may go a long way to explain the New Zealand attitude to rugby.

In the weeks running up to the next fixture at Pontypool Park, the Welsh papers were reporting disharmony between the town rugby club, local dignitaries and various committee members in relation to the use of the park facilities. Sadly, this disunity not only threatened to disrupt preparations for the All Blacks versus Pontypool–Cross Keys match, but to jeopardise the occasion altogether.

As can be imagined, the newspapers carried chapter and verse as they saw it: the problem stemming from a failure on the part of the organisers of the event to invite the chair of the urban council –a woman – to the post-match players function, allegedly to spare any awkwardness associated with her being a lonesome lady amongst a gathering of rugby men.[37] But, be that as it may, feelings were running high and with the possibility of sanctions being imposed on the exclusive use

36   *The New Zealand Herald*, November 24th 1963.
37   *The South Wales Argus*, November 6th 1963.

of the playing field, or at least rumours suggesting this, it was with relief that matters were eventually resolved to the satisfaction of all concerned.

Although a heavy win for the tourists had been expected, this failed to materialise, for the home side inspired by a man who knows more about Welsh *hwyl* than most, the indomitable Clive Rowlands, helped to keep the score to three tries and a conversion to nil. There had been moments of feisty action as the combined team, encouraged by strong vocal support, disrupted the All Blacks from breaking into their stride, but all had ended well by the time hordes of excited schoolboys spilt onto the playing area for autographs. This had been a satisfying victory and the All Blacks were now leaving Wales to play two fixtures in both England and Ireland. But there would be terrific excitement when they returned three weeks later as they would take on the country's best fifteen in front of fanatical fans.

Winter-warm tracksuits at Swansea and Wilson's gallop for glory

By the time Wilson Whineray's All Blacks returned to Wales, having defeated Munster, Ireland and two English divisional teams, they had run into form. Memories of defeat at Newport had grown more distant, whilst a return to St Helen's, the scene of a home win for Swansea in 1935 and a draw in 1953, was a reality check ahead of a full international with Wales. With the match taking place in the middle of a cold December snap, Swansea players entered the field like guardian angels, wearing full-length winter-warm tracksuits, white from head to foot.

Mike Thomas, Swansea's open side wing forward, had a lot of running and tackling to do this day against men of physical power, but he recalls his first meeting with the All Blacks being at the Gwyn Hall in Neath in 1954. The New Zealanders were attending the mayor's reception and Mike was among the school children queuing for autographs. 'I remember having six signatures from Bob Stuart,' he said, of his memorable moment with the All Blacks captain before going along to watch these same players clashing with a Neath–Aberavon team at the Gnoll. In those days school children sat on benches alongside the touchline, close enough to hear the squelching sound of leather boots in the wet mud and the thud of heavyweight packs engaging in the scrums. Mike shares his memories of the next encounter almost ten years later when he was in the thick of the action:

> We were really excited about this game, although there was doubt about it being played because the ground was so

hard. We trained, as usual, on the Tuesday and Thursday before the match, but coaching was still in its infancy then. Although many had achieved a coaching proficiency badge, we weren't instructed as such to beat New Zealand. We knew their strengths and worked to overcome them, but it was in later days that we developed more technical awareness through coaching strategies.

Mike explained that the players met at the ground. Dewi Bebb was captain and they went straight to the changing room. 'I arrived in my mini saloon,' said Mike, 'and I used to park in Bryn Road, or by the Cricketers Arms if I was early enough, before walking across the field. That day we were supplied with tracksuits and special stockings. We kept them on while the Welsh band performed and the crowd enjoyed the pre-match routines.' The game was hard going but Swansea kept in touch with New Zealand right up to the end, before another breakaway try sealed victory for the All Blacks. Afterwards, all players and officials went back to the Osborne Hotel in Rotherslade, a nearby beach location on the Gower. This is where the Swansea players shared a few drinks and a meal with the All Blacks and chatted about the game.

Mike told me that one of the Swansea fans took cine-camera footage of the action and shared this with him: 'With a bit of editing on my part,' he added, 'I later presented a copy of the film to the curator of New Zealand's Rugby Museum in Palmerston North. I had always been interested in visiting the country and, having now played against the All Blacks, I felt that I really had to go.'

In the *New Zealand Herald* of December 14th, the match report described Mike as being one of the courageous, tough-tackling forwards who 'never shirked duty in the face of the fury of many New Zealand forward attacks' despite entering play, so it is written, from offside – a case of the pot calling the kettle '[all] black', perhaps! 'But you are not offside until you are penalised,' was Mike's response, a line of thinking that the game's current top wing forwards obviously share. Such men play the whistle and the official, which makes refereeing difficult, even for a respected individual such as Meirion Joseph.

Meirion explained that he was called to officiate at the eleventh hour, having taken a phone call from Bill Clement, Welsh Rugby Union Secretary. 'Gwilym [Treharne] has twisted his knee,' he said, 'I've got good news for you.' Meirion, aged twenty-seven, was thrown into the deep end, this being his biggest match to date and certainly his first experience of a major overseas team – as it was also for Eiryn Lewis, Swansea's scrum half, who lived in Cwmafon, the same village as Meirion:

Strangely, I saw Eiryn nearly every day before the game. 'Dwi ddim yn cysgu'n rhy dda,' [I'm not sleeping at all well], he told me, 'yn meddwl am y gêm' [thinking about the game]. 'Mae'n gêm fawr ofnadwy' [It's a terribly big game].

'Paid â becso, Eiryn,' [Don't worry, Eiryn] I replied. 'Dim ond gêm yw hi,' [It's only a game], ''mond 'da Seland Newydd yn chware!' [but with New Zealand playing!]

But I must admit, over the years I had been in awe of New Zealand teams myself – in fact, ever since my father took me to watch the Kiwi Army team playing at Neath in 1945. 'We've got to go and you're coming with me,' he said, having watched the 1935 All Blacks in action and knowing there'd be great excitement at the Gnoll. So we jumped onto the bus for Pontrhydyfen, where we got off and waited right outside Richard Burton's childhood home for the Blaengwynfi bus into town.

Now, years later, Meirion was arriving at St Helen's as the man in charge, soon to step into the players' changing rooms to inspect the studs of every boot, ensuring there were no rough or sharp edges:

Money cannot buy the atmosphere and excitement under the stand. I could hear the All Blacks coach preaching to his players as if they had lost every game on tour. Being my first big match, I just wanted to get it done, and done well: 'Please,' I was saying to myself, 'no controversy today.'

Meirion had to deal with a punch from All Black prop, Ken Gray, aimed at local hero Warren Jenkins, which disturbed the crowd late on, but this was par for the course for these hard men. 'What I do remember is penalising the All Blacks heavily in the line-out,' admitted Meirion, 'and then having to explain myself to the New Zealand management afterwards.' By now everyone was warming up with a gin and tonic at the bar, before settling down for the main dinner. 'In fact, I can remember having to clarify a few more of my decisions,' smiled Meirion, as if to suggest the New Zealanders were not going to let him off the hook too lightly, 'but it was all positive and I thought we got on pretty well.' With one ball and thirty players, there will always be room for rugby debate.

That 'debate' would now be carried into the famous Welsh fortress on the bank of the Taff, where the All Blacks, although having beaten Cardiff, had failed to overcome Wales in 58 long years of trying. With twenty tons of straw tackling the frosty nights, preparations were thorough and expectations high. As a television sports programme kept Mr Kilby, the touring team manager, and Wales' Cliff Morgan busy, the New Zealand players were seen strolling around the Cardiff shops, as others played golf at the Pyle and Kenfig Hill course. Meanwhile, despite the arrival of the black-and-white televisions, the demand for tickets, so the *Western Mail* reported, was back and at its best, as was barter and exchange: £4 turkeys being traded for £1 seats in the stand!

Recognising the depth of feeling and concern back home, Wilson Whineray took time in the *New Zealand Herald* of December 21st 1963 to reassure his countrymen with a calm assessment of his team's chances. Acknowledging the recent run of victories, he felt that his side would be a tough nut to crack, especially as the All Blacks at this stage of the tour knew their opponents well. He considered the Welsh game would be more defence-orientated than attack-driven and believed that his players had now acclimatised to Cardiff Arms Park, where the singing and atmosphere greatly favoured the home team. He felt that his men were knowledgeable campaigners, well capable of overcoming the fears that afflict teams visiting this rugby landmark.

As it transpired, the All Black captain was correct. New Zealand worked hard to wear down the Welsh and won by the slender margin of 6–0, a penalty and drop goal being the difference. They had found a solution to their problem and, this evening, more so than other nights, there would be celebrations. 'Thank you Wales for giving us our best ever Christmas present,' said Mr Kilby at the official dinner – who was sufficiently excited to sing 'Macnamara's Band' with his men, before team plaques and photographs were exchanged. Equally proud was Wilson Whineray who distributed badges of the famous silver fern to players and reserves of Wales, and caps for Newport's new boys, Alan Thomas and John Uzzell. 'There was an air of friendliness [fair competition] on the field,' said the All Blacks captain, revelling in his greatest glory, 'and we respected our opponents.'

This was not a classic match; it was more of a slog, a heavyweight bout that went the distance. For certain it was

The victorious Welsh team of December 16th 1905. Furthest back: Ack Llewellyn, touch judge. Back row: Tom Williams (Welsh Football Union), Jack Williams, George Travers, Dai Jones, Will Joseph, Rhys Gabe, Sir J.T.D. Llewellyn (W.R.U. President). Second row: Charlie Pritchard, Jehoida Hodges, Willie Llewellyn, Gwyn Nicholls, Bert Winfield, Cliff Pritchard, Arthur Harding. Front row: Teddy Morgan, Dicky Owen, Percy Bush.
©*Welsh Rugby Union's collection*

The 1905 New Zealand team to play Wales. Back row: Billy Stead (touch judge), Charlie Seeling, Bob Deans, Jim O'Sullivan, Fred Newton, Alex McDonald; Middle row. Fred Roberts, Frank Glasgow, Duncan McGregor, Dave Gallaher, George Gillett, George Tyler, Billy Wallace. Front Row: Harry Mynott, Jimmy Hunter, Steve Casey. ©*Lordprice Collection*

The 1905 All Blacks perform the haka whilst Swansea players look on with curiosity, hands on hips. *©Swansea RFC. collection*

A line-out at St Helen's in the last tour match of 1905. Bill Cunningham, so it appears, sports his characteristic one white sock. *©Swansea RFC collection*

Eating the Leek

©Lordprice Collection

The tattered ball of the 1905 Cardiff international, which still bears the signatures of the day's celebrities. *Thanks to the WRU. Photo: Roger Penn*

'We have met our Waterloo,' said Dave Gallaher upon leaving the field at Cardiff in 1905. *NZ Sports Hall of Fame, Dunedin*

The 1905 official match programme. *Dave Dow, Swansea RFC*

The official WFU minutes naming the 1905 Welsh team.

The referee's inscribed 1905 match whistle. *Thanks to the WRU*

An 1887 painting attributed to H. Overend (or possibly Omrend) and L. Smyth presented by Alec Jamieson to the New Zealand Barbarians RFC, Eden Park – before the whistle!

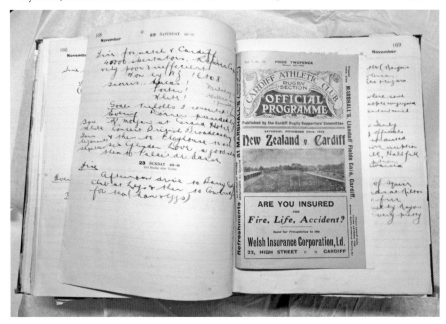

Stan Dean's Invincibles tour diary opened at November 22nd 1924
New Zealand Rugby Museum

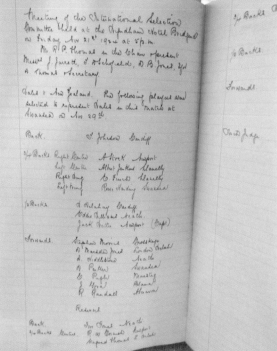

Tenby: where the All Blacks trained ahead of the Welsh match in November 1924. *Photo: Roger Penn*

Minutes of a meeting of the Welsh Football Union at the Wyndham Hotel, Bridgend, on November 21st 1924. *Thanks to the Welsh Rugby Union. Photo: Roger Penn*

Cliff Porter, George Nepia, Jack Manchester
New Zealand Rugby Museum

The Boot Hotel, Aberdare, regaled for a royal visit. A similar welcome awaited Jack Manchester's team in 1935. *R.C.T. Libraries*

Beautiful Dunedin Railway Station, which has experienced many an important rugby day during the past century. *Photo: Roger Penn*

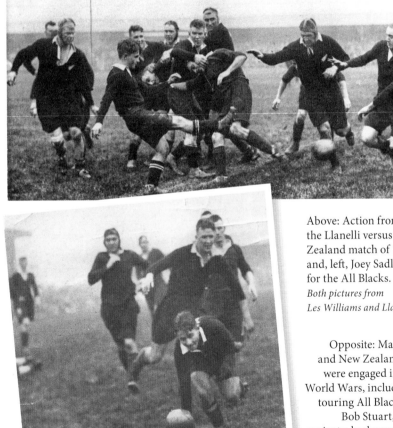

Above: Action from the Llanelli versus New Zealand match of 1935 and, left, Joey Sadler scores for the All Blacks. *Both pictures from Les Williams and Llanelli RFC*

Opposite: Many Welsh and New Zealand players were engaged in the two World Wars, including 1953 touring All Black captain Bob Stuart, pictured against a background of the War Memorial Museum at Parnell, Auckland. *Landscape photo: Roger Penn Portrait: NZ Rugby Museum*

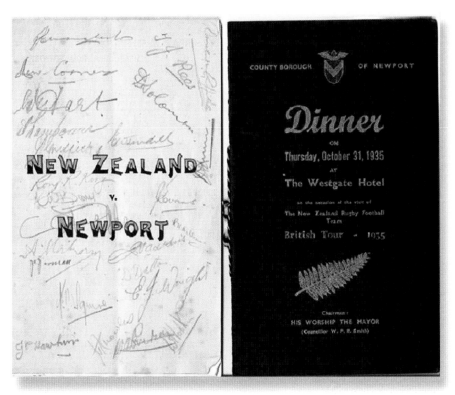

Memorabilia from Newport versus New Zealand 1935. *Mike Dams' collection*

Radio commentator Winston McCarthy. *New Zealand Sports Hall of Fame, Dunedin*

Bleddyn Williams is chaired off at the Arms Park after leading Cardiff to victory in November 1953. *Glamorgan Archives and the family of the late Bleddyn Williams*

Llanelli versus New Zealand 1953. Gethin Hughes is seen with a scrum cap, second from the right. *Picture courtesy of Gethin Hughes*

Brian Price and his victorious 1963 Newport team. *Mike Dams' collection and Newport RFC*

Action from the same winning Newport match.
South Wales Argus

Alan Thomas drinks a toast to
Wilson Whineray's men!
Picture courtesy of Alan Thomas

NEW ZEALAND					NEWPORT	
Colours : All Black					Colours : Black and Amber	
D. B. CLARKE	(1)	Full Back		Full Back	R. CHENEY	(15)
R. W. CAULTON	(2)	Left Wing		Right Wing	S. WATKINS	(14)
P. T. WALSH	(8)	Left Centre		Right Centre	J. UZZELL	(13)
I. R. MACRAE	(7)	Right Centre		Left Centre	B. J. JONES	(12)
W. L. DAVIS	(6)	Right Wing		Left Wing	D. PERROTT	(11)
E. W. KIRTON	(10)	Outside Half		Outside Half	D. WATKINS	(10)
K. C. BRISCOE	(11)	Inside Half		Inside Half	W. R. PROSSER	(9)
W. J. WHINERAY (Capt.)	(17)	Forwards		Forwards	N. JOHNSON	(1)
J. MAJOR	(16)				G. BEVAN	(2)
I. J. CLARKE	(18)				D. JONES	(3)
R. H. HORSLEY	(20)				B. V. PRICE (Capt.)	(4)
C. E. MEADS	(22)				I. FORD	(5)
W. J. NATHAN	(25)				A. THOMAS	(6)
B. J. LOCHORE	(28)				G. DAVIDGE	(8)
K. R. TREMAIN	(30)				K. W. POOLE	(7)

Touch Judge : Mr. D. J. GRAHAM   Referee : Mr. G. WALTERS - Gowerton   Touch Judge : Mr. R. T. CARTER

1st RESERVE —

NEXT HOME GAME : v. **Ebbw Vale** SATURDAY, 2nd NOVEMBER, 1963, Kick-off 3.15 p.m.

The team sheet inside the Newport versus All Blacks programme of 1963, signed by
Keith Nelson, first reserve – on the occasion of meeting Welsh supporters at
Dunedin Airport, in June 2010. *New Zealand Rugby Museum*

The 'Guardian Angels' of Swansea
at St Helen's in 1963.
Mike Thomas' collection

Sir Colin Meads and
Sir Brian Lochore. *NZ Rugby Museum*

A young Delme Thomas at Stradey Park in 1963 as Wilson Whineray, back of the picture, closes in.
Collection of Les Williams and Llanelli RFC

Policing and supporting at Rodney Parade, 1963. *South Wales Argus*

Action from Newport versus the All Blacks 1963. *South Wales Argus*

Stretching to cross the line in 'Glyn Turner's Corner' is the man himself,
a local hero and respected scrum half. *Ebbw Vale RFC*

Little work was done at Ebbw Vale Steelworks on Tuesday November 28th 1972 when
Ian Kirkpatrick's All Blacks beat Gwent at the Welfare Sports Ground. *Ebbw Vale RFC*

Phil Bennett moves the ball as 'Sosban' beat the All Blacks at Stradey Park in 1972. Roy Bergiers, try scorer, appears to the left of Phil Bennett. *Les Williams and Llanelli RFC*

Richard Moriarty's body language says it all towards the end of the Swansea–All Blacks encounter of 1980. *Swansea RFC*

An impressive haka at St Helen's, Swansea, 1980. *Swansea RFC*

Men of All Blacks rugby:
Ian Kirkpatrick, Wayne Shelford, Sandy McNicol (all courtesy of New Zealand Rugby Museum), David Kirk (a family photo), Leicester Rutledge (New Zealand Rugby Museum) and Dr Mike Bowen, the All Blacks doctor of the early 1990s.

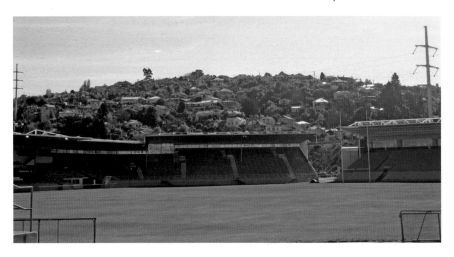

Carisbrook, Dunedin, 'The House of Pain', with its excellent running surface.
The Welsh team was invited to attend the stadium's official 'final fling'. *Photo: Roger Penn*

All Black Neven MacEwan pictured at his home with the miner's lamp that he received from Cilfynydd RFC in 2005. *Photo: Roger Penn*

To commemorate Charles John Monro, founder of rugby in New Zealand, as seen outside the New Zealand Rugby Museum, Palmerston North. *Photo: Roger Penn*

Dunedin Town Hall clock tower, which is often draped with the colourful scarves of Otago and leading rugby sides. *Photo: Roger Penn*

Eden Park, Auckland, as seen from the top of Mount Eden. The ground was a home from home for Warren Gatland's Welsh team during the Rugby World Cup of 2011. *Photo: Roger Penn*

The headquarters of the New Zealand game at the port of windy Wellington. *Photo: Roger Penn*

Sheriff John Dewar Dallas, a highly respected figure in rugby, sport and legal work. Dallas was also the referee who adjudged 'no score' after Bob Deans dived for the line in 1905.
The Aberdeen Press and Journal

a tense afternoon for spectators, especially Welshmen, who demonstrated their displeasure when, near the end of play, Clive Rowlands, Welsh captain, was tackled by Colin Meads as he made a 'mark'. Who could envy Clive, buried under a 'Pinetree' or Sir Colin faced by a chiding, berating crowd? Neither would forget this moment, as the big New Zealander recalled humorously in *75 New Zealand Rugby Greats* years after the event, stating that the crowd's hostile reaction went on and on, causing his colleagues to walk away and leave him to get on with it!

Clive Rowlands still winces. 'Menuffern i!' [Blimey!] he told me recently in his typically mischievous way, 'I can feel him hitting my backside now!' And as for Sir Colin he added more dry humour to his unrepentant stance about this incident when speaking at a rugby luncheon in Cardiff. 'When I saw him [Clive] jigging around on the dance floor later that same night – I wanted to give him another!'

There were many tired bodies and aching limbs at the end of this latest test, but when the final whistle was blown the players were tearing jerseys off one another's backs to exchange. New cap, Alan Thomas, who had learnt of his match selection when a friend knocked on his door having heard the radio news (the official letter had not yet arrived), was now caught in a dilemma because he had promised to give his first Welsh shirt to an old friend from Tredegar. 'He used to do the reporting for the local club and had once said to me, "Algy [this being Alan's nickname], I think you are going to make it; you're going to play for Wales."'

So when Waka Nathan offered me his jersey, I agreed to exchange it as long as I could find him another. I was really fortunate that Bleddyn Williams came to my rescue; he produced a Welsh shirt and the next morning Dick Uzzell and I jumped onto my motorbike and set off for Porthcawl. We went into the hotel and up the stairs. In one of the rooms the team had been having a party. I'm not sure if some of the players had even gone to bed; it had definitely been a time to celebrate, a night to remember. But I found Waka and we exchanged jerseys.

Who can blame the All Blacks for letting their hair down on this historic day? One can imagine also the scenes of happiness in Queen Street, Auckland or at the Octagon in Dunedin or on the bracing seafront of windy Wellington when the final whistle went. But, back in Wales and not many miles from the All Blacks' headquarters in Porthcawl, Grahame Hodgson, a stalwart for Neath for many seasons, was relaxing after the match. It was Grahame's recent performance against the tourists at Port Talbot that had caught everybody's eye; it was also Grahame's trusted boot that had kicked off the previous day's match. The former full back shares his memories of the occasion:

> We had a runaround on the Friday before the game, to be introduced to those who we were playing with. Then we drove up to the Royal Hotel by eleven o'clock to have lunch before the game. We had no uniform in those days and, sometimes, I wore my Neath pullover; it was a black sweater with a white Maltese Cross.
>
> As I ran onto the field I was thinking about the Aberavon–Neath game that we were unlucky to lose. That day Stan Meads, Colin's brother, was playing and as I fly-kicked the ball into touch, my shoulder happened to connect with his upper arm. It was just a momentary touch, a fleeting contact, really, but I hadn't experienced such a solid physique before. It was as if he was built of granite. I remember thinking, 'What was that?'

Grahame can recall being paid the ultimate compliment by the All Blacks in this Welsh match because, in the course of play, they kicked directly to touch (and effectively gained less ground) so as to avoid Grahame. 'Bruce Watt, outside half, was determined not to play into my hands,' he said, 'denying me the opportunity of getting to the ball. I remember speaking to Ian Clarke, Don's brother, after the match. "We didn't make you look so good today, Grahame," he said to me.'

Adding to the reputation of his colleagues who had delivered so efficiently on the field of play, Mac Herewini, who had not been selected for the Welsh match, was photographed by the *Western Mail* presenting a scrapbook to Bleddyn Williams of his days in New Zealand with the 1950 British Lions. With Bleddyn having donated his jersey to Alan Thomas, here was, perhaps, a case of one good deed repaying another. But this was no more than a brief interlude for the young first five-eighths, who was named in the team for the next match, a showdown at Stradey Park with the 'Scarlets' of Llanelli.

Still longing for a first victory against the All Blacks to accompany their triumph over the 1888 Māori side, Llanelli players were quickly into their rhythm, helped by the flying schoolboy winger, Terry Price. Llanelli's start had been excellent but, after leading early in the second half, the match slipped from their grasp as injuries began to take their toll. Shoring up the All Blacks pack, as ever, was Colin Meads, this time amusing Terry McLean of the *New Zealand Herald* on January 2nd 1964 for his strong play as he 'aroused a justifiable ire,' when persistently pushing opponents who were waiting for the ball in the line-outs as it travelled on its way.

However, this did not prevent either Delme Thomas or Hywel Jones from jumping well and securing good possession – but it was another, Waka Nathan, the All Black wing forward, who was to take the greatest praise when, forcing himself over the line for a late try, he broke his jaw. Typically humble, Waka said that he got what he deserved for failing to pass to a teammate. He returned to the Llanelli clubhouse following treatment to join in the singing of 'Calon Lân' and 'Sosban Fach' – as best he could! Only twenty-two years of age at the time, Waka had read much about the Welsh and had heard many stories from past All Blacks of a Welshman's special love of rugby. But then he heard the singing of the anthem at Cardiff, and it knocked him backwards. 'I'll never forget it,' he told me. 'It was so powerful and wonderful, especially near the end; I was totally overwhelmed – but I am pleased to say that I led the haka from there on!' Waka continues:

> It was a great honour coming to Wales and one thing I remember about the 1963 tour is that we only had a few Māori in our team. Singing has always been close to our hearts and we respect its part in the Welsh social scene. After we came from the field, we had some great times. We'd join in, strumming the guitars, playing our own ukuleles. I made some wonderful friends and, of course, I ended up returning to Wales. It was a great thrill.

Waka, who was manager of the Māori side visiting Wales in 1982, explained how he began enjoying the game from a young age: 'It was being played in primary school,' he said, 'and, when I went along, I just enjoyed it. I got going from day one, moving on to play for the under elevens and so forth, then my college first team and Auckland Colts. I soon fell into a pattern which meant a lot of jogging and sprinting for me prior to the season,' said Waka. 'This is what gave me a good start.'

There was to be little body-contact training for this natural athlete until his injury healed later on the tour. Taking his place in the team at Cardiff Arms Park on Saturday February 15th 1964, three and a half months after the All Blacks had slipped up in the drizzling rain at Newport's Rodney Parade, Waka was part of the grand finale with the Barbarians. In a match packed with pace and flair, his side scored a remarkable eight tries – two of which were his own – the home team's reply being a dropped goal from a 'mark', these 'fair catches' being awarded all over the field, from which goals could be scored directly.

But it was Wilson Whineray who was to bring down the final curtain for these popular tourists, who would play in France and Canada on their way home. Taking the ball, he shaped for the gallop of a lifetime, cheered on by a Welsh crowd who had forgotten the hard hits and tensions of earlier encounters and were now smitten by the audacity of such a magnificent display. Soon to be hoisted onto shoulders and carried off the field, this modest man would reflect upon the communal singing of a true Māori favourite by the Welsh. 'Now is the Hour when we must say Goodbye' is both beautiful and romantic and it brought a touching end to the tour. The Welsh would miss this latest group of New Zealand men, who, having broken into the Arms Park fortress, had, at last, beaten the Welsh.

Kinship and Kindness and
Two tickets for the Test

It was expected that when the Lions selectors sought men of stamina and sporting stature for four months of demanding rugby and travel in the summer of 1966, the Welsh would be only too ready to oblige. Four gruelling encounters with the All Blacks and a hazardous itinerary of provincial matches was a job for a hardy group, led by Michael Campbell-Lamerton of Scotland, a man of rising rank in the army. Among them were Howard Norris, Alun Pask, Brian Price and Gareth Prothero of Wales as well as two young workhorses heading towards the top flight, Delme Thomas and Denzil Williams.

On arriving in New Zealand unbeaten, the Lions' spirits were inevitably high, but as soon as they landed at Invercargill in the south-east corner of South Island, their winning ways were dismantled by Southland province. Bill Anderson, a well-respected figure in this hotbed of rugby, where parts of the gentle landscape are so similar to Wales, had been counting the days. 'I couldn't wait,' he said, 'and we had beautiful sunshine and a huge crowd.' Bill mentioned that rugby was now broadening its television base, with far more viewing hours and regular highlights appearing on people's screens. 'I remember going home to watch the match for the second time,' said Bill. 'In those days the cameramen were sitting at the top of our old wooden grandstand. They'd go up the stairway, through the roof. There was a covered area, also good writing space with a bird's-eye view onto the ground.'

It was difficult to recover after this painful start. However, the Lions fought back to beat many of the tenacious provincial sides, although not all, whilst losing the test matches 4-0.

This had been a long and often wearisome five months, but by the time they tackled Waikato in Hamilton, most of the hard work had been done, the tour finally drawing to a close. John Cresswell, second five-eighths for the home side, who marked Mike Gibson that day, remembers the time as being long before dieticians stopped rugby men from indulging in a traditional steak around the twelve-midday mark. As John recalls:

> I am sure the intention of a steak before a game was to build up our energy, but, in hindsight, the benefit only became apparent about two hours after the game! Rugby was so different then. While jerseys, shorts and socks were supplied, they had to be 'checked back in' after each game and we had to provide our own boots. The Lions won that day and I remember that the surface, compared to the playing surfaces of today, was like a cow paddock – David Watkins and Dewi Bebb being among the Welsh on duty.

John explained that as it was an international fixture some extra preparation was needed before the team met and had their usual training run. Then they talked through their plans and agreed the type of game they intended to play. On the Friday night everyone was booked into a hotel in Hamilton. 'That wasn't the normal arrangement,' said John, 'but it was good getting everyone together early, although, on the day, I can't say it made a big difference to the result!'

Having ghosted his way through New Zealand defences in Newport's 1963 win, David Watkins was a closely marked man. Nevertheless, the tour was an outstanding personal triumph for him, for he played in every test match and captained the side in two of these. During post-match functions he spoke for his men, the voice of a Blaina boy who had done well. As a schoolboy he was a star for Cwm Celyn

Youth XV, when he and his brother used to go to Abertillery Park to watch Blaina playing in the Ben Francis Cup. No one could lay a hand on David then and, all these years later, the All Blacks were having the same problem. David recalls:

> In those Blaina days we'd walk down the back roads to Abertillery and climb over the fence to the ground. Knowing that all the stewards were down the front, we'd break into the top of the terracing, so that we didn't have to pay, and we were rarely caught.

David looks back on the 1966 Lions tour with terrific fondness. He counts himself fortunate to have made the trip and was so pleased to be able to escape hotel life on tour by staying with New Zealand families in their homes. 'We depended upon the hospitality of local people,' he said. 'The New Zealand Rugby Union drew up a list of families who were happy to take British players into their homes. If we weren't selected for a midweek match we stayed a few more days and this made a big difference.' David explains that besides enjoying a taste of home comforts, which broke the monotony of hotels, he was shown around places of interest, generally as guest of honour.

The tour elevated Newport's outside half to great heights and one of his proudest stories relates to his own altercation with Colin Meads, some ten inches taller and far, far heavier, from which he not surprisingly emerged second best. David admits to speaking out of turn before catching a wallop from his sparring partner who was said, in his absolute innocence, to be protecting himself![38] But when David returned home to his working-class background, he was quickly brought back down to earth:

---

38 'Live and let Dai. David Watkins: A Life in Rugby'. YouTube.

I was really fortunate to go and the experience helped me in work and business and in social life. As regards the rugby, well, I thought I was God's gift. But as soon as I arrived back in Wales, I was dropped from the Welsh team – and in came Barry John!

Only a year later in 1967 the All Blacks were back in the land of the Three Feathers, where they played four matches as part of their fuller tour of Britain, France and Canada. This time the team was captained by the diplomatic, determined and already successful Brian Lochore of Wairarapa province, who had the satisfaction of leading the All Blacks, a settled side, against the recent British Lions. He was a back-row forward or lock (the term second row beginning to disappear by now) who had always loved the running game. The team was managed by Charles Saxton and assistant Fred Allen, who both served with distinction for the New Zealand Army side of 1945, which went on to beat Wales. Their arrival into the Principality was the story everyone had been waiting for, backed up by a photograph that appeared in the *Western Mail:* of a team singalong on a bus leading to Cardiff's Angel Hotel as Kelvin Tremain stood in the aisle playing his guitar.

After a thorough workout at the university ground in Llanrumney, certain of the tourists enjoyed a Rotary lunch before being shown the local sights. As for Mr Saxton, a man whose vision of rugby, as reported in David Parry-Jones' *Taff's Acre*, was to see 'fourteen men putting the fifteenth clear', his post-lunch speech praised Welsh interest in the game from the grassroots upwards. Of course he was unable to resist referring to the Bob Deans debate, but Mr Saxton saw the disputed 1905 try as a positive element in the history of the Wales–New Zealand game.

After a reunion drink with Newport players at Rodney Parade, it was down to business for the All Blacks with a difficult game at St Helen's against a West Wales team. It was at this same ground that Charles Saxton had captained Swansea in a fixture with the Barbarians during the Easter of 1946. In those days, it was common for touring players to remain in Wales where they were invited to play in matches and enjoy social times before travelling home and, on this occasion, Harry Payne, the Swansea skipper, stepped aside to make way.

Now, back in St Helen's, Swansea, on Wednesday November 8th 1967, in front of a huge crowd, it was two-try Grahame Thorne who seized the winning score, after Colin Meads, the day's visiting captain, and Sid Going had earlier crossed the line. With a young Ian Kirkpatrick racing around the field, the All Blacks overcame a strong West Wales side, captained by Clive Rowlands, to win 21–14. Tellingly, the West Wales side was coached by an astute tactician and persuasive leader whose name was in the ascendency: Carwyn James.

By now, All Blacks tours to Britain, and especially to Wales, had caught the imagination of the New Zealand public to such an extent that hundreds, if not thousands, of enthusiasts followed in organised touring parties not only to see matches and enjoy the sights, but to meet locals and share their different cultures. John Sinclair, who earlier told us about 'Bunny' Abbott and George Nēpia and who arrived in Wales for this 1967 tour with a message from the New Zealand Prime Minister, was one of many leaders of such groups. John explained to me that his contingent wanted to visit Aberfan to pay their personal sympathies to the people of the community. This is where only a year earlier in October 1966 a coal slip had spilt onto the small village school, causing devastation and the saddest loss of life. John recalls the time of his visit:

'Why can't we go to Aberfan to pay our respects?' I was asked, because of the great kinship between us and the Welsh. 'Could we go to lay a wreath?'

We went to the graves at the top of the hill, looking down across the valley to where the school had once been. We were not just sightseeing; we wanted to explain that we were genuinely sympathetic. We knew that what is between Wales and New Zealand is more than life itself.

John explained that on the way down the hill walking towards the coach, two of the ladies in his party turned to him: 'John, we were mothers before we became rugby fans. What do you think if we donate our Test tickets to the people of this valley? Please explain how much we want to do this. We know we shan't be coming this way again.'

When I discussed this with the local minister who joined us for our visit, he couldn't believe it.

'We never see tickets here,' he said, and when his message got back to the pithead, there were wild cheers of excitement.

'Two tickets for the Test!' They couldn't believe it. A raffle was organised straight away and it was this same local minister who drew his own ticket. 'Tilt, tilt,' we cried out, but he was claiming it, and was so overjoyed that he kept showing the ticket to his father.

'Now don't push your luck,' his father said, 'or you'll not have it back next time!'

The other ticket was won by a young miner. 'I alerted several of Wales' former players and arranged to meet for lunch before the game,' said John. 'The miner was with us and he had black hands like we'd never seen before. He was lost for words when he met some of his heroes. He couldn't speak. He thought he was talking to gods.'

Days later in the run-up to the Test, the All Blacks were guests at the Lord Mayor's function in Cardiff Castle. It was then that Fred Allen put them through their paces ready for the Welsh challenge. During these days when substitutes were still not allowed onto the field, it was a brave decision to select anyone less than fully fit, but Kelvin Tremain, one of New Zealand's greatest ever forwards, whether locking the scrum or playing in the back-row, got the go-ahead to play. This was bad news for a young Gareth Edwards, aged twenty, who had a brush with the Hawkes Bay captain at the beginning of the match.

'He came down on my arm and jammed it,' says Gareth in his autobiography, comparing the experience with putting his shirt through the laundry press with his arm still inside! This was Gareth's first encounter with the All Blacks, whose dark shirts 'send a shudder through your heart,' he stated. Then, giving his opinion on New Zealand's rugby outlook, Gareth cut straight to the chase: it is as 'hard as flint,' he wrote. Boys are conditioned mentally and physically to win and no grooming in this respect is 'too tough. The game is part of their body and bone', adding that losing is not a word they know.[39]

Sir Gareth's down-to-earth commentary next describes how Norman Gale, Wales' captain, motivated his men before taking to the field against Brian Lochore's team, demanding full support from his forwards especially in the first scrum. And, when the moment arrived, the two front rows crashed into each other with the loudest of thuds, each side declaring their intentions in no uncertain terms. This was a brave start and Wales, playing into the wind and rain in the first half, remained well in the hunt, until a mistake gifted New Zealand a converted try and, ultimately, victory. Barry John,

---

39   Gareth Edwards, *Gareth* (Stanley Paul, London, 1978).

the receiver of Gareth's passes, scored a drop goal after the interval.

On this occasion, the *New Zealand Herald* of November 13th praised Colin Meads for stepping between Brian Thomas of Neath and Jazz Muller, the giant All Blacks prop, when a few punches were thrown. Now, forty-five years on, Sir Colin, the peacemaker, casts his mind back to the match:

> When we went back in 1967, I don't think the Welsh were as strong. We had a powerful front row then and there were some new faces amongst the Welsh. I remember our Ken Gray, a strong scrummager, playing well and I almost felt sorry for the opposing prop that day.
>
> I can recall something going wrong with a kick-off and we were soon on the attack – and there was a scrum near the twenty-five yard line. Kelvin Tremain our wing forward, someone we called a real gannet because he was always hungry for tries, was calling out instructions. We pushed the scrum back maybe ten yards and I can remember Kelvin shouting, 'Keep it going, keep it going,' just so that he could pounce at the end for a try!

The match ended as a 13–6 victory for Sir Colin's team and this pleased the large contingent of New Zealand spectators who had travelled across the world to support their side. Before long the All Blacks were in France, where, in the course of winning the next four fixtures, one a Test match in Paris, they were impressed en route by mile upon mile of open, beautiful French countryside. A brace of matches in Scotland presented the next two challenges and the next two wins, whilst for one famous member of the team, someone who naturally belonged in the thick of the action, an enforced break would see him viewing the next few matches, to his disappointment and disbelief, from outside the field of play.

The Sweet taste of Victory
that escapes East Wales

When the All Blacks returned to Wales after their victory against Scotland on December 2nd 1967, they did so under the stigma of a sending-off. Hanging over the party's heads was the dismissal, by referee Kevin Kelleher of Ireland, of Colin Meads for 'misconduct'. At a time when a foot-and-mouth outbreak was the talk of his homeland, resulting in strict caution, quarantine regulations and the cancellation of fixtures, Mr Kelleher's actions made the headlines. Then, following a meeting of the Disciplinary Committee in Cardiff's Angel Hotel, New Zealand's leading player was sentenced, following his marching orders, to miss the next two fixtures.

This news spread across the world and in our own *Western Mail* on December 6th was the bold headline 'Board back referee in the Meads case', stating that this was the first time for a player to be immediately suspended from the field of international play. Of course, it brought back memories of Cyril Brownlie's dismissal at Twickenham in 1925, which, being the final game of that tour in Britain, conveniently avoided the greater controversies of a ban. As for Colin Meads' enforced absence, this was good news for two Welsh teams who would avoid the great 'Pinetree', now restricted to watching the action from the stand.

In the *New Zealand Herald* of December 8th, it was reported that the film of the Scottish international was viewed keenly in viewers' homes. This fuelled a wealth of opinion and debate as referees and senior officers of the New Zealand Union were asked for reaction to what was generally thought to be an innocuous lunge at the ball by Colin Meads with his feet but in immediate proximity to David Chisholm, Scotland's fly half. There were only minutes of the match remaining, the game was well won, and Chisholm was not hurt, yet, the big man's soccer skills were deemed dangerous by the referee and the Murrayfield crowd. In hindsight, one might say that his challenge appeared no more than clumsy and the decision harsh. The *Daily Telegraph* newspaper said of the incident that 'For one with Meads' worldwide reputation for robust play, this was rather like sending a burglar to prison for a parking offence.'

Certainly, overwhelming sympathy flooded in from all corners of New Zealand for the country's popular and highly capped tight forward, whose case became a precedent for future matches of this kind. And it did not end there: twenty-one years later Mr Kelleher was invited to New Zealand for Sir Colin's televised *This is Your Life* show, when he presented the infamous whistle to the great legend 'whose like will never be again,' he said.

By now all manner of incidents, stories and topical items of news were appearing in rugby journals such as our own *Welsh Rugby*, which had become a popular glossy magazine by the mid-to-late 1960s. It detailed the game from the grass roots with coverage of laws, coaching, fitness, training, player profiles, tributes and all subjects relative to the modern game in much the same way as New Zealand's *The Rugby Footballer* and *Silver Fern*. The rugby gospel was being spread; indeed, disseminating news, stories, best practice and tips was a bit of an industry in New Zealand, whose governing bodies had been sharing newsletters and best practice with provincial unions and clubs for many a day.

After fine-tuning preparations for the Monmouthshire match, which followed the Scottish Test, with cross-country runs around Cardiff's parklands, a few of the All Blacks travelled to Kenfig Hill Rugby Club, near Bridgend, to present a jersey in memory of Cliff Davies, a British Lion tourist to New Zealand in 1950. At this same time, some players were also heading in the opposite direction for a reunion with the Newport heroes of 1963. Celebrations of victories over past All Black sides were now becoming important events not to be missed by the privileged few. The Welsh team of 1935 had recently met in Cardiff before the Test and the Arms Park club side was planning its own function at the end of this current tour.

As for the next All Blacks game in Wales, the side was returning to Rodney Parade, a big event in their calendar given that this was the scene of Wilson Whineray's only slip-up in 1963. In the match programme, J. B. G. Thomas reported that Earle Kirton was hoping for a more successful return to the ground, a wish that came true with a 23–12 victory over Monmouthshire, despite stern resistance from Dennis Hughes of Newbridge and his men. Sir Brian Lochore, All Black captain, told me that as many of the losing 1963 side as possible were chosen to play. 'It was a good way of winding up the boys,' he smiled, remembering how relieved he was to have breezed in and out of Newport's ground unscathed at the time. This was all so evident in his post-match comment, when he said to the *Western Mail*, 'it is great to enjoy the sweet taste of victory after losing at Newport four years ago.'

The next game with East Wales, however, would have to wait four days because of disruption due to snow; the New Zealanders agreeing to honour the fixture by returning from London in midweek. Having by now lost matches, not to any team, but to the foot-and-mouth scare and snow, Mr Saxton was determined to play, despite the rearranged contest making it impossible to watch the varsity match at

Twickenham, as arranged, and having to cancel a soccer appointment at White Hart Lane where Tottenham Hotspur were to play against Lyon. And with his team unable to get a late hotel booking in Cardiff, it was a case of hopping aboard the morning inter-city train.

At the time Wales' scrum half Gareth Edwards had no more than a few caps to his name. Sharing a room in Cyncoed with Nick Williams, a best friend since days in Millfield School, he awoke on the morning of the *intended* match, ready to play. 'I've got to get up, got to go down to Cardiff,' he was saying to himself, until Nick, with his head out of the window, declared, 'You're not going anywhere,' for everywhere was covered with a thickness of snow. Sir Gareth remembers a lot of confusion that morning and, being captain, he had to be involved. 'I was a little surprised to be made captain [at that stage of my career],' he said modestly. 'I think it was to see if I was suitable, an idea linked to a long-term plan.' Four days later, the match took place and Gareth, in a personal telephone conversation during the preparation of this book, recalls the time:

> Dai Hayward, Cardiff's former flank forward, was coach and I remember Dai giving me a ring. The team had just been announced. There was little time to prepare.
>
> 'Look, Gar,' he said, 'let's meet up to decide how we're going to play.' So we met in the Cockney Pride, a Cardiff pub, and ordered our curry. 'Gar,' he said as we tucked into our food, 'I think it's too late to draw up plans. Let's just say we'll move the ball as much as we can.'

Melting snow meant that conditions on the rearranged match date were wet, although the home players were soon on the attack with every intention of taking the game to the All Blacks. Sir Gareth continues:

We all played out of our skins and John Hickey was amazing. I remember near the end one of the All Blacks was shouting, 'Come on guys, we've got them going now' – and John just stood tall with a forlorn look, replying with a few words of his own. He was immense that day and it was a game we could and should have won. Charlie Saxton, All Blacks manager, admitted this afterwards, but his team took the one chance they had and scored. This is what I keep saying about the All Blacks; they never give up and always find an answer.

This was a thrilling contest, and full credit went to East Wales because they were generally considered by far the better team, despite the match ending as a 3–3 draw, one try apiece. With Barry John, Gerald Davies, John Dawes and other runners in great form, the All Blacks were tested to the full, thankful for the good luck that came their way when Keri Jones, wing three-quarter, appeared to be impeded in a try-scoring chase and when Barry John's last-minute drop goal sailed cruelly wide. The home team had given the All Blacks their biggest fright of the tour, and as Brian Lochore was carried from the field, he knew that his try line had been under siege and his men had been lucky to escape.

On a night when the newly arrived breathalyser was impacting dramatically on the after-match social scene, half emptying pubs and clubs that would otherwise have been full, at least three men would drink a toast to Welsh rugby, having survived the rough and tumble of two tours to Wales in the 1960s. These were Brian Lochore, Colin Meads and Waka Nathan, all of whom had their sights set on the Barbarians match at Twickenham. However, for Waka, there was a possibility of playing against his teammates, as he explains:

Towards the end of the 1967 tour I was invited to play for the Barbarians against our team at Twickenham. I said to Fred [Allen], our coach, that I'd be honoured to play. The Barbarians side was already a huge name and I knew that I was going to retire in the next year or two. I'd experienced so many injuries and I thought it would be a nice way to finish:

'Is it alright with you, Fred?' I asked – but I remember him being pretty serious.

'Look,' he replied, 'I'm sorry to say this, Waka, but we need you as well!'

For the Barbarians match, Colin Meads had returned from suspension. After being sent off against Scotland, he had flown into Wales with his colleagues for the next match against Monmouthshire. 'I was in disgrace when we arrived at Cardiff Airport,' he said, 'and there were photographers everywhere, waiting. A great memory of mine was Kelvin Tremain throwing a coat over me for a bit of fun. He was calling out, "Here he is, he's over here," and, of course, everyone came running over, cameras ready, but no one being able to find my face because it was hidden.' Sir Colin continues:

We were lucky to have Fred Allen as our coach at the time, because he was able to smooth things over. He was good for us, especially with the press. He had toured with the Kiwi Army team years earlier and he had some great friends in Wales. Fred, Ken Gray, about six of us altogether, went along to Bleddyn Williams' place one night just for drinks. We had a great time and I formed a lasting friendship with Jack Matthews and many others. We had some fabulous times in Wales.

During his two stays in Wales as a member of Wilson Whineray's side, and later with Brian Lochore's current side, the All Blacks had lost only once, an incredible achievement. Club records at Rodney Parade remained incomplete until years later Newport invited Sir Colin to make a brief comment about the match. In this he describes the weather that day as being 'poor' and draws attention to Glynn Davidge's bravery and good work particularly 'on the ground', work that helped Newport to register a historic victory. It had been 'a mighty forward battle' against a 'competitive' Newport pack, typical of the 'ferocious battles' fought throughout the 1960s. And, as for the drop goal, 'it was a wobbly old bugger, but over it went'.

Sir Brian Lochore was another on duty at Rodney Parade that day in 1963 and reflects upon some of the battles that he encountered in Wales during the two tours of this era when the sides were so evenly matched. Why was this I asked? 'I think this is because a core of the Welsh players had tough manual work,' he replied, referring to the miners, steelmen and farmers who were the backbone of many Welsh sides over the years. 'When you are touring in a country with great rugby traditions, you can expect the home players to raise their game,' he added, 'and they did this well.' Sir Brian, a great exponent of fast and open rugby, reflects:

> Rugby had been brought up with a lot of kicking to touch and the heavy rush of forwards running downfield, the ball at their feet, but certainly by the sixties we played the ball in hand most of the time. Although teams could still kick directly for position, meaning that a lot of the time games just went up and down the touchline, we had decided to change all that completely by 1967. We preferred to be a running team. We'd moved on. The game had developed and opened up.

As a New Zealand Rugby Union ambassador who has given a lifetime of commitment to the All Blacks, Sir Brian has brought considerable advancements to the game, yet he can recall the more innocent times when teams provided a touch judge, usually one of the reserves, for tour matches. Unlike today they had no influence on the bigger decisions, although they were known to regularly grab a couple of metres if they could get away with it. And the fields on which they ran?

I recall the fields being very heavy [compared with today]. They were played on an enormous amount and I can remember when the mud went over the top of our boots. We played once a week; in Wales it was often twice.

Having said this, Sir Brian admits that Test match pitches were not a lot different in New Zealand, mainly due to schoolboys' matches being played prior to the main event, something that is not so common in Wales. 'We usually had one or two curtain-raisers before the main game,' he said, 'giving the youngsters a taste of the bigger occasions. And by the time we got out, the field was fairly chopped.' And the Welsh?

Being well received by the home supporters and the press is always the challenge you face when you are a tourist in another country, but I made some incredibly close friends in Wales – and, funnily enough, they were not always players. I had a lot of contact over the years with men of Welsh rugby. They felt that it was nice to take us into their homes, just as we took them into ours in New Zealand. We'd meet up if we could and we shared cards at Christmas time.

But all of that was off the field, of course. What a difference a rugby ball makes.

PART VI

WALES VISIT NEW ZEALAND IN 1969

Landing amongst friends
with Mascot 'Dai Debenture' on board

Wales and New Zealand were old and gracious rivals, who, in terms of their past contests, now stood neck and neck: three victories apiece. But in over sixty years of competition the Welsh national team had never set foot anywhere near the land of the silver fern. One might well ask why, but now that time had come in a round trip that combined a visit to Australia and Fiji on the way home. With rugby standards high and pride at stake, something had to give.

Wales boarded their plane in May 1969 under the diplomatic management of Handel Rogers, one of just three people who survived the Llandow plane crash of 1950, the guidance of the coach Clive Rowlands, and the captaincy of Brian Price, Newport. After a thirty-six hour extended flight they arrived in Auckland as Triple Crown holders and Five Nations champions. They were met at a packed airport by Welsh fans and expatriates, all eager to see their team, for the first time ever, facing the All Blacks on their New Zealand soil. Wales was a good team, and it needed to be for in the previous year, 1968, the All Blacks had swept all opposition aside, but, now, just a year later, these two scheduled internationals were the only fixtures of their calendar year.

Wales' expertise in coaching, spearheaded by Ray Williams, the national organiser, was bringing results. However, it was acknowledged that natural flair and ability and other proven coaching techniques were being let down by the limitation of their 'rucking'. This was a worrying factor as the New Zealanders were the masters of this aspect of the game.

Performed well, quick ruck ball allows attackers the opportunity to run at disorganised defences, putting forwards on the back foot and causing backs to stray offside. This offence, coupled with killing the ball (usually falling on it, to prevent a speedy recycle) had long since vexed New Zealanders. Such behaviour in their eyes was unacceptable, no different from tripping a player or holding someone back without the ball, and tolerances towards such offences were low. Anyone lying in the way at a ruck could expect a raking as if he were the ball itself. Technically he had no right to be there and would not be spared the 'combine harvester' as Gareth Edwards described it. The New Zealand way was harsh, efficient and something the Welsh had no answer to. When considering today's desire for a faster game, and the penalties imposed for such transgressions, it may be argued that the All Blacks were well ahead of their time.

Wales' tough itinerary of three provincial games and two Tests, starting on May 27th and ending on June 14th, was hard enough, whilst playing Taranaki before they found their jet-lagged legs, was of no help at all. But there was no point in postponing the inevitable and with 'Dai Debenture', the team mascot, on board – evidently referring to, and publicising, the issue of debenture seats at the new-look Arms Park – the team acknowledged what was expected of them in this land of rugby.

Ray Chico Hopkins from Maesteg remembers the big reception at the airport, when the singing of *Hen Wlad Fy Nhadau* and other favourites filled the arrivals' lounge. With a strong expatriate Welsh Society following the team, colourful days lay ahead, with members dressing up in costumes, taking daffodils to matches, planting leeks on the half-way line – anything to demonstrate a patriotic vigour, besides arranging evenings of varied entertainment, music and song. This helped the Welsh players to settle, to meet new friends and to maintain a bond with those who were familiar with Wales. Ray, young and carefree, was in his element and saw how New Zealand, the most welcoming of nations, had a ruthless sting on the rugby field:

> When we arrived that day in Auckland, I met a gorgeous girl whose mother was from North Wales. She was a beauty queen and her family looked after me straightaway, making me feel really at home with everyone. In later years the whole family came out to Maesteg and we're still close friends today.
>
> I loved New Zealand, the Māori and all the people. I remember the wooden houses; the narrow, bumpy roads; and the open green countryside [miles and miles of it] – but there was a lot less rugby coverage on television than I expected. In a way, the country seemed more antiquated than ours – but the rugby enthusiasm was overwhelming.

Ray lined up against Taranaki at Rugby Park, New Plymouth, on the Tuesday before the first Test, where thirty-five thousand witnessed this first match ending in a 9–9 draw, merely days after their arrival in New Zealand. By now, flowing play had been actively encouraged ever since a clever law amendment restricted players when kicking directly to touch. For this match, Ray teamed up alongside Phil Bennett, running out into an arena of excited spectators, almost all watching Wales for the first time. 'What a huge turnout,' said Ray, 'but once you are on the field you couldn't care; New Zealand or not, you just want to upset the opposition.'

In the eyes of the New Zealand public, a draw was to fall short and questions were already being asked. The Welsh had not played well (possibly because of the jet lag) and Taranaki possessed a strong, proven pack and, yes, they had demonstrated the art of rucking. Wales, still acclimatising, as well as resting key players such as Barry John and Gareth Edwards for the Test, were naturally disappointed, yet they knew that their best was to come. Welsh captain, Brian Price, who led Newport to victory in 1963 and who had experienced a Lions tour in New Zealand in 1966, was still optimistic about his team's chances.

When casting his mind back to the time, Brian told me that after arriving into Auckland at the end of their mammoth journey from Wales, he could recall having to wait for a domestic flight to New Plymouth for the Taranaki match. 'We didn't arrive at our hotel until about midnight,' said Brian, 'and after getting a few hours' sleep, there was an earthquake at about 4 a.m. It wasn't serious but it was still enough to get people out of bed and to check the buildings, bridges and other structures.' This was not a good start and having had a taste of what was to come at Taranaki, Brian was determined to put things right for the first Test.

So also was Clive Rowlands, a young coach, recently retired from playing, but without the benefit of having visited New Zealand before. Clive at this stage was struggling to come to terms with the depth of rugby enthusiasm in the country. 'I was shell-shocked,' he told me, but, likewise, he would quickly adjust and had all the experience in the world to call upon. Clive had played against the All Blacks for Pontypool, West Wales and the national team; he knew about rolling up his sleeves and he, above all others, was determined not to disappoint. But, all the while, Clive was going to make the most of this short, sharp tour and, in the run-up to the first

Test, he had met one of Britain's most influential politicians.

As it happened, Edward Heath, then leader of the Opposition, was staying at the same Christchurch hotel as the Welsh team. The *Western Mail* stated that 'he is a keen rugger fan' having last seen Wales in action at Murrayfield in February of that same year when the Welsh stormed to victory. He was spending five days on business in New Zealand and would not dream of missing the match. Clive picks up the story:

> At eleven o'clock on the morning of the first Test, I had the whole team in my room going through everything, this being part of the preparation, getting the boys pumped up, getting them all on the same wavelength.
>
> When it came to scrums, I'd call out, 'Ball coming in "Now!"' and, on the "Now!", everyone had to shout the word at the top of his voice. You can imagine with twenty-three players as well as management, there was an explosion of noise, like a piston! But unbeknown to me Ted Heath was in the next room. He was on the phone to New Zealand's Prime Minister Holyoake. We gave him the shock of his life; he thought there had been an earthquake!

I asked Brian Price if he remembered this:

> Oh yes, clearly. I may have been sharing the room with Clive that day as captain and coach. We heard this scream, we all did, and rushed out. But Ted was great with us on tour; we'd see him in the bars and have a couple of pints.

In the eyes of the New Zealand public, there was terrific expectation for this match. Wales on home ground at Lancaster Park was too good to be true and, with demand for tickets outstripping supply, extortionate prices were asked by last-minute ticket-sale profiteers. The wait had been far too long and, just as the Originals of 1905 had sensed trouble upon arrival in Cardiff, it was now Brian Price's men who were to feel the same sort of heat. In front of a fifty-five thousand crowd, Wales hoped to contain New Zealand's pack, so as to let their own talented backs have freedom to run. Now, level pegging in the Test series duel, history would surely be made this day. Brian, Welsh captain, looks back at the time:

> I remember New Zealand winning the toss, and with there being no wind advantage they decided to take the kick. Up to that point I had played against New Zealand on six occasions and every time they kicked off, the ball only went [the required] ten yards. We were prepared for this and had practised what we were going to do next. But on this occasion they decided to kick well over our heads and gave chase, which absolutely surprised all of us.
>
> The truth is that they didn't know anything about JPR. He was young and they hadn't played against him. 'Right, let's have a look at him,' they thought – but JPR was absolutely fearless. I can remember him shouting from the back 'My ball!' before running right through the All Blacks pack. 'What courage,' I thought, and spirit and this is how we played, although we lost the game.

In a recent conversation, JPR recalled that his overriding memory of the first Test was seeing black jerseys coming towards him from all directions. 'I could only do what I was taught in school [Bridgend Grammar],' he said to me, 'simply to tackle the man with the ball.' This he did memorably as, for instance, when he stopped Sid Going in his tracks with the jarring thud of his broad shoulders – reminding one of George Nēpia's crunching tackles against the Welsh in 1924. But, notwithstanding JPR and Brian Price's good line-out work and the collective efforts of the team, the Welsh pack was outplayed and the backs were forced into retreat. Wales' cause was not helped by missing vital kicks at goal, and the match was lost 19–0 in front of the large, studious and most satisfied crowd.

Most men of rugby would agree that touring is no fun without winning, and having drawn one game and lost another this was a difficult start. It would be uphill from here on. In New Zealand, where most people have considered views on the game, Wales had been put in its place and the pain of loss was lonely and punishing. However, Terry McLean in his decency was quick to highlight in the *New Zealand Herald* of June 2nd 1969 the 'futility and unfairness' of sending Wales into international combat so soon after the rigours of their exhausting travels. He had detected a missing gear in their overall performance, although others were not so generous in their honesty and most were predicting what the nation craved for most: another victory in the second Test.

But now with two provincial games to ease Wales back to winning ways and Clive Rowlands working on his men's battered egos, injecting self-belief and *hwyl* into training schedules, some winning pride was regained. Given that the buck stopped with Clive, he had questions to answer. 'We have got to win our next three games,' he said to the *New Zealand Herald* of June 2nd 1969. 'So far as my neck is concerned,' repeated Clive, 'we have got to win those next three' – being the remaining fixtures in New Zealand before moving on to Australia and Fiji. But even under this pressure he could not resist the offer of being kitted out to play in an invitation match:

> Members of the New Zealand Barbarians realised I had not played for the British 'Ba-Baas' and contacted me. They have a lovely system of playing against the schools. I was lined up against Penrose High School, Auckland, alongside

Waka Nathan, a really top man. At half-time we talked with the players, for perhaps fifteen minutes, sharing what we knew. I think I learnt more from young J. Robbins, the scrum half that day, than he learnt from me! There is no doubt about that; I liked what they did.

Clive was amazed how many school sides play rugby matches on Saturdays in New Zealand, and was even more shocked by the size of the watching crowds; they would often be in their thousands. When invited to address school assemblies Clive was equally impressed with the fitness of the children, many of whom were wearing shorts as a part of their uniform. Clive would return home with ideas for our own aspiring young players and is to this day proud to be connected with the New Zealand Barbarians Club. 'Every month I get a bulletin,' he explained. 'All the information is there for me, what's on, where people are playing golf. It's quite outstanding really, but they never leave me out.'

Otago was the next adversary at Carisbrook, Dunedin, a historic ground in the pleasing, working-class area of this small South Island city which reminds one of Edinburgh. And Wales won, bringing back a bit of confidence after their defeat in the Test. 'Chico', as everyone was now calling him, had another splendid match and a big hand in at least one of the Welsh tries, as he now recalls:

> They reckoned Maurice Richards was one of the greatest wings ever to go to New Zealand. I went blind and drew his winger and passed the ball, following him up the field (well not following really because I was 20 yards behind!). There were four or five players stretched out having been beaten, all lying in Maurice's wake. He was a determined man, a great competitor. He could also sidestep and that's what made him so good.

Wales left the stadium with a 27–9 win, vital for morale, and for raising hopes of another victory against Wellington three days later. Or would New Zealand's on-form province be too big a nut to crack? Yes, emphatically, said the locals, and with good reason, for within the last four years Wellington had beaten both the Springboks and the British Lions with a mountain of points to spare. Another scalp in the form of Wales was decidedly on the cards. It was vital that the Welsh fronted up to a big challenge in this capital city, where, ahead of the game, the team were invited to Parliament House to visit Prime Minister Keith Holyoake and other members of the Cabinet. Ray, character that he is, continues:

> By now, I had met a New Zealand girl who smoked. So when we went to a function and cigarettes were left for us to help ourselves, I'd pinch a few fags off the tables to give to her. When the Prime Minister and his Finance Minister, Mr Robert Muldoon, both tall men, looked down on me, they could see straight into my top blazer pocket, stuffed with cigarettes!

Earlier described in the *New Zealand Herald* as a 'jack in the box' the Wellington match was a personal triumph for Chico who scored virtually in the last minute of play, helping Wales win 14–6. Although Chico's display had been significant it had not been a vintage performance from the Welsh team. Yet they had stopped Wellington, and this was more than enough to put the tour back on track, auguring well for the final All Black encounter in Auckland.

Just as the old pavilions and enclosures at Cardiff Arms Park were now giving way to new concrete stands, Eden Park was similarly benefiting from progressive upgrades. Modern and efficient and still holding on to most of its old-fashioned charm, Eden Park, first and foremost a cricket ground, had seen rugby arrive in 1914. In the following half century, it had staged many of the country's epic rugby encounters besides playing host to the Empire Games in 1950.

Rob Butler, from Auckland, remembers going as a child to see provincial matches at this ground, matches which drew crowds of twenty or thirty thousand people or sometimes more. Rob recalls that his father would park in the nearby side streets, and as they walked towards the stadium they would see familiar faces sitting in the front gardens and on verandas when the weather was fine; these were people he had got to know over the years.

'I started as a mascot, aged five, for my brother's team,' said Rob, this being a group of six-year-olds competing in one of the preliminary matches before the main event. This was during the winter when he played for the eastern suburbs, often on cold, wet days when the fields were nowhere near as good as today. 'You'd be running for the line and your boot would come off in the mud,' he smiled.

> Lots of parents didn't have their own vehicles in those days, so, as my dad had a huge car, everybody piled into it and a couple of other motors, and that's how the team travelled to wherever they were playing. It was pretty basic then, I can tell you. In the stadium itself, we'd be there sitting on the grass still in our playing gear trying to behave ourselves. Around us would be stalls selling food and drinks. I can remember people coming around with trays of pies. Money would be passed to the guys in front, just as pies were passed back up the line. And there'd be the smell of tobacco like an old English pub.

Not many years before Wales' crunch match with the All Blacks in 1969 spectators stood on a gentle grass bank at Eden Park, alongside trees where the most dedicated enthusiasts perched in branches (similar to past scenes at Stradey Park) enjoying the best views. However, if they ever felt the after-effects of alcohol, they had to let go, there and then, from a great height! We can only sympathise with those below.

The Welsh completed their final practice under the glare of countless pairs of eyes, some concerned, most curious, all excited. By 1969 the shuttle trams that had, in the main, carried spectators to the ground had for more than ten years yielded to cars and car parks, but another famous match-day institution was still going strong. This was popularly known as a 'Scotsman's Grandstand', familiar to people from Auckland including rugby enthusiast Kelly Wright:

> My first recollection of a Scotsman's stand was when I was in university with a bunch of engineers. At the end of the garden was the infamous shed which housed all sorts of implements and goodness knows what else. It had a corrugated flat roof and you could lean a ladder up against it and we'd have a view of Eden Park from the north-east corner. Of course, we were avoiding paying to go in. We had a transistor radio and we listened to the commentary while we watched the action, usually with a pair of binoculars by our side.

Kelly explained that things moved on from the time when he stood amongst a few blokes on the roof with a crate of beer. 'Soon it was a case of why don't we get a couch to sit on,' he said. 'Then, why don't we invite the girls round to make sausage rolls and to winch beer up to us.' Kelly continues:

> Because six to eight guys, half tanked, could fall off, we built a sort of railing. We turned it into a mini grandstand really – taking it all down the next day. Then, over time, the whole of Sandringham and other areas overlooking

the ground developed their own roof-top stands to various levels of ornamentation. I vaguely remember one having a roof so that no one got sunburnt. Of course, our idea at the time was to throw an umbrella up and ram the foot of it into a wooden beer crate. Ours was completely rough and ready, thrown together and away you went.

Over time proprietors of Scotsman's stands started charging for the privilege of allowing others to view matches and this led to rules and regulations being put in place before the late 1960s. Such entrepreneurs were making the most of what they had, knowing that as the grandstands got predictably bigger and taller and views became curtailed, the act of allowing the Eden Park neighbourhood into the ground in this manner would eventually have to end. But this was to take time and the larger varieties were in evidence for Wales' visit. 'My phone has been ringing day and night for weeks,' explained one woman to the *New Zealand Herald* of June 16th, who had a seated enclosure behind her house. Since she had not publicised her match-day intentions, she was taken aback by the interest. 'I could easily have sold a thousand more tickets,' she said, another reflection of the New Zealanders' commitment to their national game and the draw of the Triple Crown champions who were, at last, finding their feet.

For the Welsh, Saturday June 14th 1969 would be a true rugby initiation. Sir Wilson Whineray, in his Foreword to *Eden Park: A History*, relates a conversation that reportedly took place in the Welsh changing room at Cardiff Arms Park. A new cap who had just completed his first match exclaimed excitedly: 'Now I'm an international!' to which an old stager, who had heard the words, stated, 'Yes, you are. But you won't be a *real* international until you've played the All Blacks at Eden Park.'

Could this comment belong to Brian Price, one wonders? 'No, it wasn't mine,' he replied, 'but I'd go along with those sentiments.' He, too, can remember seeing a rather elaborate balcony full of people in someone's garden overlooking the scoreboard end as he approached the ground. How did Brian feel?

> As far as I was concerned it was a huge occasion. We thought we had a chance and, although they were a brilliant side, one or two players were coming to the end of their careers. We had a choice of a young back-row: Dai Morris, Mervyn Davies, John Taylor and Dennis Hughes. We were full of encouragement and enthusiasm. As usual we sang on the bus. Clive insisted on this. It got us in the right mood.

As the players stepped out in front of the vast crowd, Gerald Davies, usually a centre three-quarter, was embarking upon a career-changing switch to the wing position, having practised line-out throws all week. 'I felt sorry for Gerald,' said Brian. 'He was worried about this and I can remember staying behind after training so that he could practise. "I don't know if I'll manage to get it to the back," he said, but he did well. And moving to the wing was the best thing to happen to him; he became twice the player.'

It was, however, New Zealand full back, Fergie McCormick, who stole the show, converting three tries, kicking five penalties and a drop goal for a record-breaking twenty-four points. As hard as Wales tried, this was a frustrating afternoon when events did not go the team's way, despite crossing the line twice and Maurice Richards' score being world class. The final score was an unenviable 33–12. However, refereeing decisions this day did not favour Wales, an issue that was described in a separate column in the *New Zealand Herald* of June 16th. In the ambiguous words of Handel Rogers, the Welsh team manager, Mr Murphy had officiated to the 'best of his ability'. But the feelings of others were not so skilfully concealed on a day when the Welsh players were maddened by many of the judgements made.

It is to the credit of the Welsh management that their policy throughout the tour was to make light of such issues and not to complain. Clive Rowlands as coach told the newspapers that he felt the experience of the tour would be the making of Welsh rugby, adding that the schools game back home needed to take stock of the ways of New Zealand and follow suit. He had been impressed by the ball-handling abilities of All Black forwards which gave him much to mull over. Then Clive, never one to shy away, put his much-talked-about neck back on the block by predicting a series victory for the British Lions touring New Zealand in 1971. Team captain, Brian Price, who was equally in demand with obligations and speeches of his own, recalls:

> At the end of the second Test, I remember having to go into the stand and make a speech. I said all the right things, I suppose, but I was thinking it was all so intense; there was such passion. We couldn't buy a paper or have a haircut without someone telling us we're going to get walloped next match. Things were stacked against us and we did what we could – but what we didn't bargain for in the second Test was the referee. He awarded some crucial penalties [against us] and, of course, Fergie McCormick kicked them all.

The All Blacks had now a 5–3 Test victory advantage over Wales, yet the Welsh could still hold their heads up high. Saddled by injuries, flummoxed by law interpretations, disappointed by refereeing decisions and driven onto the back foot from the beginning, the men had, nevertheless, dug deep, and showed ability, tenacity and the will to win. Beating Australia 19–16 and Fiji 31–11 on the way home would make the journey more tolerable. Sir Gareth Edwards, who was given the Welsh captaincy in Suva that hot Fijian day, has pleasant memories:

> It felt like it was in the eighties and I remember looking at Denzil Williams, his nice rotund face as red as a tomato; I thought he was going to burst! And every time Fiji had the ball they ran it. I can see their winger running down the touchline and JPR calling 'Leave him to me,' but he ghosted past JPR without losing pace. 'Oh no,' I was thinking; this doesn't happen too often – but on the day Dennis Hughes [of Newbridge] was magnificent for us and we came away with a win.

But the flights were just as punishing. 'We'd just be dropping off to sleep,' said Sir Gareth, 'and the air hostesses would wake us up, preparing us for another landing. I can see Brian Price and Brian Thomas sitting in the equivalent of today's economy class. They couldn't fit in; the guys were wedged into their seats!'

In another was Handel Rogers, as ever keeping the party together and spirits high. His standing of sportsmanship and agreeable, diplomatic demeanour had not only ensured him personal respect in New Zealand but it had also guaranteed that the social bond between the three feathers and the silver fern had remained close throughout their stay. However, turbulent times lay ahead.

It's Delme's day as Carwyn calls the tune

As Clive Rowlands predicted, the Welsh took great gains from their tour to the southern hemisphere. A creditable share of the Five Nations championship with France in 1970 was followed by a grand slam a year later, distinguished by a most impressive tally of points scored. Wales had, without doubt, secured a higher footing on the world ladder and this augured well for its talented pool of players when, in mid-May 1971, the latest British Lions touring party was selected. There would be two warm-up matches in Australia before the serious business of another twenty-four battles got underway beyond the Tasman Sea.

As it turned out, Wales' representation of fourteen men, including two replacements, amounted to almost half the squad. By now, players like John Dawes, Gareth Edwards, Barry John, J. P. R. Williams, Delme Thomas and Mervyn Davies felt they knew what would crack the New Zealand code, and were confident they had the right management and colleagues to do the job. Benefiting from Clive Rowlands' inspirational coaching methods during Wales' successes, the Lions' coach, Carwyn James, would take advantage of this momentum and swing by moulding it into a format of his own. His mild-mannered, softly spoken ways belied the steely, astute and formidable rugby tactician that he was. Carwyn's style was to parade up and down the training field in his tracksuit firing a series of encouraging one-liners: 'Faster, John', 'Pass it quicker, Jeff', 'Now straighten the line, Roy' – a constant torrent of attention to detail, honing the skills of a very talented group of men. With a quiet determination he would urge: 'Don't let them seize the initiative!' 'Get there first!' 'Be prepared to attack!' Such was his preparation that Carwyn knew exactly which way the wind would blow: he was, undoubtedly, a coach ahead of his time.

Although the first match in Brisbane against Queensland was lost, what followed during the next three months was a sequence of brilliant, unforgettable rugby. Five weeks into the tour, the Lions had won their second match in Australia and their first ten games in New Zealand. The rugby-savvy Kiwis knew that they were witnessing something special as the Lions' players became household names and stars. Saturday June 26th was the time for everyone to stop what they were doing and to concentrate on a compelling match against the All Blacks at an overfull Carisbrook, in Dunedin.

This day Barry John, a native of Cefneithin near Llanelli, was to play the game of his life, triggered to greatness by memories of the Welsh tour two years earlier and the ill-fated second Test against the All Blacks when he was severely angered by the referee. 'No one, before or since, has inflamed my temper so much as that man,' he stated,[40] qualifying his remarks by adding that he rarely lost his cool. The pressure on this talented outside half from television, newspapers, rival players, a back injury and even well-wishing fans, was immense. Carisbrook was living up to its epithet as the 'House of Pain'. Meanwhile, back in Wales, a nation was rousing at about 4 a.m. on match day, reaching for radios so as to listen to the live commentary, such was the game's appeal.

---

40   Barry John, *The Barry John Story* (Collins, 1974).

Barry describes the tension during the team talk at the hotel, all players raring to go and barely able to settle down and sit in one place. On the bus each man concentrated on what he needed to do, knowing that the team would do the rest. This day Barry was to be crowned 'King John', for New Zealanders had never seen such a complete outside half performance and neither would they hold back when praise was due. Roly Scott, a former rugby referee, was one of the lucky ones to have a grandstand seat and could not believe what he was seeing:

> I had never seen such pinpoint kicking over a whole game. I'd watched Fergie [McCormick] playing outstanding games for Canterbury and the All Blacks, but that day Barry John made him look a novice.

Barry John's performance may have nudged Fergie – the nation's hero when scoring twenty-four points against Wales at Eden Park in 1969 – into retirement from Test rugby, for he was dropped after a long and successful career. In those two years the wheel had turned; now the Welsh were hailed as giants amongst the Lions for their part in this 9–3 win. Another Welsh marker had been laid down in New Zealand eyes. Clearly Carwyn's hard work and vision were paying dividends, whilst away from the field of play his players were making friends. Gerald Davies, on the right wing, explained[41] that the Lions had 'struck the right balance' when it came to mixing work with play, particularly when socialising with schools. Many of the team were 'adopted' by pupils of the country's educational establishments, which meant that they took an active interest in 'their' player's tour performances, keeping a scrap book, collecting newspaper cuttings, jotting

---

41   *Gerald Davies: An Autobiography* (George Allen & Unwin, 1979).

down points scored and generally getting to learn as much about their celebrity guest as possible.

Gerald was one of a group supporting Chico when he was invited to address pupils of Gisborne Boys High School. This is a large establishment on the eastern coast of the North Island, with a strong Māori presence and a proud 'Old Boys' line-up that includes Rico and Hosea Gear. On the last tour in 1966, the school welcomed Mike Gibson as its adopted player; this time Ray 'Chico' Hopkins had the honour. Unlike some of his colleagues, who merely had to speak informally to the children, Chico was asked to talk at morning assembly. It is one thing to be a carefree and confident person but quite another when it comes to public speaking.

Chico was petrified about standing in front of everyone and, although his father had helped him to write a speech, he was more nervous about this task than facing the All Blacks. 'I was in the back of the bus reading my lines,' he said, the first of these being, 'I come from a place called Maesteg, which is a veritable paradise' – words that his playing colleagues, knowing Maesteg, latched on to immediately, creating a running joke for the remainder of the tour. Whilst Gerald felt that Chico's performance in front of the children was worthy of praise, and says so in his autobiography, the Maesteg scrum half's version of events is far different:

> I can remember standing on the stage that morning in the school. There was a lectern at the front and my knees were shaking so much that I knocked it over; I was that nervous. The children in the front row had to run for cover. John Dawes and probably half of the team came to support me. Many were lucky in that they only had to meet their headmasters and say a quick 'hello' to the children. But, as for me, I had to get up and speak.

I also remember telling the New Zealanders that when I was made captain of the Welsh youth side, Maesteg Rugby Club put on a dinner for me at the town hall. Earlier that day I had gone to Swansea to watch Manchester United playing at the Vetch Field. But because we had heavy snow, I couldn't get back home in time. So, I missed the dinner, but I was glad because I was too shy; I really didn't want to get up and speak.

Despite the Lions losing the next Test 22–12 in Christchurch, they continued on their tour until they eventually arrived at Eden Park, Auckland, on Saturday August 14th with just a solitary defeat in New Zealand. Now leading 2–1 in the Test victories, the Lions needed a draw to clinch the series and become the first British Isles team to register such an achievement. The match was colossal and was viewed from every conceivable Scotsman's grandstand – and was drawn, 14–14, thanks to a drop goal from J. P. R. Williams positioned near half-way. JPR is remembered for rock-solid defence, thumping tackles, masterful handling of the high ball, and attacking flair in entering the line, but he is not known for dropping goals. I asked him when he had landed such a kick prior to this crucial fourth Test:

> Funnily enough it was in Fiji in 1969, at the end of the Welsh tour to New Zealand. I can only remember dropping three goals. The other was on my debut for Bridgend at the Memorial Ground, Bristol, in the late 1960s.
>
> I must admit I had been practising a bit in New Zealand. Barry John and Bob Hiller were our place-kickers and when they stayed behind after training to kick some goals, I'd be behind the posts, catching the ball and getting it back to them. They insisted on me doing some 'drops' at the time and assisted me in the same way.

There was a lot of tension before the fourth Test and when I said I was going to drop a goal, I made everyone laugh! But, as Barry [John] used to say, 'Cometh the moment: cometh the man.'

Or cometh the team? JPR continues:

We used to have a split in the party. Half of us had the day off and would have a few drinks and the rest of us would be playing. The most important thing was that people like Bob Hiller and John Spencer were fantastic in the midweek side and always totally supportive. The strength of the Lions was having a strong and supportive back-up, although these players were desperately sad not to be making the Tests. Our best performance was against Wellington, one of the top sides. [The Lions won 47–9.] It was a fantastic game of rugby, lots of tries; we were running from all directions.

Along with the other players, JPR had never before experienced such crowds viewing training runs as on this tour. Often there would be thousands of people in attendance, studying the drills, making notes, all learning and remembering, such was the admiration of New Zealanders for these British rugby men and their gifted coach, Carwyn James. JPR explains:

This was unbelievable, a new experience; we'd never seen anything like it before. And Carwyn was a phenomenal coach, a real psychologist, a very intelligent man. People came just to watch him, to listen to his words; the crowds flocked from all around.

Carwyn's achievement gave him absolute respect from the New Zealand public, and his support for his players was equally commendable. Chico told me that whilst on tour he had a thigh complaint that showed little sign of healing, and it had led him to seek help from the former 1924 All Black legend George Nēpia. The famous full back, knowledgeable about good and proven Māori remedies, had a cure of his own for this type of injury and when Chico arrived for a form of consultation, Carwyn, ever supportive, was at his side:

> What a lovely bloke George Nēpia was, so modest a man. I kept writing to him for years, [said Chico]. He wanted to try to help me with my thigh. He had a special Māori leaf from a tree; it was a bit like a dock leaf, which he wet in water and put on my leg. Then he got a hot cast-iron plate, of a sort, to press down on top of it. 'Don't worry, it will be alright,' he said to me, but I made sure I didn't leave it there for too long!

It is no secret that Carwyn, who had been impressed by Chico's Lions form, persuaded him to join Llanelli as part of an exercise to strengthen the club side in readiness for the All Blacks' visit to Stradey Park the following year, 1972. And when that moment arrived Chico was in the Scarlets' changing room. Carwyn, the same intelligent coach, aided by the scientific sporting expertise of Tom Hudson, had by now prepared his side thoroughly for the arrival of Ian Kirkpatrick and his men.

Carwyn realised that Llanelli, the first team from Wales to meet the All Blacks on this tour, would be dealing with an exceptionally determined force. Losing the Lions series had been a national disaster in New Zealand and the Welsh contingent, especially Carwyn himself, were leading perpetrators. To lose out to his tactics again one year later could not be contemplated, whilst, for Carwyn, nothing could be sweeter than steering Llanelli to a triumph against the All Blacks at Stradey Park. But, all along, he had to convince his team, club officials and Scarlets' supporters that a win was on the cards.

On 31st October 1972, the All Blacks stepped from their bus at Stradey's main entrance, smart in black blazers and looking every inch a team of world beaters, before standing respectfully on the touchline watching the school boys in rugby action. But when they entered their changing room and read the match programme, they saw that Carwyn, the great schemer, was at it again.

His official written address to the fans was almost imperial, setting the last piece of a psychological jigsaw in place. Referring to past battles played by the two teams, some of which ought to have been won by Llanelli, Carwyn's words went straight into the chambers of their heart. 'In the dressing room today the Llanelli players will be reminded of those sad endings,' said Carwyn, pointing out that 'the world' and, most importantly, 'staunch Scarlet supporters' have no wish 'to know a loser.' Then he hailed his team as being one of the greatest to honour the club, adding 'of this I personally have no doubt.' As he emphasised the strength of the day's opposition – for the strongest All Blacks team had been selected to play – he referred to their powerful pack, especially at scrum, line-out and ruck situations:

> Every All Black forward is a ball winner by habit, by nature almost, and as a pack they hunt for the ball together. Always formidable, in full cry they are frightening.

Although he thought 'the Kiwi [was] a danger close to the set piece,' Carwyn pointed out that he did not expect to be threatened as much by the All Blacks in open play. But he considered their disciplined and strong forward platform had for years set the style necessary for success. Then came his punchline, executed to perfection, when referring to the 'rigid pattern' of All Black 'play'. 'The big question today is can we counter it,' he asked, 'and produce our own brand of running, attacking, creative rugby. We shall know in a couple of hours.'

Carwyn had now placed his head above the parapet, emphasising with greater detail and strength the words and feelings that had already been published by the great man in the local newspapers. This is why home supporters seemed quiet, nervous and accountable, as if sharing a collective responsibility to lift the side, ensuring their inspirational leader was not let down or proved wrong. As for Delme Thomas and his men, they had never been more determined: fire would be met by fire. Chico Hopkins felt just the same:

I can remember running out onto the field going into what seemed like a dark dell. Although it was dry it looked as though a thunderstorm was going to break out. It was very black, and the singing was like we hear in a cemetery – but it soon brightened up with 'Sosban Fach'. When we went out for a team photograph earlier, every one of us looked serious. 'Nobody is to smile,' Carwyn had said. It was a question of doing the business and getting away. We were a good side, but I've always believed that if it is going to happen, it's going to happen.

When the anthems began, the Llanelli players stopped wherever they happened to be running around in the course of their last-minute warm-up, spread across the field, bolt upright, heads held high. Within minutes came the 'thunderstorm' (of a kind) as both packs stormed forward for the ball, desperate to get the upper hand. 'Don't let them seize the initiative!' Carwyn had implored of his men. But there was one man, not mentioned so far, for whom everybody should have spared a thought. This was referee Mike Titcomb of Bristol, an experienced official but this day needing eyes in the back of his head for this was a downright violent, even brutal occasion. By half-time Llanelli were still protecting their early lead. Then, uplifted by the interval singing and music, the local heroes knuckled down to defy the odds, enacting every discipline that Carwyn their coach had implored of them, before registering the club's favourite scoreline: Llanelli 9 – Seland Newydd 3.

There was no prouder moment for Delme Thomas, whose cousin, Percy, told me that, when he called to wish him well early on the morning of the match, Delme was putting up shelves in the kitchen. This gentle giant, who began his rugby career on the wing in school at St Clears and, as stated in the *New Zealand Herald*, was 'transplanted' into the front row on an earlier overseas tour – 'I was put upfront to make room,' he said modestly – shares some thoughts forty years after the big event, the first concerning his meeting with Ian Kirkpatrick when the referee tossed the coin:

> He just smiled. We'd met the year before [on the 1971 Lions tour]. We'd spoken a lot during the series, but at this moment, we both just smiled. It was our way of showing respect.
>
> Ian Kirkpatrick is a gentleman, a great All Black. At the end of the game I went into the All Blacks dressing room, just to shake his hand. But then I could see that everyone was in such a state of shock. The result wasn't going down well. It hurt them and they just couldn't take it – so I turned round and left.
>
> Even in the evening, I could still see how much it hurt. The one thing about New Zealand is that they are not used to being beaten; they are that good. If you are on the winning side against the All Blacks, it is an honour.

Les Williams, Llanelli club historian, recalls the atmosphere before the match:

Leading up to the game there was great excitement; it was like Christmas time. What I remember is seeing the shop windows dressed with rugby memorabilia. We'd all see a photo of Phil Bennett or Albert Jenkins or another of our players; you couldn't miss them. In People's Park, someone had the idea to have a flower bed and when you looked from a distance it was arranged like the Llanelli club badge.

On the morning of the game, I was in work in the middle of Llanelli. Being a Tuesday, it was half-day closing in the town and I remember everyone making their way to Stradey nice and early, with the band marching down the street, looking smart in their red uniform.

Les explained that in the evening a 'Rugger Ball' was held for the teams at the Glen Ballroom and members of the New Zealand party were present:

Fair play, they turned up, at least a number of them were there. I remember that one of the girls who worked for me had a dance with Alistair Scown, and was terribly proud about this. The New Zealanders were good; they acknowledged they were beaten and got on with it.

Who could blame Roy Bergiers, try scorer, if he, too, had danced the night away, but this was far from the truth. After enjoying the function, Roy preferred to relax and reflect upon an incredible day, amidst feelings ranging from euphoria to disbelief. Roy remembers the team meeting for an early lunch at the Ashburnham Hotel, this, the calm before the storm; and the journey by bus to the ground with a police escort. 'By the time we got to Stradey Park Avenue, there were people everywhere,' explained Roy, 'our bus having to fight its way through. Again this was a clever move by Carwyn, each of us feeling the gradual build up, heightening the sense of occasion.'

Roy, a school teacher, remembers squeezing through a tight huddle of people at the players tunnel, before stepping onto the field and into the noise.' It just hit you,' he said. 'I also remember the spectators being packed so near to the touchline that you almost felt you were in the crowd.' Among those sitting close to the dead-ball line on temporary seats were teachers and pupils from Roy's school: soon jumping into the air as he scored his try – right in front of their eyes! Likewise, when the match was over, they were the first onto the field, as Roy recalls:

> We all remember Delme being carried shoulder high and a few friends hoped to do the same for me. But, with one being taller than the other, I was soon tipping over, legs in the air, my head towards the ground. When I eventually got off the field, our dressing room was chock-a-block, there being no security as we know it today – and this is when I caught site of Ken Jones putting away the match ball. 'Can I have that, Ken,' I asked, and I remember Ken looking at it and pausing, before eventually saying, 'Oh, go on then.'

If Roy's feet were in the air during the post-match celebrations, they were firmly on the ground the next day as he taught Class 5(c) at Ystrad Tywi School's sports field – especially as 'Aunt' Bessie's brolly was playing heavily on his mind:

> My mother did not intend going to the game, but changed her mind at the last minute. She was sitting in the stand with 'Auntie' Bessie [a close family friend] when I scored. This is when Bessie threw her posh umbrella up into the air, never to be seen again. And she hasn't forgiven me since!

Rugby loses its way
amongst the fights and the fog

When the All Blacks returned to their dressing rooms at Llanelli, the onset of shock and disbelief had already hit them. Having struggled to break through an army of spectators who invaded the field at the final whistle, and seeing Delme Thomas carried shoulder high amidst wild excitement, the All Blacks felt the stinging salt that Carwyn James had rubbed into their wounds. Over forty years later, lock forward Andy Haden, sadly now departed, a veteran of 117 appearances for the All Blacks, explains

> All Black teams are always shocked to lose. The expectations of the fans and I suppose the players, too, are very high. It's a big wake-up call when things don't go well and it doesn't matter who the opposition is. The measure of those expectations is the way that opposition teams react in victory. They would certainly, prior to the match, have aspired to play well, but I suspect many would have thought that to win would be a bridge too far – but, when they do win, they all, in turn, respond with enormous celebration. Those very celebrations help to stiffen the resolve of All Black teams that follow on.

And 'resolve' is what Andy and his teammates would need to face Cardiff at the Arms Park in four days' time. But, before then, they found time for golf in Caerphilly, a visit to Cardiff Castle, a Lord Mayor's gathering, and a tour of the new Cardiff Stadium, a totally different venue to the one Brian Lochore visited in the late 1960s. Enjoying a stay in the Angel Hotel, whose good neighbourly links with the famous ground date back to early internationals, the All Blacks would have noticed an unwelcome billboard near the entrance; it bore the score of their game with Llanelli. Carwyn's psychology was catching!

In the *Western Mail* the day before the match was the news that a former Welsh referee who had moved to Brussels was bringing a party of children to Wales to play some rugby of their own before attending the big match. Little did he know, however, that this was not to be the best advertisement for the game. Despite some running of the ball and three tries for the All Blacks, the match is remembered for fighting, bad blood and the prostrate body of All Black prop Jeff Matheson when stretchered off after a punch. Cardiff lost by 20 points to 4.

Only days earlier, Terry McLean, writing home for the *New Zealand Herald* on November 2nd, had been gracious in defeat with the headline 'Magnificent play by Llanelli', supported by the words 'All Blacks Out-Thought, Out-Fought'. But following this Cardiff match was the equally telling statement: 'All Blacks win amid ugly Cardiff scenes.' He cited some of the unsavoury incidents of the day, which included the private punch-up of a cluster of players that continued whilst Ian Kirkpatrick crossed for a try. But what also upset Mr McLean was the unruly behaviour of certain elements of the crowd, whose unsporting gestures were provocative and rude. It was perhaps just as well that the All Blacks left Wales for three weeks to honour their next fixtures in England, Scotland and Ireland, as tempers needed to cool.

Could it be that sixty-seven years on from Dave Gallaher's Originals the goodwill and friendship between the two rugby nations was slipping away? Admittedly, the refereeing rumpus affecting the Glamorgan match of 1905 had caused an ugly and heated exchange at the time, but the ill-feeling now being expressed by fist and boot was overshadowing the play and creating a state of discord and stubbornness that had never previously been seen. Clearly, the highly publicised Lions series win had a bearing of some sort and doubtless the bruises of the heavier encounters stung painfully – but, somehow, the game, which had now become highly commercialised, was beginning to leave one or two essentials behind.

The whole rugby edifice seemed to be at some sort of tipping point. Llanelli's match, for instance, was a bonanza for media, social and business activities, as it was a rich honey pot for rugby itself – although, of course, not exclusively for the host club. Yet, on the day, the referee had to step into a cauldron of emotion, had to handle players bigger, fitter, better than before, each driven by an iron will and backed by fanatical support, but with touch judges devoid of all power, with viewing officials having no capacity to cite serious indiscretions, and with the added anxieties of spectators positioned yards from play. It is to the credit of Mr Titcomb that he controlled the match in such circumstances when supremely fit, strong and utterly motivated players were happy to get away with whatever they could.

Rugby's sheer physicality and competitiveness has never offered a soft option and its rivalry is strong and raw and unashamedly so. From the grass roots upwards, old battles are carried forward just as players leaving a club know what to expect should ever they return in different playing colours. Likewise, the view of Mr Meredith, All Black tour manager in 1935, about giving and taking knocks and shutting up about them, continues to be upheld by players – well, at least until next time!

Yet, judging from the Llanelli and Cardiff encounters of 1972, it was apparent that the standard and appeal of players that fans looked up to, and the nature of the game itself, had moved on to such a degree that the administration was lagging badly behind. Equally, a more rugby-sophisticated, and paying, audience was justifiably correct to feel a sense of unease with the rawness of the on-field contests.

Gareth Jenkins played flank forward for Llanelli in that match of 1972 and, even without the benefit of his later coaching experience, he recognised at the time that changes had to be made to the game. Walking off the field at Stradey that day 'aching from head to foot', he would not have dreamt of harping on about the nastiness of the battles. 'When you step onto the field,' said Gareth, 'it is part of the deal. You are entering into serious physical confrontation and need to be prepared.' That said, playing issues still needed tightening up. Gareth continues:

> In the 1970s rugby was at the height of its physicality because we had big crowds, always rivalry and just one referee – meaning that what went on (as we players used to say) on the 'blindside' [behind the referee's back] went unnoticed.

Clearly, Gareth and his colleagues did not know what the outcome would be against New Zealand on that particular day other than knowing both teams were hell-bent on winning. 'It was head-on,' he said, 'the match was brutal.' And, as regards the referee, Mr Titcomb, highly placed in the international game, 'he held it together,' said Gareth, 'he got the eighty minutes played. And, of course, the crowds were thoroughly entertained and got their money's worth, but if parents wanted to see their children playing the game, things had to change.'

When the All Blacks returned to Wales, it was to tackle Gwent, captained by Newbridge's Dennis Hughes (hero of Wales' win in Fiji in 1969) at Ebbw Vale, the rugby stronghold of a team familiar with big match atmosphere and well versed with the complexities of serving-up first-class rugby union. Interestingly, in the early 1900s, the locals chose to give rugby league its chance, organising matches whilst players travelled to and from the north of England. This was to last a period of about five years, ending around 1909,[42] by which time the travel on limited resources was, in the main, deemed just too wearisome.

Roy Lewis, who described his earlier journey in a Jones bus, and a long-serving Ebbw Vale club member, was excited to see Ian Kirkpatrick and his side performing at Ebbw Vale's Welfare Sports Ground. He was thrilled that such a strong visiting team had been chosen – players such as Andy Haden, Keith Murdoch, Alan Sutherland, Ken Stewart and Grant Batty being in the line-up – and he had never before seen so many people packed into the ground.

> It was great to see the All Blacks in our area, on our field. This was the wonderful thing about the old tours. We used to look forward to the players arriving and getting to know them.
>
> On the day we saw an exciting match but the All Blacks were too strong for us, especially as they fielded almost a Test pack. But we had our moment at the end when Glyn Turner, scrum half, was unstoppable. He nipped round the blind side of the scrum, managing to evade the brilliant Sid Going. That part of the ground is now known as 'Glyn Turner's corner', and there is a photo on the clubhouse wall of him scoring.

The match, played on November 28th 1972, ended with a

---

42   Abertillery/Ebbw Vale *vs* All Blacks match-day programme 1963. Article by Len Coldrick, club secretary.

16–7 victory to the All Blacks. Despite losing, the men of the county had given a good show of themselves, causing the beer to flow. Roy told me that most rugby receptions at this time were held at Ebbw Vale's Lever Hall. These were big affairs, with the best of everything – food, drink, guest speakers, entertainment – showing just how strong clubs were in those days. 'The next step up was a full international,' said Roy. 'And what we have to realise is that the local players were going to work in the morning and playing the All Blacks in the afternoon. They were unforgettable occasions, bringing crowds along in their thousands.'

It was no doubt early to bed for the All Blacks who faced Wales at Cardiff days later on 2nd December. By the standards of their predecessors, Ian Kirkpatrick's team, having already lost to Llanelli and England's North Western Counties, were not doing well. They needed a big win and beating Wales, at this time a strong, settled, talented team, would do the trick. The All Blacks relished the opportunity, especially as their countrymen would now be watching the match live via a direct satellite telecast.

Wales had trained well under coach Clive Rowlands in the fresh air of Aberavon Beach, where the Afon Lido, just like the Waterston ground in Bridgend, had become integral to the team's preparations. However, Arthur Lewis, the captain, was injured and Jim Shanklin of London Welsh came in as centre, giving Delme Thomas the responsibility of leading the side. Delme has never forgotten the honour:

> We were in the Angel Hotel, which is a wonderful place to stay, right by the ground. We had an early lunch and we met up in one of the rooms to go through everything. Clive [Rowlands] had a few words to say and then it was up to me to motivate the team.

Delme was known for his rousing pre-match team talks and his men were prepared to give their all for the big man. So when Wales trailed 13–3 at half-time, at Cardiff Arms Park, Delme sounded another battle cry to great effect. However, the All Blacks responded by tackling everyone who moved, and that in a fair manner, for this match saw no nastiness. Wales' final twenty minutes was deemed worthy of victory itself, and there was a feeling of hard luck because JPR was denied a try similar in technique to the one awarded to Keith Murdoch earlier in the match. As Wales trailed 19–16, Phil Bennett, who had kicked well all afternoon, stepped forward to save the match for Wales; but, this time, the ball narrowly missed its target. 'It was the most disappointing day of my career,' said Delme. 'We had a great Welsh side. We should have won; it was a golden opportunity. But that's sport.' New Zealand walked away with the prize and now the gap between the teams extended to three clear victories.

It was four weeks later, December 30th 1972, when the All Blacks returned to Cardiff to challenge East Glamorgan. This day was so foggy that the match became a farce, for both the players and the ball disappeared into a wilderness of white. Added to the disappointment of losing 20–9, the home team also suffered the loss of scrum half Gareth Evans (a South Wales Police player) to a heavy hit when, following some pushing and shoving, he was caught by an unfriendly fist. New Zealand's Terry McLean said he could feel the clout from the press-box! His words in the *New Zealand Herald* of January 2nd 1973 do not hide his hurt and disappointment in stating that the two rival nations had hit a bumpy patch. 'Rightly or wrongly,' he added, his team's reputation in Wales, and particularly in Cardiff, was at an all-time low.

A Gem of a Try in the Greatest Game of All

As the All Blacks prepared for their last three matches in Wales, they were welcomed back to the Seabank Hotel, Porthcawl, by John Bowen and his staff. Hosting the All Blacks was a lively experience as the hotel had been inundated with people calling, phoning – indeed, blocking the phone lines – wanting tickets and requesting meetings, as well as bringing 'rugby balls and autograph books' to be signed. Not only had they to find rooms and space for all thirty-five of the group along with 135 items of general luggage, but satisfying the men's enormous appetite was another major task. All in all it was an enjoyable headache for Mr Bowen and his staff, who, according to the *Western Mail* of December 1st 1972, a day or so after the All Blacks' arrival, saw the men appearing in 'their pyjamas' in the hotel passageways: not in any way playing truant, but responding to a fire alarm scare, caused by a technical hitch which proved unfounded.

Handel Rogers, the manager of the Welsh touring party of 1969 and, more recently, a liaison officer for touring teams entering Wales, was another admirer of the All Blacks. This gentleman, who was soon to be president of the Welsh Rugby Union, had taken time to get to know the men and was enjoying their company as much as any previous tourists, especially the young players in the group. The 'changing of the guard', as Sir Brian Lochore referred to it, had taken place a year earlier following the 1971 Lions tour, when the likes of Messrs Meads, Lochore, McCormick and others had quietly left the playing scene after years of service.

The men of Newport were next into the fray, soon to challenge the All Blacks from the first blast of Air Commodore Larry Lamb's whistle. Taking the lead with a penalty was a good start. But the All Blacks seized control as the game progressed, being comfortably ahead when Newport scored a last-minute converted try. This took the final score to 20–15, a creditable return for the home team's labour. Nevertheless, there was that underlying and explosive tension between both sets of forwards, with the most notable incident of the match, in this respect, being the wrestling bout between Peter Whiting and Lyn Jones as play continued far away. Both had entered into a stubborn private duel, culminating in this prolonged tussle, for which they earned a reprimand from the man in charge although being allowed to play on.

When the All Blacks moved on to Neath, they were on another gentle roll, gathering pace and a momentum not easily stopped. A combined Neath–Aberavon side would bear testimony to this. It was a talented unit, carefully selected after much consideration to the feelings and strengths of both clubs but, try as they did, the All Blacks had the game well won early on, scoring seven tries in all, six converted by Joe Karam to win 43–3. This was exciting rugby, full of good quality movements, with Bob Burgess, first five-eighths, in splendid form. What is more, there was no nonsense.

Playing that day was the now-sadly-departed Sandy McNicol, a big, strong prop forward from Wanganui, with a friendly, smiling countenance and long sideburns. Sandy was such a nice guy, full of humour and so easy to talk to, that one wonders if he really did fit into the tough world of rugby players. This is a point that was apparently picked up by French sports journalist Denis Lalanne, who is understood to have described Sandy as the sort of bloke to help an old lady across the road. Be that as it may, he had been flown to Britain to replace the injured Jeff Matheson, who, in the Scottish Test, had suffered another injury, this time to his ribs.

Sandy arrived in time for the East Glamorgan game and was then selected for the Newport match, where he thought the referee was correct in allowing the two warring lock forwards to play on. 'They were rolling one on top of the other,' said Sandy, 'nothing too serious, but it went on for a while. Afterwards, someone said, 'Ref, why didn't you stop that?' And I remember him smiling, as if to say, 'Look guys, I had it under control.' I asked Sandy how he received news of his invitation to All Blacks duty; was it by way of a phone call?

Yes, on Christmas morning, and my father, a rugby nutter, just walked around the garden for the rest of the day. He couldn't believe his ears. Up until then I couldn't do anything right but, after this, things changed!

The next day the press quickly got hold of me, 'How are you keeping fit, Sandy?' they asked. 'Flying my son's kite,' I replied, jokingly, but it still went into print.

Later that Christmas Day we were trying to find the All Blacks' tailor. He'd gone away to his beach hut in the north.

When I got a blazer, Bob Duff, the 1956 captain, gave me an old [All Blacks] bag to use. It was very generous of him and then I was ready to jump aboard the plane. It was the first time I'd done such a long journey on my own. I stayed in a flash hotel in Los Angeles and I remember it was near a six-lane highway. The next day I went shopping for shoes.

Then, at Heathrow, a liaison officer met me, a really nice guy, and we went down on the train into Wales.

Sandy explained that the All Blacks were soon travelling to Neath to play the combined Neath–Aberavon team. From what he could gather, there could be huge resentment about who got chosen for the home side – eight from one, seven from the other, this sort of thing – although the selected fifteen is not always the strongest in the end. Sandy enjoyed his full part in the emphatic win and in the after-match function he met a Welshman who seemed to be on his own, as Sandy recalls:

'Good day to you,' I said. 'Good day to you,' the Welshman replied. We had a few drinks as we were pretty well free to do what we wanted in those days.

'What are you doing next?' the Welshman asked.

'Oh, I'm going to go for a meal,' I replied.

'Come and have a meal back in our house,' he said. 'My wife's a good cook.'

I remember going through the door and there was a wonderful smell of food.

'I've brought somebody round to see you,' he called out to his wife. 'I've got a bit of a surprise.'

But all of a sudden, a doorway opened from a room under the stairs and, at this point, the old lady of the house appeared:

'Ethel, what's going on?' she called out loudly to her daughter. 'I've told you before; we're not having strangers in this house!'

She was running the show alright. She must have seen our haka or something and got scared. All of a sudden, I was feeling a bit like a spare part. 'I'd better disappear and be out of here,' I thought, so I was soon on my way!

The following Saturday Sandy was on reserve duty, kitted out in a tracksuit, sitting in the North Stand at Cardiff Arms Park as his team faced the Barbarians, a fixture that had the potential to be a thrilling match. Captained by John Dawes and made up mostly of British Lions from 1971, this was close to being a fifth Test selection from that record-breaking tour. Admittedly, there were one or two omissions, and no Barry John, but in his place was Phil Bennett, exceptional and dazzling and, in such talented company, capable of setting the world alight. From the outset this game was going to be a ticket sell-out. Not only were the Barbarians committed to flowing, running rugby, they now had the added attraction of two hardened prop forwards, Sandy Carmichael and Ray McLoughlin, both injured on the last Lions tour and prevented from playing in the Tests. What is more, Carwyn James had helped to prepare the side and John Dawes, whose winning record against the All Blacks is admirable, was captain.

This game was transmitted live to New Zealand and it proved to be one of the greatest games of all time. Starting with magnificent singing – heard by the players when changing under the stand – the stadium erupted when the two teams ran onto the field. Within minutes of the haka, there was the most breathtaking of scores. All Black Sir Bryan Williams told me when I visited New Zealand that he was singularly, and rather modestly, proud to have been part of this 'greatest try of all' because it still brings him fame! This, of course, is only by virtue of him taking a pass from Ian Kirkpatrick and, after running upfield, 'putting in a beautiful centring kick' which, when bouncing awkwardly beyond the Barbarians' defence, gave his team the opportunity to attack. 'But Phil Bennett had other ideas,' he said with a smile – resulting in Gareth Edwards scoring in the opposite corner.

Sir Bryan Williams CNZM MBE, past president of the New Zealand Rugby Union, legendary wing and scorer of 66 tries for New Zealand, was enlightening as we drank a glass of beer in Ponsonby Rugby Club, Auckland. Ponsonby, which runs eleven senior sides, 50 junior teams and a women's section, is Bryan's club, as it either was or still is to so many All Blacks. A large painting of the great man in action appears high on the wall by the main bar and many items of memorabilia in the abounding display cabinets relate to Bryan's outstanding club, provincial and international achievements.

Clearly, scoring tries is Sir Bryan's subject and he recognises the brilliance of this one which, all these years later, is enough to bring tears to one's eye. Phil Bennett actually stopped and turned on a sixpence causing Alistair Scown to overrun his tackle. There then followed the mesmerising side-steps that threw, in turn, Peter Whiting, Ian Kirkpatrick and Ron Urlich. JPR did not flinch when Bryan tackled him high around the shoulders and the move was well under way, the ball in John Pullin's hands. John Dawes straightened the direction of the run, in the way that was so distinctive of his style, and by the time Derek Quinnell, having received the ball from Tom David seemed to pass to John Bevan near the 25-yard line, Gareth Edwards, going like a train, was intercepting the pass and heading for the line.

Was there ever a louder or more long-lasting cheer at Cardiff Arms Park than when Gareth dived early and low, so as to evade the covering tackle of Grant Batty? With a mere split-second difference in timing of their runs, this could have been an explosive mid-air collision, both men diving at terrific pace into the corner from different angles. It was an amazing try, and everyone knew that they had witnessed a truly wonderful score. Cliff Morgan, the player and this day the man with the microphone, spoke for all in his famous BBC commentary: 'Oh, that fellow Edwards, what can touch a man like that? If the greatest writer of the written word would have written that story, no one would have believed it. That really was something.'

Judging by the shocked expression on Gareth's face as he returned to his position, it appears that he felt exactly the same. But had he noticed Grant Batty, one wonders?

'Yes, in my peripheral vision,' Sir Gareth told me in a phone conversation, 'but I didn't look. I had my eyes glued on the corner, doing what I was taught, which is to dive; this way it wasn't so easy to tackle me.' What about the prolonged applause? 'We all try to shut out the crowd,' he added, 'but that time, as I walked back, I realised there was a huge cacophony of noise, the likes of which I had not heard before.'

How could the rest of the game better such a start? It would require sustained stunning running rugby from start to finish – and this is exactly what transpired, for the excitement never subsided. Early in the match, after a wonderful passage of play, John Bevan was denied a try by Alistair Scown's tackle – and what a score that might have been! John Dawes at the culmination of another storming run also managed to cross the try line, but the score was disallowed because of a forward pass. Ireland's Fergus Slattery then squeezed across the line to put points on the board before the All Blacks hit back when their two wings combined at speed: Bryan Williams, who was concussed following the weight of JPR's tackle, burst into the line and sent his good friend, Grant Batty, on his way.

Having now had a taste of the ball, Grant Batty was not content with just the one try. Next, he gathered a colleague's chip ahead as he neared the touchline, facing the might of JPR's broad shoulders getting closer. This was enough to make anyone chip ahead, but only one as sharp and talented as the electrifying winger could dash around him, gather the ball and walk a few paces nearer to the posts in such little space. In his biography, Grant refers to this try as being one of his best, yet he was disconsolate to hear the crowd jeering as he went back to his position. This was another example of the intense rivalry and hostility that had shrouded so much of this tour – as was his momentary spat with the much bigger Tommy David towards the end of the match.

The final try began when David Duckham of England produced a dazzling run allowing J. P. R. Williams to swerve past Joe Karam and dive into the corner. This left Phil Bennett to end a glittering rugby performance with a conversion from the touchline – as the referee, Georges Domercq, barely seen all afternoon because of the quality of the rugby, signalled the end of play. Barbarians 23, New Zealand 11, a scoreline that sparked enormous excitement in Cardiff, but far away in New Zealand, questions were being asked. Cynwyl Davies, a West Wales farmer from St Clears, was at the time gaining experience with the New Zealand Dairy Board, living and working on a family holding:

> We all got up in the middle of the night and watched the match on a black-and-white set and, of course, Phil Bennett was sparkling, jinking about all over the place.
>
> Everybody knew about Barry John after all he did for the Lions the previous year, vowing when they lost, 'This will never happen again!' But now it was Phil Bennett bringing them down, another danger man. 'Who's this Phil Bennett?' they were asking. 'Where's he come from?'

Sir Bryan George Williams who was in the thick of the action this day, could gauge better than most the likely reaction in his homeland to this defeat. But all these years later, in the bar at Ponsonby Rugby Club, he was philosophical and self-deprecating when he assessed his performance, especially as his two sons, both first-class players, have studied a recording of the game. 'My two sons enjoy ribbing me about the tackles I missed in the Barbarians match,' he said. 'John Bevan, another great Welsh wing, also managed to push his way through me that day.' Then, admitting that he had lived through 'some good days and through some not so good days', Sir Bryan implied that, despite the supreme nature of the rugby and sportsmanship, this Barbarians experience would not be ranking as one of his best. He added:

> For the All Blacks, it's almost sacrilege to lose and it doesn't happen often, but I've actually found that these clouds have a silver lining. When I look back over the years I realise that it is through losing that I made close friends and this is why I find myself invited to places where the All Blacks have been beaten – and this includes Llanelli.

Leicester's Memories of an Unbeaten Trail

In November 1974 a *Welsh XV* was defeated 12-3 by the All Blacks at Cardiff, before far greater attention was switched to the 1977 Lions squad touring New Zealand. Llanelli's Phil Bennett, proud to follow in the footsteps of John Dawes as captain, went in the hope of decent weather and fine conditions allowing him to get his talented backline moving. Sadly, however, he was out of luck, for atrocious weather virtually from start to finish made the going difficult, despite the playing performances being consistently of a high standard.

After winning all but one of the non-Test New Zealand matches, losing the series 3-1 was a bitter blow, for the playing standards of both teams were closely matched. In the first Test, won by the All Blacks 16-12, Grant Batty's interception cruelly snatched victory from the Lions, whilst one point was the difference in the last encounter at Eden Park as New Zealand scraped home 10-9. But few could begrudge that All Black all-out desire to win. The good news was that the keen rivalry, as enjoyed by Welshmen on this tour, was soon to continue when Graham Mourie and his men returned to Wales a year later, in 1978.

In their first game of the tour, three days before checking in to the Royal Hotel, Cardiff, the All Blacks had beaten Cambridge University comfortably, 32-12, setting themselves up nicely for another Arms Park showdown. Six years earlier the bodies wearing the famous 'blue and black' shirt had turned *black and blue* following the game's ferocity. All hoped that this encounter would not see a repeat of similar scenes. In their line-up was Bryan Williams, again making headlines, this time for reaching his 100th All Blacks game, an achievement that Colin Meads and Ian Kirkpatrick had managed already. Honouring the occasion, Cardiff chairman, John Davies, presented 'a silver salver' to the flying wing three-quarter before the match, which was good-natured sport, deservedly won by the All Blacks 17–7 on account of their lively second-half performance. It was a positive result for Graham Mourie and Russell Thomas, captain and manager respectively, both of whom received a miniature miner's lamp during the course of the evening dinner.

Before the following encounter at Swansea, certain All Blacks visited Stradey Park, where officers and team members of the Llanelli club showed them around the ground – although in many ways it was like visiting the scene of a past tragedy! Then they were hitting tackle bags on the open fields of Swansea University ahead of their next assignment against West Wales. With the world of rugby putting emphasis on gaining quick ball and ensuring continuity of play, the visitors had the right man in their flanker Graham Mourie. Never far from the action and with the uncanny knack of appearing just where he needed to be, Graham played the complete game, inspiring his men, in this case, to a 23–7 victory.

By now rugby lawmakers had celebrated more than a century of pulsating on-field action since the first *Rules* had been updated in 1862. But instances of serious injury were causing administrators to consider the safety of players more carefully than ever. As Gareth Jenkins suggested in a previous chapter, new strategies and laws had to be formulated for the good of the game. On-field concerns centred around the setting of scrums to prevent collapses; setting bigger gaps in line-outs so as to lessen the dangers of outstretched elbows; eradicating stamping in the rucks, a feature that was often induced by players killing the ball; reducing the unstructured pile-up, which was an unnecessary trait; and, most importantly, ensuring that players on the ground rolled away from the scene of a tackle. Each proposal would see the game prosper and the integration of all these ideas into rugby's framework, alongside future changes in match management, would be a matter of interest and a cause for debate in future years.

Seventeen days after defeating the West Wales side, New Zealand were to face the Test team. The Welsh, undeniably hampered by injuries ahead of the match, delayed the announcement of their final selection, giving added impetus to a subject that was again well covered by J. B. G. Thomas in his *Western Mail* column. JBG's words carried a hefty punch, enough to have people striding to newsagents on Monday mornings to read his back-page spread. But now JBG was taking time out from defending the Welsh cause to pay tribute to Terry McLean, the veteran rugby correspondent of the *New Zealand Herald*, on his forthcoming retirement.

Mr McLean was JBG's long-term counterpart, the voice of New Zealand rugby just as our man was the voice of the rugby people of Wales. It is understandable that passionate readers of the game might, as a consequence, sense a difference of opinion between the two, a rift even; but how wrong they would be. That day's *Western Mail* piece belied the idea, for it emphasised their ease at being together and their many shared rugby moments, stating that their rapport was, most certainly, in the best of health.

On the day of the match, JBG's message was that he and Terry were going to enjoy a drink irrespective of which team triumphed: a friendly gesture that was put to the test given that a controversial late line-out penalty incensed the Welsh supporters. Spectators close to the incident and television viewers – with the benefit of the new replay facility – were convinced that Wales were being penalised for a deliberate

New Zealand dive from the line-out. As it transpired, the referee had blown his whistle for an earlier infringement, but at 12–10 in Wales' favour it was a match-settling decision, for Brian McKechnie, the Kiwi full back, rarely missed his target. As expected, he sent the ball between the posts and if ever there was disappointment at the end of a brave performance, this was it; the final score read 13–12 for the men in black.

Television replays were now the luxury of the day, so it was bad news if a referee slipped up. And with the weight of the watching world bearing down on his decisions, arguments continued for touch judges to be given more powers to intervene, ensuring that bigger games were influenced by another pair of eyes each side of the field. Just as goalposts were now padded, giving protection to players, it was high time that referees were helped to safeguard their own situation in the modern, demanding game when controlling men of considerable speed and power.

A match against Monmouthshire County XV at Rodney Parade, more than a fortnight after the Test match, had the potential to be another difficult outing for the tourists. Captained by Charlie Faulkner, an injury replacement for the Lions on the 1977 tour to New Zealand, and coached by an earlier Lion (of 1971) Arthur Lewis, this team contained the fearsome trio known across the world as the 'Pontypool front row'. It was hoped that if Messrs Price, Windsor and Faulkner and their forward colleagues could build up a sufficiently powerful platform, the back division might just do the rest. But this proved not to be the case; the overall result going the way of the All Blacks, 26–9.

It was now left to Bridgend, two weeks later, under the captaincy of J. P. R. Williams, to represent Welsh interests in halting the progress of Graham Mourie's side. Bridgend were so far nigh-unbeatable in this their centenary season; they were strong and local belief and expectation were high, but they had never before played the All Blacks. If ever a man had the measure of these illustrious opponents, it was JPR – whose performances for Wales in 1969 shocked New Zealand, whilst his part in the 1971 Lions triumph was colossal, as was his presence for the Barbarians two years later. Everybody was wondering if he could lead his team to victory in the centenary year, on the Brewery Field, complete with recent and improved stand and terraces.

Meredydd James was in the front row and feels, all these years later, that if the match had been a cup final it would have been postponed because the playing area resembled a paddy field after so much rain. But, as everybody at the club had worked to stage the event and others of the community had offered support, the game went ahead. For the Bridgend squad, keen to train in the days leading up to the fixture, and wanting also to protect their pitch, this meant using the town's open green expanse known as Newbridge Fields. But this venue also happened to be popular with dog lovers – which proved to be the reason why Meredydd was nowhere to be seen for the last few scrum practices before the big game.

> Big Billy Howe basically fell into some dog excreta, [explained Meredydd] and although I am a farmer's boy, the smell turns my stomach. It didn't matter that we were due to play the greatest team in the world, I wasn't rejoining the forwards until Billy replaced his jersey and that ghastly smell had gone away!

Meredydd, a head teacher, knew how much in demand the All Blacks were in this last week of their tour in Wales, being inundated with requests to visit schools and clubs and accepting as many invitations as they could. Days ahead of the match, they were popular visitors at Llangewydd Junior School,

Bridgend, where they taught the children how to perform the haka, before being treated to some of Welsh rugby's favourite songs by children of the school choir. I asked Meredydd when he first experienced the All Blacks in his youth:

> I had a fleeting appreciation of Wilson Whineray's side of 1963, but it was Brian Lochore's later team that really gripped my imagination. Players like Waka Nathan, Kelvin Tremain at their best, gave me a belief in the game and what it was all about.

As it happened, Meredydd saw Graham Mourie's men before they arrived at the Brewery Field:

> I went out to take a few tickets to some friends, last thing, as you do, and saw the All Blacks' bus arriving. There were hundreds and hundreds of people clapping as they got off. The aura was certainly there but, as an opponent, you get this out of your mind. You can't let yourself be swamped by the tidal wave that comes with the All Blacks. You have your part to play; we had good players. It was a case of a stiff resolve to meet fire with fire. We're going to beat them; this was the mindset that day.

Meredydd explained that in the weeks leading up to the game, Bridgend put in some weekend training sessions that were uncommon at the time, as well as some extra midweek runs. But it was, for the majority of the team, the biggest game of their careers. Now Meredydd takes us onto the field, where the action was extremely competitive:

> Beyond the physicality, there was a mental toughness about the All Blacks; this came over. We were a footballing side, but in the monsoon conditions it was always going to be a forward battle up front. I gave it my all and stood up when the forwards had a bit of a disagreement under the stand.

At the end, as we left the field, Graham Mourie caught hold of my arm: 'Tight head, you're a hard man,' he said to me, which I can only hope was a compliment.

With playing conditions so difficult, this game never produced the flowing rugby expected. But it was a hard, fiercely fought encounter, epitomised and best remembered for JPR with his face covered in blood directing his men when leaving the field for treatment before returning later to action. The All Blacks held on to win the game, 17–6, but it was neither the showpiece sporting contest hoped for, nor the outcome that would have crowned Bridgend's centenary season.

By now, Gareth Williams, back-row forward for the home team, but today sadly departed, was being touted as a future Welsh international, a tall, athletic player, powerful with driving ambition. 'I was knocking on the door,' said Gareth, 'but that's not enough. You have to knock the door down,' he smiled, recognising that this match was another step nearer his dream:

> The game was just massive in our minds and the intensity of the training increased as the day got nearer. We were a close-knit outfit, performing well; we deserved our chance against the All Blacks.
>
> By now we took to the habit of going to Ogmore-by-Sea before important matches. We were there by mid-morning and spent a few extra hours together, having lunch before the game. I can remember looking out onto the sea. It was grey and wet and miserable.

Gareth also remembers getting to the ground and seeing the field looking wet and muddy. 'We were a running side,' he said, 'and the weather had let us down.' But, taking his place amongst two packs, neither budging one inch, helped push him nearer to his first Welsh cap. 'The game was something of a catalyst for me,' said Gareth, who admitted he'd have done anything to play for Wales. Ironically, his moment arrived two years later in Cardiff – against the All Blacks – having by then toured with the Lions of 1980 in South Africa. But, as he left the Bridgend quagmire that day, he was looking forward to a special night at the Recreation Sports Centre, where the top table for this post-match function had been laid across the length of the room. Meredydd James was there:

> Ivor John, a senior official of Bridgend club, was sanctioned with responsibility for the top table. For a decade or more, Ivor had given great service to the club and was a highly recognised figure. In many ways he was the main man and was looking after the guests that night.
>
> I remember calling the waiter over once we'd finished our free samples, and ordering a plentiful supply of red and white wine. We were signing slips of paper and by the end of the event there must have been about ten different signatures, all booking drinks down to Ivor's name. Needless to say we had a free night courtesy of the great man, God bless his soul, without him [as yet] knowing about it.
>
> At the next training session, Ivor came along wanting to address the players: 'I thought I was the only Ivor John around here,' he said, holding up the chits.
>
> Initially we all pleaded ignorance, especially as Ivor suggested the money come from the players' fund – but then there was an outbreak of laughter!

No more was said and the bill was paid. But there was now a serious grand finale awaiting the tourists at Cardiff Arms Park, for the Barbarians, on December 16th 1978, were aiming to repeat their never-to-be-forgotten 1973 performance, and the quality of the players suggested that this might be a possibility. The *Western Mail* highlighted the back-row contest between Jean-Pierre Rives and Jean-Claude Skrela and their All Black counterparts. It was suggested that the two French stars, at the time thought to be the world's best in their positions, might now be eclipsed by the All Blacks captain and Leicester Rutledge, the latter being in exceptional form as blind-side flanker.

Leicester – who made available to me a ticket for the Springboks Test in Dunedin in 2012 – hails from Christchurch, but has lived in Invercargill, at the foot of South Island, for many years. He played in every one of the tests on this tour, each one a victory. He had been rested for the Bridgend match, but now he was raring to go again for this much hoped for feast of tries. He was neither disappointed with the occasion nor the result, and his superlative form was maintained up to the end. His comments about his team's unbeaten trail through Wales bear repeating:

> Playing against Wales was something that I was lucky enough to experience. Seeing the Welsh supporters and hearing the singing, with the grandstands full was very special. Wales led for most of the game, then Brian [McKechnie] kicked the late penalty and the crowd was stunned.
>
> We trained at the clubs. We didn't have a lot of equipment with us. There were certainly no scrum machines. We had two forward packs, so we did scrummaging against each other. After our games, we couldn't wait to get into the beer. As soon as we got back to the changing room, there was no water, or energy drinks, for us. We believed water made you bloated. If we were lucky enough, we had orange segments at half-time.

Leicester has, of course, seen the game change greatly since the days when the presentation of a Test tie was important.

But he admits that, more recently, there has been greater emphasis on the official handover of the jersey. 'In our time, we were given two shirts for Test matches,' one to keep and one to swap,' said Leicester, who, alongside his colleagues, tried hard to get on the right side of the press. They were aware of the difficulties encountered by the 1972 tourists, and, wanting to redeem the All Blacks standing in the public eye, they had, to a great extent, been pleased with results. But mistakes can and will occur and woe betide those in the public eye who slip up because the merest sniff of a story, the slightest hint of gossip, will end up on the front page. In the less tolerant and more belligerent world, these men were ever mindful as they went on their way. 'None of us are perfect,' Leicester said, 'but if we learn from mistakes, it is healthy.'

The superb 1973 Barbarian performance was not to be repeated – how could it be? – and the All Blacks won 18–16, helped by Leicester when he powered over the line for a try. However, it is a measure of the respect both sides showed each other that, in the post-match dinner in the Royal Hotel, Cardiff, Graham Mourie, in the presence of Sir Douglas Carter, the High Commissioner for New Zealand and many other distinguished guests, was made an 'Honorary Barbarian'. And, as for the Welsh contingent, there was more good news, for Mr Mourie and company would be returning to Wales in less than two years to celebrate a rugby milestone.

PART VIII

CENTENARY CELEBRATIONS IN 1980
AND A RUGBY WORLD CUP IN 1987

A Referee's commentary and Terry's dream tour

As part of its centenary celebrations in 1980, the Welsh Rugby Union invited New Zealand to play the four Welsh clubs that had defeated the All Blacks over the years. Swansea, Cardiff, Newport and Llanelli would therefore have plum fixtures on their home grounds, with the tour culminating in a full Test against Wales at Cardiff. A turnstile-and-money-spinning three weeks would provide excitement and entertainment during the autumn months and it would be a huge achievement if just one of the sides were to repeat its past success.

The visitors, led by the manager Ray Harper, Eric Watson, a seasoned coach, and Graham Mourie, an inspirational captain, were again a strong force. With big, powerful forwards and creative, fast backs, the All Blacks seemed to be getting better by the year. A worry for the opposition was that older players of exceptional ability were being easily replaced by bigger, athletic players of equal talent. At the All Black recruitment factory productivity was remarkably good!

Besides targeting five victories, manager Ray Harper's clearly publicised intentions were to make this an enjoyable tour in the hope that any unsavoury incidents or disappointments in previous years were laid to rest. Arriving in Wales via Vancouver, Seattle and London, the team had already enjoyed a run-out in North America, with matches against the United States and Canada. Observers now saw that their preparations extended to performing pre-training warm-ups before the main sessions, a fine-tuning that Malcolm Hood, a member of the side's medical team, was responsible for, and, as the *Western Mail* four days before the Cardiff game suggested, this was an initiative that was fresh to Wales.

Cardiff players were again first to face the haka and as they did not, in the opinion of rugby experts, have the top-quality performers of previous years, it was anticipated that they would struggle. Their performance, however, spoke volumes for the determination and will of the home players, and, even though they lost 16–9, Cardiff's accomplishment, especially in denying the All Blacks a single score in the second half, gave other clubs real hope.

For 92 years Stradey Park had never given New Zealand rugby teams an easy time; Tuesday, October 21st 1980 was to be no different. With the usual Scarlet passion and enthusiasm lifting Ray Gravell and his team to higher powers, Llanelli led the way 10–3 at half-time, courtesy of a Mark Jones corner try. Such had been the attacking determination of the home team in that first half that the score flattered the visitors, but it was a different story in the second half as the All Blacks crossed the line twice to steal the game. Then, as the clock ticked away into the last minute of play, drama unfolded when referee Alan Hosie of Scotland appeared to signal the dismissal of lock Graeme Higginson for dangerous trampling – as a three-man judiciary of Ray Gravell, Phil Bennett and Graham Mourie arrived on the scene.

In this commendable act of sportsmanship both Welsh and New Zealand camps it seemed were protecting the goodwill of this tour. Also, without realising it, spectators witnessed the reliving of a rugby vignette from earlier days when two captains assisted by an 'umpire' consulted each other as players stood around, waiting for a verdict. But, this time, as it transpired, the match had already run its course, as Mr Hosie, concluding his thorough discussions, signalled the end of play and the beginning of bar activities.

With two big hurdles out of the way, the All Blacks, four days later, moved on to the grass version of a billiard table at St Helen's, Swansea, which was favoured by Duncan McGregor of the Originals more than any other field he played on during the 1905 tour. This day another large crowd filled the ground to see the All Blacks in try-scoring mood, running the ball from all corners and crossing for six tries. Swansea, led by international Geoff Wheel, took the 32–0 defeat on the chin, acknowledging the class and clinical work of a great side as it coasted towards the end of its tour.

Ahead of the important international with Wales was another midweek clash at Rodney Parade, where Newport, not as strong as in past years, put up an excellent performance in difficult, wet conditions to stay close to the All Blacks throughout. This time there were no mud-wrestling side-shows, just non-stop action from the brave Newport heroes, who went down to a somewhat severe scoreline of 14–3, due to a try being conceded in one of the final acts of play.

A senior official from England, Scotland, Ireland or France had refereed the four club matches, but it had been left to the All Blacks to make their choice of referee, from one of the four, to control the Test. Bearing in mind the feast of rugby seen at St Helen's and the well-controlled manner of the game, many tipped John West of Ireland, living in Dublin but a Cork man, to be given the nod, as indeed he was.

John, an international referee for eleven years, was no stranger to the All Blacks. It was he, in 1979, who had the honour of being the first neutral official to take charge of an international match in New Zealand – a surprisingly late date so it would seem. The occasion was a two-Test series between New Zealand and France, but as John says, 'there had been some rugged encounters down through the years so a neutral referee was requested'. Only a year earlier, in 1977, the important test matches between the All Blacks and Phil Bennett's British Lions had been refereed by New Zealand's three top officials, so it was high time for a change in this respect. The move by rugby's administrators was good news for all top grade officials who recognised the opportunities of far greater travel when pursuing their love of refereeing.

That French tour was a great success and the matches were played in good spirits. Now, a year later, John had clinched the main prize in Cardiff on this centenary occasion. Speaking by phone from his home, John told me that he had thoroughly enjoyed his outing in Swansea on a field where Jack Manchester's men lost in 1935 and Bob Stuart's All Blacks were held to a 6–6 draw in 1953. He felt that the latest score between the two teams, 32–0, gave no indication of the even contest during the eighty minutes. 'Swansea did a lot of the attacking,' he said, 'but the All Blacks broke from defence to score their tries. And John's reaction to the forthcoming Welsh match?

> I was immensely proud, although you try not to show this. It was a brilliant honour and it's just wonderful to be involved with these occasions. In the first place it's good to go along, but to be selected to referee is mind-blowing, a great opportunity to participate, to back your judgement and to help a game flow for the enjoyment of players and spectators alike.

At the forefront of John's mind was doing the job to the best of his ability and maintaining the standard that got him selected in the first place. He told me that lots of fitness training is important 'which, in part, brings along the mental side of match preparation.' John trained with his school side, being coach of the under-15s at the time. Then, when it came to match day, he kept to a tried and tested routine:

> The first thing for me was, I suppose, keeping pretty well to myself. I tended to stay in the Angel Hotel when in Cardiff. It has a fantastic buzz, always jam-packed, the foyer flooded with supporters, all passionate about the game. I would go for a walk early in the morning. Then I'd stay in my room until it was time to go across to the pitch. I'd have to go through security and then I'd walk onto the field – before a chat and a cup of tea with Bill Hardiman, a lovely man who looked after the ground.

If John passed a player in the corridor before the match, he would say a quick hello but he would not deliberately get involved. 'I suppose I was keeping my distance, also respecting privacy,' he said. 'Players prepare themselves differently. Then I would have knocked on the door of the changing rooms for the captains to toss the coin. I liked to perform this ritual early, returning later to inspect the studs. I would have wished both teams well, hoping that they enjoyed the game.' As for the reception that awaited players and officials as they emerged from the tunnel, John had this to say:

> Going out onto the pitch brought a tremendous cheer: firstly for the All Blacks followed by even more noise when the Welsh emerged, a brilliant feeling. Then came the haka, a wonderful spectacle to observe, especially at close quarters.

As regards the match, played at an enormous pace with high-quality rugby from both sides, New Zealand scored four tries but the Welsh supporters were generous in the way they applauded. 'I can remember Wales being on the attack,' said John, 'David Richards sprinting for the line before New Zealand caught him and broke from deep. Moments later, Graham Mourie was scoring in the opposite corner. He was a splendid captain; he had a clear view of the ethics of the game.' Such a player takes responsibility for his men and this is enormously beneficial to a referee. John had another fine match that day, making the job seem easy but the battle of wits is constant:

> I will always remember the All Blacks attacking and Jeff Squire got injured and it took a while before he left the field and was replaced by Eddie Butler, perhaps three minutes passing before we restarted play with a scrum.
> 'Whose ball is it Ref?' asked one of the Welsh players.
> 'It's an All Black put-in,' I replied.
> 'It couldn't be Ref,' was the response.
> 'No, you're right; I gave them a penalty, didn't I?'
> Then a hint of a grin accompanied the words, 'Scrum it is, Ref; All Black ball!'

Despite the score favouring the All Blacks 23–3 there was great camaraderie between the Welsh and New Zealanders in the evening function at Cardiff's City Hall. Cliff Jones, president of the Welsh Rugby Union, was delighted with the good-natured way both teams had reacted on and off the field and John was delighted to receive his personal thanks. 'The tour was an undoubted success,' said John, 'a triumph for rugby – and much of the lingering bitterness of previous tours had been swept away. This had been his main ambition and everything had gone well.'

In the *Western Mail* the following Monday, J. B. G. Thomas described the evening event as being the most high-profile and sparkling of rugby occasions held in the country. Staged at Cardiff's City Hall, with five hundred in attendance – mostly players who had worn the red of Wales – this was a night to celebrate Welsh Rugby's proud 100th birthday and to honour those connected with the afternoon's play. Among the celebrities were rugby league players who, having crossed the big divide, had, nonetheless, helped to lay cornerstones for the union game's greater success. Attending the function was Hector Monro, Minister of Sport, alongside guests who had travelled from all over the world, but it was the New Zealanders who made these celebrations possible; it is they who crowned the Welshmen's day.

Following such a glittering occasion it was sad to note that Wales' standing in the Home Championship's order of merit was not at its highest. When it came to the choice of Lions for the 1983 eighteen-match tour to New Zealand, Welsh participants were lower than usual for what became a series whitewash: four straight Test defeats. However, this did not stop the enjoyment of hordes of rugby supporters who left Wales for the opportunity of a lifetime in flying into Auckland to support their team.

Organising one of the touring parties for the supporters was Jim Strachan, who today has his own sports travel business in the middle of Cowbridge. Jim, who has vast experience of travel, has no doubt that when it comes to being genuinely welcomed to a new country, where rugby tops the charts, New Zealand is out and out the best.

Jim remembers that in 1983 a young man by the name of Terry Morgan came to support the tour that was, incidentally, organised by John Cory Travel. Terry, a talented sportsman, had, a few years previously, suffered a serious spinal injury whilst playing rugby, and although now he needed constant nursing care he had become a bit of a celebrity. Jim recalls:

It was fantastic. The first day we arrived in Wellington I had a phone call. 'Good morning, Mr Strachan. I am the prime minister's private secretary. Can you spare a few minutes?' The prime minister invited about 120 of us to the parliament building, known as the Beehive. This made the national news. We were singing 'Calon Lân' at 8.15 in the morning. Then former All Blacks came out of the woodwork, real legends like Colin Meads, giving Terry kit, jerseys, shirts, you name it.

Andrew, Terry's brother, explained to me that, like so many Welsh people, Terry was determined to go to New Zealand despite being confined to a wheelchair. 'He wanted to see for himself what the country was like,' said Andrew, 'he wanted to know what was there.' Andrew was amazed at the welcome Terry received. 'I couldn't believe what people did for him,' he added. 'They were bringing gifts and presents, offering hospitality and gestures in so many ways. They couldn't have done more.' Andrew continues:

> We went to a Māori school and they performed the haka, just for Terry – but, not only that, when the same school toured our country in later years – by which time my brother had sadly died – certain members got in touch with us and came to see my parents. Then they went to the grave-side and sung their school song alongside Terry's grave.

John Sinclair, to whom this book is dedicated, was active in making arrangements for his guests. On the subject of the above story, he shed greater light, explaining to me that Te Aute College, a school in the Hawkes Bay region of the North Island with a strong Māori representation, made Terry an honorary prefect, and, when its members later toured Wales with a Māori team, they asked if they could be taken to the town where Terry was buried. 'The Māori are magnificent singers,' said John, with tears welling in his eyes. 'They got out of the coach and sang him his old school song. It was a song for their former prefect.' The rugby bond goes no deeper than this and it is these deeds that reveal John's former niche in rugby life: planning schedules for touring parties, filling time between matches, visiting interesting places, meeting past players, sampling local delicacies, tasting beers, no matter what: every activity geared to pleasing tourists who had taken time to visit New Zealand.

Occasionally, however, a free afternoon was granted to everyone – and John Sinclair and Jim Strachan had adventures of their own. On one occasion in 1976, Jim's first visit to New Zealand, whilst preparing an itinerary for the 1977 Lions supporters tour, they went on a jaunt from Auckland to Whangarei, the northernmost city in New Zealand. It was a long, arduous, winding road, so to make things easier they decided to fly back, for John knew that at Kerikeri there was a little airport and that Mount Cook airlines had a flight to Auckland. As well as running mainstream flights this well-respected company carried passengers from remote to central locations which included transportation to the airfield; a valuable service. Jim can recall a woman in smart corporate uniform collecting them; soon, they were on their way:

> I remember going off the carriageway and onto a single road, and off the single road into a lane and the hedges were getting higher and higher as we went along. Then we stopped by a gate that led into a field, where there was a sort of concrete pillar box. 'Welcome to Mount Cook Airlines', was the notice, with the friendly greeting 'If the telephone rings, please answer it', or a message to this effect!

In no time, the two men heard a small aircraft, a six-seater, buzzing over the trees and hedges, coming down to land in this same field. Then the captain stepped outside: 'I hope you're not in a hurry, gentlemen? I've got to make one more collection; I've got to visit a farm to pick up some oranges.' Jim continues the story:

This was all great fun as we landed somewhere near an orchard. There were six sacks to be taken to Auckland to catch an Air New Zealand flight. 'Do you mind giving me a hand?' the captain asked, as we started to spread the load evenly in the aircraft. 'John, you sit in the front, in the co-pilot's seat,' he said. 'Jim, perhaps you'd like to sit in the middle.' There I was, amongst the oranges.

'How will we find our way back to Auckland?' we asked.

'We'll follow the main road,' was the reply. 'That's no problem; I've even got a road map here!'

I remember we had to fly around a big cloud, because we couldn't go over it, but we found our way back and in good time. And when we arrived, there was a big 747 ready to take off – but, firstly, it had to wait for a little plane carrying one Welshman, a New Zealander and six sacks of oranges!

When I visited John at his home in Palmerston North he had boxes of rugby programmes, cuttings and general memorabilia all around him as he spoke of his vision for a rugby museum and of his pride in securing premises for the venture. John was most knowledgeable about the Wales–New Zealand connection, and one of his favourite stories relates to the time he took a bus full of his countrymen to the home of Willie Llewellyn, the last Welsh survivor of the 1905 international. This was in November 1967, when Willie, aged 89, waited at the entrance to his home in Pontyclun as the bus arrived, carrying Māori greetings on a flag draped across its front.

I took my group to see him [said John]. We treated him like a king for the day at his home. We gave him an All Blacks supporters tie and performed the haka. We were given coffee and cakes by the family. They were a cross between a scone and a pikelet. Whatever they were [they were Welsh cakes], they were delicious.

This was big news in the *Western Mail* of November 8th 1967, appearing under the heading 'New Zealanders pay homage to Willie.' In all, thirty-three members of the touring party arrived on the bus and were welcomed by Willie's wife, their children, grandchildren and great-grandchildren. Willie was handed a written message from Billy Wallace, who had exchanged his rugby shirt with Willie at the end of the 1905 match. According to John, calling on Willie meant as much to him and his party as going to Cardiff for the Wales clash.

Stephen Berg, curator of the New Zealand Rugby Museum founded by John, is aware of many of his mentor's interesting stories and the visit to Willie Llewellyn ranks as a favourite:

This is one of the most beautiful of them all. To think that the New Zealand supporters, sixty years later, were still honouring Willie for playing in that great game, and doing an impromptu haka outside his house, is just amazing. And there being All Blacks amongst them; and John's description of Willie crying, and of his grandson speechless – it is all so emotional. They basically put Willie, an old man, on a pedestal for the day, a special thing to do.

But the story doesn't end there. When John returned to Wales, probably at the time of Ian Kirkpatrick's 1972 tour, he revisited Willie, now in his nineties, shortly before he died.

'This second time we wrote ahead,' said John. 'Willie was getting old now. "We are only coming to pay our respect to the last survivor of the 1905 Test," was our message to his family. "You must come," was the reply, "because he's living for it. It's all he's talking about."

"After our meeting, and as I was walking to the bus," said John, "Willie put his arm around my shoulders."

"How would you like my 1904 [British team] jersey for your museum?'"he enquired.

"That would be marvellous," I replied, "but doesn't your own museum want it?"

"Well they do, but I have always had a soft spot for you New Zealanders." '

The same jersey which Willie, no doubt, wore in the Test at Athletic Park, Wellington, in August 1904 (an All Black victory, 9–3) arrived, inadvertently, at Rotorua, miles from Palmerston North, but carrying clear instructions that it was to go to *no one other* than John Sinclair. In a later exchange of letters, Mrs Llewellyn, Willie's widow, conveyed her pleasure that it had arrived safely. 'He had such happy thoughts of his visit to your country,' the lady added. 'He was thrilled when you paid your two visits to us.'

The pleasure John Sinclair felt when he returned to New Zealand with Willie's note for his old pal Billy Wallace was enormous, for he enjoyed nothing more than having some news to share with the legendary All Black and players of his generation. Billy Wallace was, of course, the star of the 1905 Originals' tour and it was he who had cut a pathway through the Welsh defence to give Bob Deans his dash for the line. Billy often spoke of the match, especially of this incident, and detailed it in his memoirs, published in the *New Zealand Sportsman (Wellington)* some thirty years after the match. In the run-up to the fourth Wales–New Zealand game in 1953, the *New Zealand Herald* published an extract of Bill's words so that the famous story was retold. They are précised and retold here from the moment that Bill prepared to launch a counter-attack after Wales had kicked in his direction from a line-out won near the half-way mark:

'I dashed in [and] scooped up the ball in my stride,' he said, leaving the forwards behind, before somehow slipping past Nicholls and Gabe so as to face Winfield near the 25-yard line in a move earlier described as 'a mackerel' – that is, going 'through a shoal of herrings!' Thinking about chipping ahead and chasing, or throwing a dummy pass, Wallace heard the cry 'Bill! Bill!' to his side. This was Deans to whom he threw a long pass allowing the big centre to sprint up the touchline. However, in veering towards the posts, Deans allowed Teddy Morgan to gain ground and tackle him around the legs at the line (where Gabe was even more closely involved as we know). This was, according to Wallace, eight yards to the left-hand side of the posts – and not far from the spot where Phil Bennett turned and side-stepped for the Barbarians against the All Blacks in 1973.

Interestingly, *Fields of Praise* makes reference to Willie Llewellyn bringing down Wallace after he had made his pass to Deans, so denying Wallace (who stated that it was a score) the best of views of what happened next. 'Neither he nor I could form an opinion,' said Willie, of an incident that was too distant for viewers positioned on the ground.

So, did Deans score or not? The record, as we know, says he didn't, but, intriguingly, according to more of Wallace's words from his memoirs, also appearing in the *New Zealand Herald* of 1953, Teddy Morgan, Wales' try scorer, returned to his medical duties at Guy's Hospital, London, that same night and told a Dr Pat McEvedy that Deans had scored. Surely, Rhys Gabe would have been livid – but had John Sinclair known about this?

Sadly, John Sinclair is no longer with us, but he told me about the day he travelled to Wellington to meet Billy Wallace and to learn from the great man all that he could. Although the exact date of the visit is unknown, Billy was young enough to be active because John found the great All Black up a ladder outside his home: 'I'm Bill Wallace,' he replied. Then, they both spent time catching cushions in Wallace's sitting room. 'He was demonstrating the flick pass,' said John, 'lamenting the fact that it had gone out of the game.' Over many years the two spoke often and John knew how deep a disappointment the disallowed try had been to Wallace. Had the try stood, the great kicker would have backed his own trusted boot to have converted the score, so as to return to New Zealand undefeated. As for John Sinclair, he did not give a dime for the match details, as is apparent in this statement:

I say 'good' on the bloke who pulled him [Bob Deans] back. It was confirmed in many ways that it was a try; but that's what it's all about. It was good for the game that he didn't score: good for the Wales versus New Zealand fixture.

And who, we might ask, was Dr Pat McEvedy, mentioned in Wallace's memoirs? The answer is captivating. Born in New Zealand but having studied medicine at Guys' Hospital, London, Dr McEvedy represented the British rugby team that toured his home country in both 1904 (alongside Willie Llewellyn and Rhys Gabe) and in 1908. When he returned to his roots it was to continue medicine in Wellington. As a sportsman respected for fair play, he was also a distinguished President of both the Wellington and New Zealand rugby unions. He donated the McEvedy Shield for Wellington schoolboys to compete for in a major annual athletics competition. And to crown his sporting achievements, his name is linked distantly to the entanglement and intrigue of the famous 1905 'no score!'

Bill's biggest thrill as Wales visit Invercargill

Wales' mediocre form in the mid-1980s would have benefited from an All Black clash to set interest alight; but, for the first time in many years, there was a barren spell in this respect. Off the field of play, developments were, however, continuing to lift the game as coaching standards assumed far greater levels of sophistication across the now big wide rugby world. It had been generally recognised that conditioning, nutrition and all categories of fitness – from aerobic, stamina and speed to mental agility – were rising. However, on comparing the Welsh and New Zealand game one saw a definite gap between the standards of the two countries that would be confirmed or disproved when the long-awaited next clash took place.

It was also recognised that New Zealand, by virtue of a thoroughly efficient and progressive outlook to its national game, was quietly gearing up – and ahead of time – to an inevitable professional era. With better television coverage and general media attention having catapulted the fast and open modern game into an appealing package, corporate interest and all that it entailed was growing with great rapidity. Rugby hospitality was becoming a popular vehicle for international business deals. Those who had the foresight and money to buy the first issues of Cardiff Arms Park debentures in the 1960s were now reaping the benefit of this well-chosen investment as demand for match tickets continued to rise.

In essence we were experiencing the modern-day equivalent of Prime Minister Seddon's vision for New Zealand in 1905, when he recognised the value in terms of economic growth of the publicity generated by Dave Gallaher's Originals. Now, some eighty years later, Alan Thomas, of

Newport's winning 1963 team, had accepted an invitation from Leicester Chamber of Commerce to join like-minded businessmen and women in exploring the possibilities of trading overseas, but when he and Jane, his wife, landed in Auckland for a conference they were in for a big surprise:

> When we stepped off the aeroplane and were taken into a large conference room full of business people, my spirits dropped when I heard an announcement:
>
> 'Ladies and gentlemen, is there an Alan Thomas from Newport in the room?'
>
> 'Oh no!' I thought, 'something's happened at home.' Fearing the worst I telephoned the number I was given.
>
> 'Is that you, Alan?' a voice enquired.
>
> 'Yes . . .'
>
> 'Good. It's nice to know that you've come to a country that knows how to play rugby!'

Alan explained that when he filled in the form with his personal details – age, address, nearest big town and so forth – accompanied by words to the effect of 'We beat you in 1963 . . .' – this prompted rugby minds to take a closer look. The spoken words on the loudspeaker belonged to Sir Wilson Whineray, who wanted to extend a welcome to Alan and Jane by inviting them to a social get-together at the Barbarians Club. At the time, this was a small building – not unlike a typical detached New Zealand residence – situated alongside Eden Park, full of interesting rugby memorabilia and frequented by All Blacks and big personalities of the game. For Alan and Jane, this rugby interlude made a welcome change from the business aspect of their stay and led to a lasting friendship in the country they admired so much.

At the time, Wilson Whineray, a lifelong pillar of New Zealand rugby, was setting his sights on giving his fullest support to the game's first World Cup due to start in May 1987. The concept of a tournament along the lines of football's glittering event had been discussed in general terms years earlier, but a concentrated drive throughout the 1980s brought things to a head. The International Rugby Board set the scene for sixteen rugby nations to stake a claim for the Webb Ellis Cup. There would be no qualifying rounds and it would be co-hosted by New Zealand and Australia, kicking off with a match at Eden Park between the All Blacks and Italy.

Winning the match 70–6, New Zealand breezed through these early stages, beating Fiji 74–13 and Argentina 46–15, before securing a 30–3 quarter-final win against Scotland, which meant that a semi-final encounter with the Welsh awaited them in Brisbane, Australia – provided Wales cleared its own hurdles. The Welsh, who were made to feel at home in New Zealand, were on form, beating Ireland 13–6 in Wellington and Tonga 29–16 in Palmerston North, before flying down to Invercargill at the foot of South Island to play their final pool match. It is there at Rugby Park on June 3rd that Wales beat Canada, a victory that cleared the decks for a long overdue game with New Zealand: the last clash being against Graham Mourie's men seven years previously.

Bill Anderson, who earlier shared his memories of Southland's victory over the 1966 Lions, was now the rugby liaison officer for Southland with responsibility for hosting the Welsh squad, a privilege he will not forget. 'The biggest thrill of my life was to share with the Welsh team the presentation of their playing strip before the game,' said Bill. This took place in the upstairs of the Grand Hotel, each player having to walk down the aisle to the front of the room when his name was called out. 'It was a private occasion, a proud moment, and what intrigued me was the way the kit had all been carefully laid out,' said Bill. 'You don't have the opportunity of seeing this sort of thing very often.' Bill explained that Wales flew into Invercargill well ahead of their game and he was on the spot to welcome the party from the plane:

> When you come down to Southland, you must taste the oysters. They are a delicacy around here so we took the team down to Bluff and they had plenty of feeds. We gave the party the chance to meet the people of New Zealand. We took them out to the seaport of Riverton and to some of the pubs, also meeting people not connected with rugby.

Bill remembers Clive Rowlands well. 'He was an excellent organiser, the ideal man to lead the team.' People who had toured with the All Blacks knew him to be a passionate Welshman who loved the game. 'And he could sing, too,' said Bill. 'We'd be going round in the bus and the Welsh party would break into song; this happened quite regularly.'

In being appointed manager of the Welsh team, Clive had completed a unique 'full set' in relation to New Zealand rugby: spectator, player, captain, coach, selector, now ambassador for his country – a remarkable accomplishment, and crowned when he later became president of the Welsh Rugby Union. On being reminded about his stay in Invercargill, his response was full of more cheeky humour:

> We went to the end of the world. When I think about it, not many of our players have played an international match in Invercargill – there's not a more southerly ground – the complete opposite of Murrayfield in the north!

Wales won the match against Canada emphatically, 40–9, Ieuan Evans scoring four tries, setting up a quarter-final against England which the Welsh also won. Confident and enjoying a formidable unbroken run, Wales' semi-final against New Zealand would be the definitive test. Earlier results had made the host nation hot favourites, although Brian Lochore as coach was ensuring that no one in the squad got carried away. In an interview with the *New Zealand Herald* on June 11th 1987 ahead of the Wales match, Sir Brian expressed his thoughts on substitutions at international level. He suggested that consideration be given for up to two tactical replacements to take place and, stressing that injury delays were proving disruptive for viewers, he proposed that it was more advantageous to all concerned for such players to be replaced more readily.

How interesting that law changes such as these can simply be the response to a suggestion by one of the game's thinkers, before being later discussed by law committees and eventually implemented. However, the number of substitutions later allowed by the game led Sir Brian to feel that the changes had gone too far. 'The game has now gone from fifteen a side to twenty-three a side,' he told me in July 2013. 'I don't think we've got it quite right. The game is about fitness as well as ability, and fitness doesn't come into it so much when you can, let's say, rotate your props. It's very disruptive, and that's not what rugby is about.'

In preparing his men for this first World Cup, Sir Brian had to overcome problems of his own. In the weeks before the tournament, his captain Andy Dalton's hamstring injury prompted New Zealand's manager to hand the skipper's arm band to scrum half David Kirk. Then, when Dalton was declared fit before the final, Sean Fitzpatrick got the nod and, as the world knows, did rather well! He claimed the hooking berth for the next ten years and ended up captaining the All Blacks for fifty-one tests.

For the semi-final clash with Wales, David's parents, Dr Murray Kirk and his wife, Diane, made the journey to Brisbane, where they stayed in the same hotel as a crowd from Wales. This reminded them both of old times in Glamorgan where Murray worked in Sully Hospital and when their children were small. By coincidence, both encountered Welshmen who had 'spotted' young New Zealand lads with All Black potential – but would either have believed that David would now be captaining the All Blacks in the World Cup semi-final against Wales? As Diane told me when I met her and Murray near their home in Palmerston North:

> Here I am in Penarth, Murray off doing his doctor's work, three children, two little boys – one in a push chair, one on a tricycle – on my way to the Bank in Sully, trundling up the road. We pass the butcher and, being Welsh and friendly and welcoming, he said, 'Hello', and so did I.
>
> 'Your accent,' he said, 'you don't come from around here, do you?'
>
> 'We're from New Zealand,' I replied.
>
> 'Ah,' he responded, 'I wonder if there's a future All Black there?'

Murray's story is similar and concerns Meirion Roberts, a 1962 Welsh international who, as a pharmaceutical representative, visited the hospital where Murray worked. 'On one occasion, he gave me one of his first two rugby jerseys for my boys,' said Murray, 'because one day one of them might be an All Black.' But now, in 1987, Murray and Diane were amongst the Welsh at their hotel, as Murray recalls:

> We had great empathy with the Welsh. When it came to the match we had to get out to the field. 'Get on the bus with us,' they said, and we did. One of the fellows did a bit of a sweepstake. A paper was passed around and we had to put down the likely score. Then it came to us. I was thinking

we'll beat Wales by fifty points, so I thought we'd better decline to comment – and not say we're David's parents.

Diane continues the story:

When it came to returning to the hotel we did not catch the same bus or else we'd have been shrinking into our seats!

Murray has another lasting memory of match days in Cardiff, when the All Blacks were visitors in the early 1960s. He happened to be down an alleyway between the shops, near the city centre. At the time it was snowing and with no traffic noise the city was strangely quiet. 'There was a man down there singing,' said Murray. 'It was about ten o'clock at night. A crowd had gathered around this tenor who was singing beautifully. It was a warm winter scene and it was just wonderful, and it has stuck in my memory for about fifty years.'

Murray's prediction on the bus was close; Wales lost the match 49–6, a routine victory in the eyes of New Zealand's loyal fans that cannot be disputed. But with minutes to go the Welsh were clearly disadvantaged when, following a private duel between Gary Whetton and Neath lock forward Huw Richards at a maul, Wayne 'Buck' Shelford stepped in with a punch that knocked Richards to the ground. This resulted in Huw, one of Wales' hard men, being sent off when he regained his senses! Rough justice, one might say, especially when Buck was allowed to get away with his action and play a week later in the World Cup final.

It was now obvious that after eighty years of competition the gap between the two countries was widening. New Zealand went on to beat France and win the tournament emphatically, whilst Wales, having later beaten Australia by one point in the play-off, came third.

Buck's beefed-up haka
flattens Welsh Feathers

By the late 1980s, professionalism in rugby union was just around the corner. As top-performing players made great sacrifices of time and money to train, play, travel and take knocks, whilst attracting crowds and television cameras, it became inevitable that full financial considerations had to be addressed. Over the century, money issues for running club bars, driving team buses, coaching the youth, writing newspaper columns, receiving book royalties or speaking at after-dinner functions were regularly questioned. Each payment brought its own peculiarity that fell either inside or outside the rules of amateurism, but, before long, the so-called boot money would be an offering of the past.

The ramifications of future earnings would not be straightforward and would impact dramatically on players, coaches, team managers and backroom staff. The game as it had been known for a century and more was about to change. Indeed, the door to a professional model was already ajar, for the Rugby World Cup of 1987, with its publicity, sponsorship and advertisement deals, had accelerated an irreversible development. Its skills, thrills, drama and scintillating scores had laid the financial foundation for the next world exhibition of rugby in four years' time. No sooner had New Zealand lifted the coveted trophy than preparations began for Twickenham in 1991.

David Kirk's earlier-than-expected departure from the All Blacks team, to undertake studies in Oxford in 1987, saw Wayne Shelford become captain of the side. Wayne is a proud Māori with a 'hard as nails' playing physique and psyche and this had already helped him to earn the Tom French Cup (best Māori player award) on numerous occasions. But his mission during the World Cup of 1987 was to beef up the haka which, as interesting as it had been over the years, lacked a distinctive punch. This was not good enough for such a tough nut as 'Buck', who had his team practising until the haka changed from being part of the All Blacks' repertoire to a coat of armour.

The 'Ka Mate', the words used in the haka in the 1987 World Cup, is said to have been spoken by Te Rauparaha, a Māori leader, as a celebration of life over death. In 1821, as we understand, after a close escape from his assailants, he went into hiding in a pit, while his wife sat at the opening to this same hollow. He, believing his capture was inevitable, cried 'Ka mate!' [It is death!], but when the enemy disappeared his message was a mightily relieved, 'Ka ora!' [It is Life!].[43]

Buck's on-field play and tenacious standards were just as exacting as his pre-match haka. As Wales found out on a summer tour to New Zealand in 1988 he had taken levels up another notch. Getting to grip with the silver fern, now invigorated by World Cup glory, was an experience that the Welsh would not relish; it also confirmed that the widening gap between the two teams had dulled the keen sense of rivalry that had once existed.

In tackling the world champions on their patch, the Welsh gained a taste of sporting euphoria the New Zealand way. Still cock-a-hoop from the manner of victory over France, rugby followers were as excited to see Wales arriving for an eight-match tour in 1988 as when Wales flew into Auckland in 1969. In acknowledging their Triple Crown credentials and

---

43 A memorable display about the history of the 'Ka Mate' can be seen at Dunedin's most impressive Flemish Renaissance-style railway station.

third-place tag in the World Cup, the country was not going to underestimate the Welsh in any way.

When it came to rugby mania the hype in 1988 was extraordinary and *Western Mail* reporter Robert Cole was able to see at first hand how good marketing filled the terraces. In his column of May 21st, Mr Cole described the great excitement, which saw 'street parades' as well as 'schoolboy coaching clinics' and 'rugby awareness' slipping into a festival of rugby, enhanced by shop window promotions and the All Blacks mascot 'Leo the Lion'. Although we in Wales know how to party on the back of a rugby boom, New Zealanders tend to push to the limits and that is why it is not unusual for airports to be decorated in team strips, or town hall clocks to be draped in sporting scarves, whilst ribbons and balloons continue the tribal show of colours of earlier times.

As touring players will testify, the New Zealand welcome is second to none, but that greeting stays off the playing field or the 'paddock' as it is known. This represents the flipside of the deal, a torrent of rugby warriors, immersed in strong traditions, intent upon punishing every weakness, inadequacy or error in one merciless assault for rugby perfection. The Welsh were spared nothing on this tour of 1988, Waikato striking the first blow, winning 28–19 at Rugby Park, Hamilton (today's Waikato stadium), where Warren Gatland, the current Welsh coach, took his place as hooker in the front row. Warren remembers the time:

> I think that we [in Waikato] have always had a pretty good record against international teams, going back to 1956 when we beat the Springboks. Because of this we are guaranteed to have a full house and this is why we have often been given touring teams to play on a Wednesday afternoon. That year, 1988, was no different and we weren't

a bad side ourselves. For me it was fantastic to play against Wales. They came over as Triple Crown winners and deserved a lot of respect. Afterwards, we had our usual post-match function and with us winning it was always going to be a late night!

Warren mentioned that in those days the Waikato players never got to keep their jerseys unless they won, so this was a big bonus, even though they had to wait until the end of the season. A modest Warren omitted to say how well he played; his performance, when coupled with an earlier trial match, helping him knock down that door as previously described by Gareth Williams of Bridgend. This launched Warren into an All Black career and onto an early tour of Australia. Wearing the coveted black jersey for the next three years, Warren made seventeen appearances, heaping more pride onto Waikato, a province of the North Island which has an enviable rugby record. Besides toppling the Springboks and Wales, there have been wins over the British Lions, Argentina, Australia, France and many other countries in the past fifty years.

Recovering from their early setback, the Welsh beat Otago and drew with Taranaki, just as their predecessors of 1969 had done. There was also a win against Hawke's Bay before losses to Wellington and North Auckland. Being on the back foot from the beginning, Wales could not break into a rhythm to prevent their opponents from scoring a big pile of points. In the Test matches, Wales fell 52–3 and 54–9, unheard of in earlier contests between the sides when losses, keenly as they were felt at the time, were by narrower margins.

For the Welsh players, the tour offered invaluable experience, but the drubbings came as an unwelcome humiliation in their careers. In the course of their four weeks of travelling and playing, injuries were costly and besides losing tour captain Bleddyn Bowen early on with a fractured wrist, vice-captain Bob Norster was forced from the action later on. This opened the door for Jonathan Davies to lead the side, a job that earned him great praise, especially in the second Test at Eden Park. Saturday June 11th 1988 saw Jonathan step up to the plate in all aspects of the game. Leading by example, he tackled like a Trojan; players such as Wayne Shelford, Michael Jones, Gary Whetton, all a lot bigger, were sent crashing to the ground by the Welsh outside half, who earned the man of the match award and a standing ovation. 'I ran almost the length of the pitch to score a consolation try,'[44] said Jonathan, to win this unique accolade.

During that particular Test, Grant Fox kicked goals from all around the field whilst John Kirwan and Terry Wright, with two tries each, were amongst many try scorers. By coincidence, the heavy blow of this defeat landed when Wales and New Zealand officials were about to finalise fixtures (through the regulatory channels, of course) for the following year's All Black tour to the British Isles. This would give the Welsh players an opportunity to strike back, whilst the tour would also bring renewed contests with four of the Welsh clubs. But, at a time when the All Blacks were pulling ahead so rapidly, many were wondering when this privilege would end.

When the time came round, in October 1989, the All Blacks looked world class in every respect as they performed their training drills at Sophia Gardens, Cardiff. Today's Welsh coach, Warren Gatland, was amongst them competing with Sean Fitzpatrick for the hooking position, also injecting variety into the daily runs with his own brand of fun rugby games. But the All Blacks were challenged hard by a Cardiff side which surprised many, attacking their opponents at

44   Peter Corrigan, *Jonathan Davies Code Breaker* (Bloomsbury, 1996).

every opportunity. Clearly, the numerous concerns, letters and suggestions flying around the sports pages following the disappointing 1988 tour were bringing results. The spirited manner of Cardiff's 25–15 defeat was both heartening and uplifting to a rugby nation in crisis, whose international game had plummeted to a sad and low level.

In moving on to Gwent, these latest All Blacks were making history by challenging Pontypool, as a sole club side, for the first time. They were assured of a rapturous welcome from the twenty thousand crowd, Ray Ruddick, today's club historian, amongst them. Ray can remember arriving at the ground early. 'I wanted to be on the bank where I normally stand and with the usual people around me,' he said, but, riveting as it was, a 47–6 scoreline was a bigger deficit than expected: 'It's just a shame we did not do ourselves justice,' said Ray. 'This came two seasons too late. Our 1987/88 side would have given them a better game. But we were playing the first ever official World Champions and they were superb.

After the match, the All Blacks went back to Pontnewynydd Cricket Club, less than half a mile from the ground, to escape the crowd and the media for a few hours. It is there that they analysed the match video before moving on to the Parkway Hotel in Cwmbran for the official dinner. Ted Stevens and fellow cricketing members of the club remember waiting in the car park for the bus so that a hero's welcome could be extended as the All Blacks stepped off. John Gallagher, full back, went straight to the boot area and produced cans of lager for the police motorcyclists to drop into their pannier bags, a 'thank you' for having escorted the team from the ground. Ted, who remembers the pavilion decorated with flags and bunting courtesy of sponsors Steinlager, recalls:

That day, my wife was one of the ladies taking plates of sandwiches down to the All Blacks in their room. Immediately one of the team noticed that she had a plaster cast on her arm – it may have been one of the Whetton brothers, I cannot be sure – but he made a big fuss of her. 'Come over here with us, my lovely. What have you been doing?' he said. Five minutes later she came out chuffed to bits: every player's signature was on her arm!

Ted explained that the All Blacks had a large following of fans this day, many being from North Harbour. 'I think they had heard on the grapevine that the All Blacks were coming back to us,' said Ted. 'They were certainly enjoying themselves in our club where they could get really close to the players. When they left we were presented with an inscribed dinner plate, and it is behind the bar today.'

In his *Buck, the Wayne Shelford Story*, the All Blacks captain mentions the team's visit to Pontypool Rugby Club before returning to their hotel in Cardiff.

'They wanted to pay homage to the local players by going there,' explained Ted Stevens. 'In no time the players had their guitars on their laps and were singing Māori and Welsh songs, led by Joe Stanley and John Perkins, our former international. I remember Inga Tuigamala, one of the try scorers, having a conversation with Ray Prosser, our former coach, and we all realised that this sort of occasion didn't happen too often.'

Wayne's story provides a straight-talking and enlightening account of events, taking readers into the nitty-gritty of top-class rugby. Mentioning visits to Cardiff Castle and a Welsh colliery, he also describes a helicopter ride which he enjoyed when invited to the headquarters of British Steel, Port Talbot, a tour sponsor, where the team also trained.

Days later the All Blacks were heading to St Helen's to meet an in-form Swansea whose strong second-half performance gave them a shock. In front of an eighteen thousand crowd on a windy and showery day, spectators were treated to a wealth of well-worked tries, three from the All Whites, courtesy of Paul Arnold, Ian Davies and Kevin Hopkins, and six from the visitors, the scorers being Mike Brewer (two), Craig Innes (two), Bruce Deans and Wales' own Warren Gatland.

No more than six miles away, the All Blacks were due to play in Neath, where the open green fields of today's Gnoll ground had facilitated much sport over the years. On Wednesday October 25th 1989 the ground was buzzing in anticipation of the biggest game in the club's history. Neath's home of rugby had grown and developed alongside the elegance of early Edwardian houses, slotting into the street patterns of old, a snug fit and a close bond with a community that has rugby in its bones. A big crowd this day was inevitable, the local heroes stepping into the small arena to do serious business with the world champions.

Neath, the 'Welsh All Blacks' by virtue of their similar playing strip, had been crowned 1988/89 Welsh Club Champions during the previous season and were now on course for a repeat of this success. Neath was the side to beat: hard-hitting and fearless up front, with strong and straight runners, every one of them believing this match was to be won. The club had never experienced so much excitement. Hearts were pounding and hopes raised as referee Fred Howard of England invited the two sides onto the field.

The home team were led by Kevin Phillips, a Pembrokeshire farmer. In a conversation, Kevin told me that he and Brian Williams, a neighbour and a regular prop for Neath – whose early passing shocked the close Pembrokeshire community – travelled to the game together. 'We met in Blaenwaun, a small village three miles from where I live,' said Kevin. 'This is where we usually got together for training. I was driving that day.' For the first few miles the two front row forwards talked about farming before the subject changed to rugby. 'What a chance we have to make history,' they were thinking. 'That was a totally different journey from any other I had previously made to the Gnoll,' said Kevin, who in the fullness of his career played against top-tier teams like Australia on this same ground. 'But now it was the All Blacks,' he said proudly. 'They are something special.' Kevin looks back to the match build-up:

> We all met up in Neath, early, and had a light buffet at the Glyn Clydach Hotel. Then one and a half hours before kick-off we walked from the town centre [about half a mile] straight into the dressing room. That was something special. There were crowds everywhere, all going to the match, everyone wishing us well. The atmosphere was tremendous.
>
> We were in the dressing room when the All Blacks arrived. We heard the crowd; we knew something had happened.

'Beaten but unbowed' was the headline in the *Neath Guardian* the next day, describing a titanic effort by the local men. Trailing by just one point midway through the second half, Neath thought the unthinkable and piled on the pressure. This forced the All Blacks to up a gear, always a sign of a great team, and they scored two late tries to win the match 26–15. Kevin continues:

> We had good fun together afterwards and a dinner at the Cimla Court Hotel. We all sat down in mixed company, so that we could have a chat and a laugh as we got to know each other. They told us we should have won that day but it was good to be with them, to hear what they had to say.

Mike Price, Neath's long-serving secretary who doubles up as club historian, will never forget the atmosphere at the Gnoll. 'You could cut it with a knife,' he said, 'a wall of noise with chants of "Neath, Neath, Neath!"' Mike, who remembers Kevin and his team acknowledging the fans with a walk around the field at the close, said he was reminded of a funny incident by Sean Fitzpatrick when the great All Black hooker returned to the club in 2012, over twenty years later:

> Sean was invited to speak at our club dinner and I met him at his hotel in Neath in the afternoon. Then we went over to the Gnoll ground where he wanted to walk across the field. Sean could remember details of the match, such as the cheering of our supporters and the jam-packed open stand on the opposite side. 'I remember this,' he smiled, when I took him down to the changing rooms. 'Good to see you've fixed the door.'

Sean was referring to the arrival of the All Blacks at the ground, when they found their changing room door unexpectedly locked. This may have been a bit of sporting psychology on Neath's part – a distinct possibility from what Mike recalls – although Alex Wyllie's men may also have arrived early. Nevertheless, whatever the reason for the locked door, it was soon off its hinges, with non-playing All Blacks standing in the gaping doorway when their team talk got underway.

At that same time, Kevin Phillips was firing his men to a fever pitch, but, all these years later, he was amused to be reminded of the door incident, which, according to recent rugby folklore at Neath, centred around the All Blacks coach, also a highly successful Test player who is admired as a great character in the game. Certainly, he is not the type to be intimidated by a locked door to his own team's changing room when there was no time to play around! Kevin shares the story as described by his friends at the Neath club, which, in the context of rugby's no-nonsense and territory-driven ethos, really explains what the game is all about: 'Alex Wyllie said, "Open this door before I knock it down" – but before he had finished saying it, they were inside!'

On the day of that match in 1989, Neath players wore a specially embroidered white jersey with a black band extending across the chest and elbows displaying in the usual place the club emblem, a Maltese cross, as well as a New Zealand fern. It represented the winning design of 160 suggestions from a Neath community that was totally involved with its rugby club, a state of affairs that was reflected down the road at Stradey Park, Llanelli, where preparations were underway for the next tour match.

Despite temporary stands having been erected to satisfy the demand for tickets, they could not be used because a freak storm of gale-force winds and driving rain almost blew away the afternoon's rugby. Forced into the classic 'game of two halves', Llanelli were first to play into the lashing elements in a match that was as predictable as it was farcical, although strangely absorbing. In the second half, Llanelli drove the ball down to the All Blacks line before their opponents, retaining close possession, forced their way back upfield against the odds. Then, when Llanelli regained the ball, the process was more or less repeated; they kicked ahead and back everyone went. The upshot was that the All Blacks sneaked away with a 11–0 win, moving on to Rodney Parade for one last date with old rivals Newport.

Newport's 54–9 loss demonstrated clearly the difference between a club side and world champions aspiring towards a professional model, despite players still having to earn their living away from the game. The result also virtually ended a tradition that reached back to 1905 of the All Blacks playing leading Welsh club sides. There would be one exception but the sad truth is that the fixture was no longer a match.

In terms of brute force and physicality, this encounter did, however, live up to the standards of earlier slogs between the two sides. Two of the Newport team had broken noses and there were some missing teeth, as the All Blacks also felt the physical impact of the Black and Ambers' hard, determined and sometimes desperate tackling. 'Shall we say we saw some bruised and broken parts to the body that day,' said historian Mike Dams, who refers to a far-sighted post-match comment from club captain Glenn George about the playing standards. New Zealand 'took passes at speed and showed us what can be achieved playing sound basic rugby,' said the powerful forward, before adding, 'I cannot see how it is possible to close the gap against such fitness, strength and professionalism.'

Newport's past players Alan Thomas, David Watkins and Brian Price, who have each provided stories in the earlier sections of this volume, and who cherish their 1963 win, felt the sadness of this latest occasion. But equally, the fruit of their earlier glories lives on, as Alan reminds us when, one day around this time, he picked up the telephone:

'Hello, again, Alan. It's Wilson Whineray here.' But I honestly thought it was David Watkins teasing me, so I said 'Thanks Dai' and put the phone down – before it rang again.

'Alan! *This is* Wilson Whineray. My daughter, Sue, is in Worcester, touring Britain with her boyfriend. She's got something for you. Please tell her how to get to your home.'

When they arrived, Sue presented Alan with a signed copy of her father's book, *Willie Away*. Inside was a message: 'With fond memories of our match against Newport in 1963 – and your own splendid contribution to the victory . . . Wilson

Whineray.' This was the moment for Jane, Alan's wife, to repay past kindnesses to the Whineray family, for she and Alan would be taking their guests out to dinner, and there would be home comforts when they returned.

It remained for the Welsh side to cheer up their countrymen by rolling back the years and winning the biggest contest of all, the full international on their favourite patch of grass where great things had happened in the past. But the 34–9 score that transpired on November 4th tells the sad, discouraging truth that All Blacks supremacy had already gone too far.

This tour had produced some engrossing encounters, some breathtaking scores, whilst occasionally the game's rougher edges had re-emerged with heavy punches giving rise to battered bodies and bruised egos. It is said that crowds jostled two of the visiting referees upon leaving the playing area and not even the All Blacks were spared hostility of an off-the-field nature from the general public.[45] Such incidents are always unwelcome and regrettable, but the story of this tour of Wayne Shelford's World Cup winners speaks for an era struggling with the consequences of the migration from amateurism to professionalism. As ever, the All Blacks had enriched the Welsh rugby way of life, leaving much to admire and to discuss and, most certainly, to aspire to.

---

45   Wynne Gray and Wayne Shelford, *Buck, the Wayne Shelford Story* (MOA Publications, Auckland, 1990).

PART IX

THE START OF A PROFESSIONAL ERA IN 1995

An outing to Johannesburg and an All Blacks doctor from Wales

For Wales, a determined rugby nation, the latest run of heavy defeats to its New Zealand friends was a heavy load to bear, and it was little wonder if during these early 1990s the team stood back, regrouped and watched others giving the All Blacks a game. Ireland and Scotland were struggling as well, both without a win to date against the New Zealanders. But the same could not be said for England, whose latest victories had seen them beat the All Blacks on four occasions to Wales' three. The next Wales–New Zealand clash, as fate would have it, was destined to take place in South Africa, where the two teams had been drawn to meet each other at the pool stage of the 1995 Rugby World Cup.

Wales were one of a number of serious challengers hoping to produce what was necessary to carry home the Webb Ellis Cup. They had a good team, led by Mike Hall of Cardiff, and had disposed of their first opponents, Japan, with a comfortable 57–10 scoreline. Under the guidance of Alex Evans, the Australian head coach, Wales even had an upbeat manner and self-belief when they stepped forward to meet Sean Fitzpatrick's team in Ellis Park, Johannesburg, at the end of May. The All Blacks had also won their first game against Ireland, 43–19, a score which gave the Welsh reason to hope for a decent contest. Little did Wales know, however, that the All Blacks were soon to rip open the history books by swamping Japan 145–17. This was the difference!

At times of major tournaments, New Zealand has inevitably risen to the occasion and at least one player has shown sensational form. On this occasion, Jonah Lomu was that man, who, having enjoyed wreaking havoc on unsuspecting defences, knew that his demolition work was far from done. Although brave Welsh defence and determination succeeded in stopping Jonah from crossing the line, the winger was only one of many threats that Wales had to deal with on the day. A combination of his giant presence coupled by the might of the rest of the team proved too great for the Welsh, who lost 34–9, a score identical to the last encounter in Cardiff in 1989. A little consolation could be sought in the fact that only three tries were conceded, but now each carried a five-point rating, courtesy of an extra incentive introduced in 1992 for teams to cross the line.

This showpiece World Cup more or less coincided with the disappearance of the 'amateur' game at the top level and all that the word once entailed. In the sports pages of the *New Zealand Herald* of May 31st 1995, the day Wales played New Zealand, D. J. Cameron reported that the structure of a competition between senior sides from New Zealand, Australia and South Africa, the 'Super 12' series, was being finalised, whilst the national teams of the three countries would also be engaged in an annual Test match competition of their own. Only a few months later, on August 26th, the big day arrived; the door had finally opened to professionalism. Suddenly new challenges and horizons emerged for the Welsh and other nations, whilst the past concerns of players drifting to the northern code seemed to slip quietly away. As for the conventional All Blacks tours of old, sad as it is to say, these had finally come to an end.

Gareth Jenkins, a former Welsh team coach, had predicted this outcome long before the day:

There were too many examples of professionalism evident in all areas of the game. By now, some countries around the world were not respecting amateurism any more. Vernon Pugh, chairman of the International Rugby Board, was left with no other alternative; he had to bring rugby into the open. But we hadn't prepared for the consequences. We just opened the door and let it run. Wales became destabilised within the game for a long time. It is only in more recent years that we are back on a firm footing.

In hindsight it was obvious that changes needed time to take effect and, in the absence of a more gradual transition, rugby lost its bearings. Gareth continues:

We had a situation of a coach being amateur one day and professional the next. But things had to evolve to make a coach professional; it called for training, leadership, people skills and so on besides rugby issues. Support workers and back-room staff were necessary and a lot more. Back in the 1970s, there would have been one coach and, perhaps, an assistant; nowadays, top sides have a team of experts.

Twenty-three years before that professional door opened, the year Llanelli beat the All Blacks, the rugby world was a different place. At the time, Gareth was working for Duport steelworks, a huge employer in Llanelli with 3,500 workers. 'It was a steel-smelting business,' he said. 'Iron was poured into furnaces and out came steel.' On the Tuesday of the match, Gareth had a day's leave and although his engineer wasn't particularly happy, Gareth was, at least, expected back at work on the Wednesday. But the bruising encounter with the New Zealanders had, by now, left him with two black eyes, which led to a chance meeting with a gentleman in the patron's bar after the match:

> I didn't know him from Adam although since then we have kept in touch. 'I've been a boxer in my younger days,' he said. 'I can assure you the best cure is to put [raw] steak on your eyes.' Then he put his hand in my pocket and left something and, when I checked, it was a £20 note. It was the first time I had ever seen a £20 note. I was earning £29 per week at the time and I told my wife, 'You're not going to believe this.' It meant that I could afford to have three days off. The £20 paid my wages for the rest of the week.

As one would expect, Gareth was glued to the World Cup action in South Africa, and he was disappointed that Wales lost by a single point, 24–23, to Ireland at Ellis Park, thus ending Welsh hopes of progressing further. Then a week or so later, he saw the glittering, treasured prize passing from Nelson Mandela, regaled in a Springboks jersey, to South African captain, François Pienaar. It was an astounding moment in both sporting and African history and was watched by the world. The All Blacks had been defeated by a Joel Stransky drop goal in extra time.

That day, Dr Mike Bowen, a Welshman who had moved to New Zealand in the mid-1970s (and who is thanked in the Acknowledgements section of this book), was on duty as the official doctor of the All Blacks and was soon to be introduced to the South African president. 'We all met Nelson Mandela,' he said, 'this was not a long chat but I felt that I had been in the company of someone special. It made me think, "How did this happen to me and how should I be so lucky to have such an opportunity?"'

The answer is that when he and his wife Diana arrived in New Zealand, Mike discovered there was a sports medicine society near his home. When he went along, he was the new boy on the block. 'Will you be secretary?' he was asked, and when he agreed, things moved along from there. Mike then had a call inviting him to look after Melville Rugby Club; and when Waikato heard about this, he was encouraged to go along to help out on the bigger provincial scene. 'This was way back in 1976,' said Mike, 'and I continued this post with Waikato for twenty-five years until 2001.' It was towards the end of the term that Mike had a big surprise:

> In 1994 I was trekking on the South Island with my son and I had a call from the New Zealand Rugby Union asking me if I would like to be medical doctor for the All Blacks team, whereupon I was duly flattered and excited and couldn't believe my luck.

'Looking back I was probably the first doctor to go onto the field for Waikato province,' said Mike:

> We were entering into the professional era and, up until then, physiotherapists attended to the players: doctors being called on only if injuries were serious. Certainly I was one of the first [All Blacks] doctors to wear gloves for potential blood injuries.'

> By association with the All Blacks I was launched into different fields of contact. It seemed to me that they were welcome visitors wherever they went. There was terrific excitement about being with the team.

> I remember Dame Kiri Te Kanawa being invited into our dressing room under the stand after beating Scotland in the quarter-final [of the same 1995 World Cup]. She sang 'Pokarekare Ana' [a traditional Māori love song] and it was the most tingling and moving off-field moment I'd experienced with a rugby team and she got all the boys to join in.

Mike brought a touch of the Welsh *hwyl* into the All Black camp and he enjoyed himself with this elite band of rugby men. He told me about the times he had to physically tackle the giants to pay his dues in the squad's court sessions and there were frequent instances of the men playing pranks on each other. What impressed Mike greatly was the strong sense of tradition and proven values that are a part of the team's ethos. To this end he quickly learnt never to sit near the back of the bus which 'belonged' to the senior players and which was in every respect a 'no-go area' for anyone else, especially the greenhorns – the new boys.

Would any of this change, we all wondered, when the game stepped out from the shades of amateurism into a more professional brighter light? The answer would be both 'yes' and 'no'. Under the new model, leading fixtures would be bigger, better supported and bound up in television deals as commercialism in its fullest sense was prioritised. There would be time aplenty for relaxation, fun and frivolity, but beyond the new disciplines of training, travelling, playing, recovering and resting – the apparent core constituents of success – time would have to be made for agents, personal and public appearances, as well as corporate promotions.

Dr Mike Bowen has seen both ends of the rugby spectrum that connects our two countries and he, more so than most, appreciates that beyond the undeniable links of kin, kith and communities, the biggest common ground stands between two vertical sets of parallel posts one hundred metres apart. But if the final whistle was to blow for the end of a professional game, would there be the flow of beer that was once synonymous with post-match functions, and would ukuleles and guitars spark a sing-song of hymns, arias and Māori songs that once bounced around clubhouse walls? Would hardened prop forwards continue to forge friendships in the murky tunnels of front row play? Would Cliff Morgan's story, derived from the Cardiff–All Blacks match of 1953, ever repeat itself in some form? [46]

I remember Stan Bowes, our tough naval prop, playing opposite 'Snow' White, an equally rugged New Zealander. They struggled and hit and fought in that front row all through [the] game, and yet until the day that Stan died in the early nineties, Snow White would come across to see Stan, or he'd pay for Stan to go and see him in New Zealand, and they kept that friendship going for thirty-seven years.

It is a story belonging to a different age. The big difference from now on, of course, was that players were not only travelling extensively to play against distant teams, but they were also travelling the same distances to play *for* them. When I spoke to Wales' former outside half Stephen Jones, he told me that he had been amused when he last visited Carisbrook, Dunedin, with the Welsh side, to see the faces of two young men who he had got to know well, appearing in team photographs on the walls of the stadium's rugby rooms. These faces belonged to Kees Meeuws and Simon Maling, men who at this stage of their careers, in the mid-1990s, were breaking onto the scene with the New Zealand Colts. Yet, much later down the line, *both* – not one of them – were destined to wear the Scarlet jersey of Llanelli and so play alongside Stephen, another well-travelled professional man. Indeed, Regan King, formally of Waikato Province, was another and stayed at Llanelli for many seasons.

---

46   Cliff Morgan and Geoffrey Nicholson, *Cliff Morgan the Autobiography: Beyond the Fields of Play* (Hodder & Stoughton, 1996).

In this new age the world really was the oyster of talented and dedicated players although many also appreciated that the same open door to the game's new framework had let a lot of rugby's old charm and innocence escape. Innocence such as when Chico Hopkins and Carwyn James visited George Nēpia for a dose of the Māori's traditional cure during the Lions tour in 1971, or the similar innocence as shared by former Welsh Rugby Union president, Harry Bowcott, when he travelled to Wellington for the screening of George Nēpia's *This is Your Life*.

When appearing on the programme, Bowcott, a Cardiff, London Welsh and Wales centre, explained that he had watched George playing in Cardiff, and it was George who had influenced him to adopt the spiral form of 'torpedo kick'. In 1930 the two men had played against each other in the same British Lions match versus the All Blacks that saw Ivor Jones making his memorable break for Jack Morley's winning score. These men had a lot in common and could have talked all night, but before the Welshman left the stage, he had just one important question to ask the famous full back: 'One thing, George,' he said in a quiet, soft manner, 'I'd like to know why *five* South Wales clubs are pleased to have in their museums a jersey given by George Nēpia: in fact, *the actual one* that he wore for the All Blacks against Wales in 1924?'[47]

These are memories from the good old days and long may they live on. Of course, George, like Chico Hopkins, and many others mentioned in this work, had tasted both the 'union' and 'league' codes. This may have been another reason why the two remained such good friends after their meeting in 1971, prompting Chico to be amongst the crowd when George, touring with his countrymen eleven years later

47 *This is Your Life*, George Nēpia: Television NZ, as at March 31st 2013.

in 1982, was honoured by a standing ovation at St Helen's, Swansea. Chico's last meeting with the legendary player, who died in 1986, was in a Cardiff hotel where he was one of the few admitted to see the great man whose health was failing at that time.

Of course, many years before this date, Chico had made the transition that George had made, a transition that once caused past players to be ostracised from their communities. Would those men have ever believed what was happening to their beloved game? Probably not. The wheel had turned a full circle: rugby union was also switching codes.

Sharing more than a
Walk down Wembley Way

During the months that followed the World Cup of 1995, a rugby-loving New Zealander was at work as principal of Kelston Boys High School, Auckland. He had been a player and a cricketer and had also taught at Auckland Grammar School not a mile from Mount Eden, another highly regarded seat of education also acclaimed for sport. Besides his academic responsibilities, he was immersed in rugby's great cause, particularly at Eden Park, with everyone connected to the game and all things existing for its purpose.

Graham Henry's coaching career had for years been fuelled by his characteristic energy and ambition. Following success in New Zealand's National Provincial Championship, he was soon to direct Auckland Blues towards exciting times in the Super-12 series, today's Super Rugby. However, throughout all, his sights seemed to be set on becoming the All Blacks senior coach. But with the post occupied by John Hart, Graham was, understandably, considering an alternative situation to challenge his proven sporting pedigree in the new world of rugby.

In November 1997, Graham would have taken note of New Zealand's latest triumph over Wales. On this occasion, there was no series of matches with Welsh club sides – those days had gone for ever; there were just three fixtures, one being the international. As a consequence, there was a different feel to the arrival of Sean Fitzpatrick's All Blacks team, who had, by now, pitched their game higher still, helped by regular Tri-Nations rugby.

This was all too evident when the All Blacks swept aside Llanelli 81–3 (and who could possibly have predicted *this*?) before walloping Wales 'A' 51–8 after the Welsh had played superbly for the first hour. As if these were not big enough blows, Cardiff Arms Park was out of bounds because the ground was being restyled for today's Millennium Stadium. This meant that the two sides and a 76,000 crowd were heading to Wembley, whose stately structures had witnessed most of a century of sport. But even its famous twin towers could not compete with the warm hearth of a nation's favourite arena on the banks of the River Taff in Cardiff. Having come into this match on the end of a run of victories, Wales had been feeling hopeful, but the body blow of a 42–7 defeat made their journey home a difficult one.

Playing this day was Mike Voyle, a tall, powerful second row forward who stood up to the challenges of Ian Jones and Robin Brooke in the line-outs. Mike, who had played for a number of top-class sides in Wales, fitted the mould of the modern player: a smart man with celebrity looks, punctual for training, careful in managing his body and driven to new levels of fitness and playing ability. He certainly impressed Les Williams at Llanelli's ground, where training took place on most days in the new era – a regime far removed from the mandatory Tuesday and Thursday nights of old. Rugby was now a different game for Les: 'Everything changed from that moment,' he said. 'I can remember some of our players having good cricketing careers. Keith Jarrett was one, a leading Welsh international, also a first-class batsman for Glamorgan; but these things changed with the new set-up. When Jeff Wilson visited Stradey [Park] in the late 1990s, another combining the two sports, I remember asking him how he was managing both. I do believe he was the last of the dual internationals.'

In this new rugby world, rumour was rife and before long news was making its way from New Zealand that Graham Henry was responding to the challenge of a coaching appointment with the Welsh Rugby Union. By taking his proven formula and skills into the northern hemisphere, Graham was not only linking once again the fortunes of these two rugby-driven nations, but unknowingly establishing a precedent for later activity of this kind. Likewise, in extricating himself from commitments in his native country he was demonstrating the mobility and will of a modern-day professional.

Graham Henry's immediate impact sparked a revival in Welsh rugby's fortunes and New Zealand's loss was quite clearly seen as Wales' gain. It was only a question of time before Kelston's former headmaster had transformed the Welsh nation's belief in its own sporting stock by achieving an outstanding run of consecutive wins. With this revival occurring at the same time as the completion of the new stadium, Wales was fast returning to rugby's land of milk and honey. Hopefully there would be no stopping the national team as it faced the challenges of the next century.

Time had proved correct an innocent comment made by Danny O'Shea, the coach of North Auckland (a side that beat Wales in 1988). His message, as reported in the *Western Mail* of June 8th that year, was that if Wales had been blessed with a good coach, such as New Zealander John Hart, then the team's fortunes would have been different on that particular tour. Clearly, those in authority in the Welsh Rugby Union were of like mind and, in supporting Graham Henry with the key personnel he needed, no stone was left unturned in a desire to return the once proud rugby nation to its former glory on the international field – despite voices of disapproval emanating from certain quarters.

Wales' ambition was, and still is, commendable and, in living the professional ethos to the full, every consideration was given to the growing young talent which would one day carry the nation's ambitions. Rugby within the schools and youth set-up, and beyond this into the more senior groupings, had long provided the bedrock of future talent, and when a junior World Cup competition was staged in Wales in 1999, Welsh rugby followers saw for itself the healthy future of the nation's game. Entertained by enterprise and dash, there was great excitement in seeing the young Welsh going all the way to the final, held at Llanelli's Stradey Park. But it was hardly surprising and equally worrying that their biggest rivals – once again – would stand in their way when it came to seizing the main prize.

The *Western Mail* of April 5th 1999 gives an account of the match, played in front of a crowd of 12,000. Well led by Adam Jones, Wales secured a good deal of the possession and ran well with Jamie Robinson and Ceri Sweeney in a gifted backline of attacking players. Welsh full back, Rhys Williams, a talented runner, was brought down near the tryline on a few occasions in an absorbing encounter that spoke volumes for Wales' future stars.

The New Zealanders had shining lights throughout their side as well: Jerry Collins, Aaron Mauger and Junior 'Mils' Muliaina all being prominent, whilst Tony Woodcock, substitute, entered the match in the sixty-sixth minute. But it is another, described as being a 'human dynamo' and seen 'everywhere', who would one day be the cause of much future Welsh despair. This young man, a try scorer on the day, would soon heap lots more hardships on the Welsh. His name is Richie McCaw.

PART X

ENTERING A NEW MILLENNIUM

Neven's night out in Cilfynydd

Despite some impressive Six Nations displays in earlier seasons, Wales were far from at their best when, having crossed into the new millennium, they met the All Blacks at Cardiff in November 2002. This was effectively the start of the fuller and more meaningful series of autumn internationals, with the Wales–New Zealand fixture being every Welshman's pick of the bunch. Many aspects of the old game were unrecognisable now, and even the Arms Park field had experienced its own paradigm shift by being rotated ninety degrees. There were certainly no All Black visits to Abertillery Park, let alone to Aberdare. Yet, these latest matches offered compulsive viewing, filling the new stadium, complete with all its modern amenities, whilst fuelling the old rivalry.

It is ironic that when Graham Henry presented match jerseys to the Welsh team on the occasion of this 2002 encounter, he was no longer head coach. By the time he called to see his former players, a generous courtesy, he had already secured his release from duties with the Welsh Rugby Union after a four-year stay. In his place was Steve Hansen, a fellow New Zealander, causing one to smile at the extraordinary affiliation between Antipodeans and the Welsh rugby flag. Playing hosts to a younger looking All Blacks team with a number of new caps, the Welsh were destined to meet Keven Mealamu and Tony Woodcock in the front row for the first time at senior level. Their early Cardiff Test baptism was a close contest until the last few minutes of play, when Wales ceded three tries to lose 43–17.

With the Rugby World Cup squeezing into an already packed programme, there was no autumn match scheduled for 2003, but this did not stop Wales flying to New Zealand to test conditions 'down under' with a 'light' warm-up in Hamilton – if there is such a thing against the All Blacks. Certainly, it proved to be a heavy defeat, 55–3, and there was no avoiding the hurt of this rout for the latest Welsh Kiwi coach. But the occasion did, at least, provide the Welsh with an inkling of what could be done before facing these same opponents in the World Cup in Australia later that same year.

When the time arrived so did a new Wales, for what came next was an absolute treat. Whatever Steve Hansen told his men as they stepped into the final pool match with New Zealand at the (formerly named) Telstra Stadium, Sydney, should have been noted for future use. The verve, nerve, fight and unfailing spirit of those in red was a joy to behold, causing everyone to salute the Welsh effort.

The words of the World Cup's anthem, 'As we climb to reach our destiny, a new age has begun', defined the Welsh performance this day, as they reinvented themselves on this great stage. Having absorbed the first two blows – the earth-trembling Haka and Joe Rokocoko's converted try – a third came when Garan Evans was stretchered off. But then came the scoring of try for try, virtually tit for tat, in a thrilling exhibition of seven-a-side style rugby from two teams of fifteen men. This match was about possession and passing, running and ball retention, and sparkled with counter-attacks and good use of advantage ball, thanks to referee Andre Watson from South Africa. By half-time, Ali Williams, Joe Rokocoko and Leon MacDonald had scored tries with Mark Taylor, Sonny Parker and Colin Charvis replying for Wales.

When play resumed, the score was delicately balanced at 28–24 to the All Blacks. Then Wales grabbed the game by the scruff of the neck with a Stephen Jones penalty and a try by Shane Williams, which was converted. Now, winning 34–28, Doug Howlett, playing on the wing, replied with a try at sizzling pace before Stephen Jones struck a penalty. This moved the score to 37–33 to Wales as both teams went for glory. It was breathtaking rugby, all the way through to the final whistle, by which time the All Blacks had reclaimed the high ground, clinching victory 53–37.

Those who attended the match had hardly stopped talking about it when November 20th 2004 brought the two teams back to Cardiff for another finely balanced contest. Events surrounding this latest fixture underlined the merry-go-round taking place at the top of the game, for Graham Henry was now the head coach to the All Blacks with Steve Hansen as his assistant. David Moffett, formerly of the New Zealand Rugby Union, had also crossed the world to be the Welsh Rugby Union's chief executive. Mike Ruddock, a Welshman and national coach, must have felt the odd man out!

With the shock news that Tana Umaga was being rested, Graham Henry made a bold statement by giving Richie McCaw the captaincy. Only five years since serving his apprenticeship as a winning member of the Junior All Blacks at Llanelli, Richie had already proved himself to be tailor-made for the senior 'Number 7' jersey. The day also brought a first cap for Piri Weepu at scrum half, who entered the field with not only pride but disbelief on his face. In his *Piri – Straight Up: Cups, Downs & Keeping Calm*, he said he was, in fact, looking for his brother – an optimistic hope, surely, despite a banner being held aloft to attract Piri's attention!

Both Piri and Richie were no doubt impressed with the Welsh singing this day, including the lonesome voice of soloist Wynne Evans, who, in something of a novel act to boost choral activity, stepped forward, microphone in hand, singing *Guide me, O thy great Jehovah*. This set the scene for the latest episode, another nail-biter of a match that continued from the last encounter in 2003 with the score swinging like a pendulum. But the sad news for the Welsh was that New Zealand's flying left wing, Joe Rokocoko, was just too good on the day, tearing through the Welsh defence, ensuring the visitors recorded a one-point win, 26–25, in this the twenty-first official meeting of the two teams.

Far away in Palmerston North, New Zealand, former All Blacks second-row forward, Neven MacEwan, was taking note as the players exchanged their jerseys at the end of the game. Many years had passed since Neven had played for the All Blacks against the 1959 Lions when he battled hard with two of Wales' strong second-row forwards, Rhys Williams and Roddy Evans. 'I was up against Roddy in each of the first three tests at Dunedin, Wellington and Christchurch,' said Neven, 'and no quarter was asked or given.' Neven, who set his heart on Wilson Whineray's 1963 tour to the British Isles, France and Canada, was prevented from going by a cartilage injury, causing him to wait over forty years to visit Cardiff's famous ground.

Neven, fully aware that the last touring Lions sides to his country in 1993 and 2005 had been humbled by more recent All Blacks combinations, explained that for many of these years one of his jerseys had been displayed at Cilfynydd Rugby Club, near Pontypridd. Wanting to recover it for the MacEwan family, Neven's son Angus contacted the club secretary asking if he could have the jersey back. 'Yes, we'll gladly release it,' was the reply, 'but we'd like you to bring your father here so that we can honour him.' Neven continues the story:

I went over with my son in 2005 and my old friend Roddy [Evans, British Lion] was the first person to phone me when we arrived in Cardiff. We met up and it was just as if time had stood still. Then we had an absolutely unbelievable night in Cilfynydd. The club put on a function and members of the Welsh Rugby Union were present.

It was a touching occasion, one that I will never forget. I was blown away by the many addresses and presentations. I was given a Welsh miner's lamp; it was absolutely unbelievable.

In return, Neven gave both a Wellington and an All Black shirt to the evening's hosts, the latter having previously belonged to Joe Rokocoko. It was a special night as Dudley Lloyd, chairman of the Cilfynydd club recalls:

Neven is a lovely, lovely man and it was a pleasure for us to have him with us. I must admit that at first I was concerned that some of our younger players would be a bit raucous, but as soon as Neven started to talk – and he was a good speaker – they all kept quiet. He had the entire audience in the palm of his hand and I can tell you they were mighty big hands!

Dudley also remembers the visit coinciding with the latest November international between the two countries on Bonfire Night, 2005. This was the evening when Neven fulfilled his long-standing wish to visit the new-look Cardiff Arms Park to watch his colleagues in action. But this was no routine Test; the occasion marked the hundredth anniversary of David Gallaher's 'Originals' playing at Cardiff in the titanic struggle of 1905. All week the newspapers had been looking back on a century of rugby, marvelling how the two countries had slogged it out on the field throughout this era, yet had remained on such excellent terms.

When the players arrived at the ground a hundred years earlier they would have been ushered into the pavilion amidst chaos breaking out in all directions. With the ground entrances closing early, people were trying to catch a glimpse of the action from every vantage point, including passengers who had arrived late into the city aboard the Devon and Torquay excursion, who paid, so it is said, between three and five shillings, a lot of money in 1905, for the privilege of climbing onto 'the roofs of hansom cabs in Westgate Street'.[48] How very different it was when the recent teams of Gareth Thomas and Tana Umaga made their entrance in 2005 and filtered into the spacious, secluded and modern changing rooms that awaited them.

It is with thanks to personnel of the Welsh Rugby Union who, in the knowledge of this book being written, invited me to the Millennium Stadium for a brief visit, that I was able to see two treasures from the past. The first is the dear old match ball from the 1905 game, and how hard it is to believe that this battered and much-kicked piece of leather, which bears the signatures of players alongside a gaping, ugly hole, commanded every pair of eyes that day. The occasion could not have taken place without that priceless object and every player's bump and bruise was received in pursuit of it. It passed through Teddy Morgan's hands for a score; likewise, it passed through Bob Deans' hands for the no-score.

Situated alongside the ball I was also able to see the day's match whistle. This silver, shining piece of equipment bears the inscription 'New Zealand v Wales, December 16th 1905, J. D. Dallas' and had been passed on to the Welsh Rugby Union by the family of Sheriff Dallas many years after the

48   Bob Howitt and Dianne Haworth, *The 1905 Originals — The remarkable story of the team that went away as the Colonials and came back as the All Blacks* (HarperCollins Publishers, 2005).

game. Again, how amazing it is to consider that this small instrument was blown at 2.35 p.m. on that winter's afternoon to start the proceedings and to follow the action throughout the game . . . but not closely enough for the likings of George Dixon, New Zealand's tour manager!

In an extract from his tour diaries Mr Dixon voices his disappointment – although not in a harsh manner – about Mr Dallas' performance on the day. He 'was not what could be called first class according to my standards,' he states, for the reason that Mr Dallas was often found behind the action. Mr Dixon cited his apparel as being the probable reason, for he appeared 'in heavy clothing', part of which was 'the orthodox stiff collar' and on his feet he wore 'ordinary walking boots, no buttons or bars.'[49]

But Mr Dallas was doing no more or less than was deemed appropriate for the occasion, dressing in the customary manner of British officials at the time. Gil Evans, for instance, who Mr Dixon admired greatly, and who refereed most of the New Zealander's matches in Wales, would have appeared in similar clothing, usually a jacket, breeches, boots, cap and often with a big white handkerchief protruding from one of his front pockets. Mr Dixon had been surprised by all of this formality, again stressing in his diary entries that this could not have been more different from the ways of senior referees in New Zealand.

A century later it was all so different in the 2005 clash of the rivals as Chris White, the man in charge, having travelled the short distance from Gloucestershire, looked immaculate in the latest range of smart, light-weight referee's gear. With memories of the Welsh players responding to the haka by

---

49   Bob Howitt and Dianne Haworth, *The 1905 Originals — The remarkable story of the team that went away as the Colonials and came back as the All Blacks* (HarperCollins Publishers, 2005).

singing the National Anthem all those years earlier, the order of events for this occasion was altered to mirror that significant, distant day. And with the roof being shut so as to contain the noise, and everyone encouraged to be in their seats and singing early, the spine-chilling crescendo of 'Mae Hen Wlad fy Nhadau' was enough to make everyone tremble.

Unfortunately, the absence through injury of six of Wales' leading players – too many to lose to an All Blacks clash – was a downbeat factor on an otherwise wonderful day. For a nation who in the past two years had been close to clinching the long overdue victory, this 41–3 thrashing was a profound blow. And for Neven, viewing from the stand, the score was a painful reminder of how far back his Welsh friends had fallen behind.

One last visit to Carisbrook for the Welsh

The All Blacks know better than most how difficult it is to remain on top of the sporting ladder having in the first place worked so hard to get there. Heavily engaged in Tri-Nations matches and demanding schedules nearer home, they had effectively become the hitmen of rugby, flying into Johannesburg or Brisbane to do serious work before returning to the British Isles to add to earlier successes. Of course, it is extremely challenging when every team wants to lower their colours and every capacity crowd turns up to cheer the home side. At this stage, 2005, neither Scotland nor Ireland had beaten the All Blacks, whilst England on six occasions and Wales on three shared the international victories so far gained by the Home Countries.

It was, however, a sad reflection of the times that Welsh rugby, steeped in rugby values and customs and true to the red shirt, three feathers, choral singing and a 'ten-point' anthem, had by now discarded some of its rugby treasures. The thought of Stradey Park closing and later reduced to rubble for a housing development had broken many a heart and, with facilities being shared with footballing friends, most Welshmen felt the sadness that former first-class grounds rich in the memories of All Black encounters with the Welsh were being denied representative rugby at a high level. Cardiff's return to the Arms Park may well have lifted some spirits in this respect, but one wonders if the wearing of patterned kit in the past – and more recently green socks – was a sign that the Welsh were letting go of certain traditions.

Today's All Black playing strip, admittedly refashioned for comfort and appeal, is to all intents and purposes the same black jersey and silver fern that David Gallaher's men wore in 1905. And neither is it likely to change, fundamentally, because its design fits a purpose, and sponsorship logos fall respectfully into line. When New Zealand beat France in Marseille some years ago – wearing white, as was necessary to avoid clashing with France's dark blue – Richie McCaw, when putting on a black jersey for the post-match interview, was making a major statement before he uttered a single word.

Paddy O'Brien, a former international referee and rugby administrator, once explained to me the significance of the All Black tie. This is not a readily available item and it finds its way only to the elite of the New Zealand game. According to my understanding, if a tie becomes soiled or worn, it must be handed back before another is granted in exchange, a simple principle defining the essence of 'value,' just as the haka speaks for the New Zealand way. The haka is, of course, an essential part of a powerful machine, indispensable to a nation whose rugby is influenced by Māori customs. Its place in the game is not for change or negotiation – as Wales realised fully in the autumn fixture of 2006.

On that November evening, the Welsh had both requested and hoped to respond to the haka by singing its national anthem, altering the usual pre-match order of events to be consistent with the previous year's revised centenary match timetable. And when the two parties could not agree to this, New Zealand performed the haka in their dressing room. This incident was a defence of, what had become, accepted practice over the years and Richie McCaw's endorsement of the action was emphatic. As reported in the *Western Mail*, his message was that the All Blacks would carry out the ritual in privacy if necessary, which also attacked the suggestion of worldwide dissenters who were advocating the haka's discontinuance – because the place of this traditional ritual in the game is absolute, not to be altered but to be left alone.

New Zealand went on to beat Wales 45–10, with three tries from Sitiveni Sivivatu, a replacement for Joe Rokocoko, before the success story was repeated in Cardiff in 2008, although by a reduced margin, 29–9. By now Warren Gatland was Wales' man in charge, with Graham Henry and Steve Hansen, two former Wales coaches, opposing him. Warren was responsible for driving Welsh momentum forward into the following autumn, 2009, when the All Blacks squeezed home to victory by a far closer 19–12 margin.

The two teams travelled thousands of miles from Cardiff for the next match on June 19th 2010 to a much-loved stadium that was on this same day scheduled to officially bow out of the international game. A changing world had now caught up with Carisbrook Park in Dunedin, a delightful old international ground that had been in existence since the late 1800s. It was initially built for the playing of cricket – as was Eden Park – before becoming the hot bed of Otago rugby.

Ever since the All Blacks and British team in 1908 kicked a heavy leather ball in square-capped boots on its extended berth, Carisbrook with its open terraces and somewhat sheltered position had enjoyed the hallmarks of a genuine rugby landmark. Its excellent playing surface and feeling of limitless room to run around on has hosted the greatest players in the world and many of Wales' former internationals have fond memories of the old stadium.

Sir Gareth Edwards had the chance to return there in 1983 as a match analyst for the BBC. 'There is a lovely feel to Carisbrook,' he told me, 'it felt a natural place to play the game'. But he can also remember being thrown flying out of the rucks in the Otago match of 1971 and feeling quite bruised by the close of play. Yet it was not malicious, he added, just another example of a country's no-nonsense approach to the forwards' role. In the first Test that followed a few weeks later, Sir Gareth was forced to leave the field injured, giving Chico a chance to enter the fray and make his mark. Welshmen have never been strangers to this famous sporting landmark where almost two-thirds of the Lions team that day were Welsh.

For an atmosphere of fun, Carisbrook has always taken some beating, boosted by a growing student population who were known to walk down Princess Street and onto the open terrace carrying wooden crates upon which they would stand. Beyond one set of goalposts is the most famous Scotsman's stand of all, extending across the residential site on the nearby hill. This has been a popular and convenient viewing spot for ticketless fans keen to enter into the spirit of matches from a distant lofty height. Indeed, with the country virtually shutting down to support its team at Test time, this elevated area was alive as trains, passing nearby, stopped to watch the game, passengers spilling out, nobody wanting to go anywhere, to do anything, until the match was over and won.

The inevitable demise of Carisbrook serves to remind us of the passing of the years. We can only wonder what the old tub baths of earlier days were like as the players put a shine on their appearances before donning stiff collars and ties for the greater officialdom of post-Test match dinners. Thereafter it saw the days of cine-cameras, radio commentaries and television recordings, before 1987's World Cup and later professionalism breathed a different, corporate air along with the finer accoutrements of our modern game.

For the final act in the old arena this night, Dan Carter would choose to forget the tackle he made on Welsh replacement Martin Roberts when the teams last met in Cardiff, a tackle which earned him a citing. Now, geared up on this historic night, Dan, the supreme All Black, having already scored 1,000 points for his country (a feat first achieved for Wales by Neil Jenkins), was set to slip into overdrive. He scored two tries, three penalties and four conversions (27 points) in a colossal contribution to his team's 42–9 victory. Was there a finer way of saying farewell to the old stadium?

And so it was that on a night of sentimentality the final curtain fell. As people trickled from their seats and standing spots beneath a sky coloured by exploding fireworks, a long and fascinating sporting era came to an end. Less than a mile across the city, a new stadium, named the Forsyth Barr, stood in wait, built to accommodate thirty thousand spectators with a roof to keep everyone dry. This is where former All Black, Jeff Wilson, would be transplanting a clod of earth that he had this night dug from Carisbrook, a gesture signalling that the passionate voice of provincial rugby had a good and safe home well into the future.[50]

It is significant that it was the Welsh who had the privilege of sharing 'Carisbrook's final fling', as Brent Edwards of the *Otago Daily Times* described the event – not knowing that the All Blacks and Fiji would return to play one more fundraising match a year later. After stating that everyone had been saying goodbye to 'more than a rugby or cricket ground', Mr Edwards then offered his own farewell. It came in the form of a touching tribute to a dear old friend from someone who knew 'her' well. His words simply said: 'rest in peace old girl.'

---

50   *Otago Daily Times*, June 21st 2010.

But on the morning after the night before, Jim Strachan, who had enjoyed the entire night's proceedings, was flying back from Dunedin to Christchurch with members of his supporters touring party from Wales. Unfortunately, torrential rain swept in preventing their plane from flying. 'It was just hopeless,' said Jim. 'As we sat in the airport lounge, everyone was feeling miserable, and looking glum, glancing at me as if to say, "What are you going to do about this, what now?" But, by a stroke of luck, everybody's mood was suddenly lifted as the entire All Blacks squad walked into the room. Talk about clouds having silver linings! Soon everyone in our party was chatting away and mixing freely and taking photos.'

As if that wasn't enough, later, when Jim was standing in a queue, the gentleman in front of him turned round to enquire if he and his party were from Wales. 'You won't know me,' the gentleman added, 'but I am an All Black. I toured Wales with Wilson Whineray's side in 1963.'

'Hold on a moment,' Jim said, and off he went to find Roger Batten, a member of his supporters party from Newport who had the official Newport–All Blacks match programme on him, a programme he was due to present to the Rugby Museum in Palmerston North. As the group looked through it, all eyes focused on the team photograph in one of the pages and then back up to the gentleman standing by their side – and, true enough, the gentleman was Keith Nelson, an All Black with eighteen appearances to his name and he had been first reserve in Newport that day!

Rugby World Cup 2011 and
a certain French connection

A week after Wales and New Zealand shared the after-match festivities at Carisbrook, the two countries were meeting again in Hamilton. This, a closer contest, ended in a 29–10 scoreline, paving the way for a third successive encounter within six months, on, by now, familiar territory at the Millennium Stadium. The game in Cardiff, in late autumn 2010, started following a minute's silence in memory of the miners who had lost their lives in the Pike River Mine disaster in New Zealand, a sadness that the Welsh could relate to.

Casting one's mind back almost a full century, a similar occurrence took place at Killan, in Dunvant near Swansea, only days before the two teams met in 1924. On the morning of the match, detailed newspaper columns describe the rescue attempts being made to recover Welsh miners in their difficulties. Many of those attending the match did so with a heavy heart, this a tragic situation dreaded by all, but not uncommon in those days of heavy coal mining in South Wales.

On November 27th 2010, Wales, having benefitted from the two recent 'summer' tests in New Zealand, were quietly confident that they were now good enough to win; however, confidence was not enough and although thrilling tries were enjoyed by both sides the All Blacks won 37–25. Again, it was a case of being beaten, but not by a mile, and Wales would take comfort from the emergence of a young and talented team under the influence and direction of Warren Gatland.

The following year, there would be no autumn matches due to the Rugby World Cup, beginning at Eden Park, Auckland, in mid-September 2011. This glittering showpiece had long been awaited in New Zealand for a multitude of reasons, not the least of them being to ensure that the home team did not fall short in this event again. Having won the inaugural challenge in 1987, the All Blacks, indisputably the world's best rugby team during most, if not all, of these intervening years had fallen short in this major knock-out competition. But, it was felt that this time round, as they were playing on home territory in front of home supporters, the result would be different; the All Blacks would go all the way to claim what many throughout the world believed was their rightful prize.

At the start of the competition experts who predicted the likely results, setbacks and permutations saw that Wales had a chance of contending the final with New Zealand. This would, of course, depend upon the two teams overcoming many strongly-performing nations along the way, one of these being the unpredictable, yet often inspired French, who had shown that they could perform miracles in the World Cup when it mattered most.

In the tournament of 1999, Taine Randell's All Blacks under head coach John Hart seemed nigh on invincible. Leading 24–10 in the semi-final against France at Twickenham, with Jonah Lomu waiting on the wing for more of the ball, the All Blacks seemed almost certain to win and win well. But amazingly, against all odds, the French whipped up a tornado of footballing brilliance to turn the match on its head and triumph 43–31. 'Never underestimate the French,' is now the mantra in all corners of international rugby.

What caused such an extraordinary change on that day is difficult to explain, but its effect meant that senior men in the All Blacks administration had to consider their position. And when, by an unbelievable twist of fate, the same scenario was repeated in Cardiff in the Rugby World Cup quarter-final of 2007, it astounded the entire rugby world. Grown men wept unashamedly. A French team, comprehensively out-played and marooned near its own goal line for long spells, inexplicably broke free like runaway roosters to steal the match. Understandably, the New Zealand coach Graham Henry found his 'neck on the line', to use Clive Rowlands' 1969 phrase, and, once again, this failure on the big occasion led to major inquests in New Zealand. Whatever the findings, the impact of the result was severe; it created a countrywide despondency, although Graham Henry was deservedly given a vote of confidence to continue his work.

So the stakes for the 2011 Rugby World Cup in New Zealand were high and this time the New Zealand public was going to have a big bearing on events, starting by cheering the Irish to victory against Australia in an early pool match. This not only wobbled the Aussies – an excellent side, capable of winning the cup – but it sent them into an earlier than expected 'battle of the Titans' against South Africa in the quarter-final. This kept one of these two major competitors away from Richie McCaw and his men, easing the host nation's passage to the final by a considerable measure.

Despite the ever-alive memories of the disputed try of 1905 and the brawls of the 1970s and the ups and downs of rugby's never-ending controversies, the New Zealanders had welcomed the Welsh team and supporters warmly. Spare bedrooms had been opened up to accommodate their long-lost friends, and camper vans were invited onto driveways to share essential facilities. Warren Gatland, the Wales coach and a Waikato man, had already in June of 2010 led his team on a successful public relations exercise around his home town when playing the All Blacks at Hamilton a week after Carisbrook's farewell. This same Waikato stadium is where some of the early Welsh World Cup matches would be played, and this ensured that the Welsh players felt at home.

The remarkable form of Warren's men in beating Ireland 22–10 in the quarter-final at Wellington inspired the Welsh and the build up to the semi-final with France a week later filled the *Western Mail*. Not surprisingly, politicians and religious leaders took advantage of the nation's optimism to show solidarity and to canvass support. Wales' flowing and enterprising style of play was winning admirers from across the globe, whilst back in Cardiff over sixty thousand people gathered in front of a big televised screen at the Millennium Stadium to cheer on their heroes in the semi-final.

Likewise, New Zealanders at Eden Park were also lifting the Welsh who, in their eyes, were firm favourites against the French. As New Zealand had dispatched of Australia in clinical fashion only a day earlier, a Wales–New Zealand final was definitely on the cards. However, eighteen minutes into the game with France, Sam Warburton, the Welsh captain, was dismissed for a dangerous tackle. The French had now an obvious advantage, but true to form they proved to be unpredictable. They laboured under withering Welsh attack, often at a loss and on the back foot, but they hung on by a thread to win 9–8. It was a solitary point that was enough to take them into the World Cup final.

Few could have possibly predicted this sequence of events, but it meant that the seventh Rugby World Cup would see the same two countries battling for honours as in the first final staged on this same ground in 1987. For certain, a vast majority of the Welsh remaining in Auckland for the game were supporting the All Blacks, whilst the Welsh players, knowing that they had seriously wobbled their Gallic friends, had in a manner of speaking also aided the home team's cause. Nothing was now more predictable than seeing fans from our two countries sharing the best of times in the hectic wind-down to this astounding rugby occasion.

Running the line in that final would be Nigel Owens from Mynyddcerrig, Llanelli. As a young referee he visited Tycroes Rugby Club, where, amazingly, a 1905 Originals jersey had been in the possession of the club for more than fifty years – although it had been kept in a bank vault for a long time. When it saw the light of day, the Welsh Rugby Union was particularly interested in having it displayed at the Millennium Stadium, Cardiff. Ian Thomas, a member of the Tycroes club, explains:

> When the press got hold of the story, we ended up being interviewed live for a New Zealand TV programme. The next thing we knew was that someone from New Zealand wanted to come and present us with a replica jersey.

This 'someone' is Robertina Downes, who, alongside a colleague at Massey University and in collaboration with Manawatu Knitting Mills and the New Zealand Rugby Museum was commissioned to reproduce the 1905 jersey. This was a conservation exercise aiming to get as close to the Originals shirt as possible, in terms of design, texture, material and weaving methods, which included adopting the techniques used on period machines. It was decided that one of the jerseys be donated to the Tycroes club following news that the club's treasured possession had moved on. Robertina, or Tina as she is known, came over to make her presentation, where she was hosted by Irfon Hughes, another committee member, and his wife. Irfon had been well looked after by New Zealanders when he visited their country with the British Lions of 2005 and wanted to repay the compliment:

> When it came to guest houses in Christchurch ahead of the first Test, it was a no go-area; every one was full. But someone suggested trying a friend. Then it was a case of, 'Come and stay with us,' and it all worked out well.

We were thrilled to have Tina as our guest. My wife and I showed her around. Then she made her speech and presented the replica jersey. It has pride of place in our trophy cabinet today.

Nigel, experienced and able official that he was, would have known that this World Cup tournament had begun with the shrill blast of a famous whistle which had been used to start the first match of every World Cup tournament since its inception in 1987. The whistle once belonged to Gil Evans, the man preferred by the Originals' manager, George Dixon, to control the Welsh matches in 1905 following the big refereeing rumpus of the tour. Gil had used this same whistle when he was in charge of the England versus New Zealand match in Crystal Palace in 1905, before handing it over to Mr Freethy, of Neath, to use in the corresponding fixture of 1925 when Cyril Brownlie was sent off. The whistle, which was later given to Stan Dean, the tour manager, was safely back in its home in the Rugby Museum of New Zealand when the 2011 finalists were preparing to step onto the field.

Everybody with the slightest interest in rugby tuned in to this latest World Cup final. Television coverage had never been so good, whilst those lucky enough to be in Auckland experienced a city buzzing with excitement and tension as the New Zealand nation prayed for success. Graham Henry, Richie McCaw and their team carried more weight on their shoulders than we can imagine. Diane Kirk, introduced earlier, whose own son David lifted the trophy as the All Blacks captain in 1987, summed up the nation's craving for a victory in a few words: 'The country needed World Cup success. We'd had earthquakes and mining disasters and it had been so long since winning in 1987.'

As both teams entered the field, it came as no surprise

that the French had a trick or two up their sleeves. The first and most obvious was their response to the haka. The French formed their players into an arrowhead and moved slowly, precisely and menacingly towards the All Black huddle. With the team clad in an all-white strip and moving in perfect symmetry, this was a well-planned and impressive retort to the war cry just as the challenging slapping of thighs and gesturing was coming to a climax. The French, devastating and dangerous during world cups, had turned up!

Memories of making his appearance as a substitute prop in the Junior World Cup Final at Stradey Park, Llanelli, in 1999 were far from the thoughts of Tony Woodcock as he raced through an opening in a line-out to score unopposed. This was a good start, but a failed conversion and then a few missed penalties, followed by an injury to first five-eighths Aaron Cruden (the latest of so many New Zealand players in this pivotal position to be sidelined during the tournament), moved momentum the way of the French. It was an extremely anxious time for all New Zealanders to say the least.

Only a few weeks before this match, Stephen Donald, first five-eighths, was a contented fisherman, but having answered a late call from Graham Henry – and now in response to this latest Aaron Cruden injury – he was thrust into the limelight of the final. As the game hit a critical period in the second half, Stephen was lining up a difficult penalty goal from around half-way. Who can imagine his reaction when the flags went up, for the whole of Auckland erupted in celebration. It was a mixture of unrestrained joy, relief and hope. And what a hero Stephen Donald had become.

Now 8–0 in front and knowing that France had to score twice to gain the lead, the All Blacks could, at last, settle down a little, that is until Thierry Dusautoir, the French captain who shattered New Zealand in 2007 with a try, scored again and, what is more, by the posts. Advantage was swinging towards the French and they were only one point behind.

Spectators and television viewers could hardly bear to look. One of these was Greta French, widow of Tom, remembered by the Tom French Cup that is awarded in his family's honour each year to the best performing Māori. Tom was from a strong rugby family, whose father had lost an arm fighting in France in the Great War before becoming a Māori coach and selector.

Greta told me that she had attended the earlier match against the French in the pool stage, when New Zealand won convincingly. 'I was right down in the front where the lovely Jock Hobbs presented Richie [McCaw] with his hundredth cap,' she told me. Eden Park had given Greta great memories over the years: 'I remember the really old stands and then I saw the building of the next lot of stands,' she told me. 'Rugby was a wonderful social life. Sean Connery was with us on one occasion. He brought his tumbler of whisky to the box. All of us were taking it in turn to shake hands with him.' And in 1953 she remembers a woman with a transistor sharing the breaking news that Edmund Hillary had just climbed to the top of Mount Everest. What had Greta planned for the final?

I had gone over to my daughter with Nancy Boggs, widow of former All Black, Eric. I had persuaded Nancy to wear Eric's cap. It is of black velvet, with a silver fern image, white coving and a tassel.

We had our meal and we were drinking champagne. No one could forget 2007 – but this was going to be different. Then came the last twenty minutes. It was hideous; I felt so sick. My daughter said, 'It's turning to custard; we're going to lose.' We were hanging on by a point. We had waited years for this, but now we just wanted it to end.

Not far away, Janis Nathan, wife of the famous Waka, felt just the same. 'My heart was in my mouth,' she said. 'Waka was at the game, but two of the brave rugby men watching with my daughter and her friends had to slip out of the door. They couldn't look. They came back later to find out what had happened!'

And how did our Welsh rugby heroes see the match going? Would New Zealand, plagued by injuries and feeling the fatigue of a hectic twelve months of rugby – let alone the strain of winning the tournament – hold on?

Clive Rowlands: 'Clive,' I asked, 'did you think the All Blacks would tire?'

'Tire?! Listen . . . I've never known an All Black side to tire. They never tired against Wales, that's for sure, and they certainly wouldn't in a World Cup final at Eden Park. They were always going to win.'

Sir Gareth Edwards: 'Gareth. Did you think that one point would be enough?'

'Knowing that France seem to find another gear against the All Blacks, I thought they might win – but I also knew the All Blacks *always* find an answer when it matters.'

And what were the thoughts of Sir Brian Lochore at this critical stage of the match? 'Sir Brian, knowing the French have a tendency to upset the All Blacks when least expected, did you feel that your team would hold on?'

'The French only upset us in the important matches,' he smiled. 'With twenty minutes to go it was very even. You wouldn't have put money on either team. But I felt certain that New Zealand would not freeze.'

Richie McCaw is understandably idolised in his homeland. I spoke to Richie as he stepped inside the entrance of the All Blacks hotel in Wellington as he returned from a training run. I took great pleasure, as a Welshman, in reminding him that before hitting fame he is remembered for playing in the Junior World Cup Final at Stradey Park. 'Yeah, we beat you,' he said with his handsome smile and characteristic nod of the head. 'Twenty-five nil, in [19]99. It was great.' Beating our Welsh boys in the final had been a thrilling victory but it was also a dedicated mission. There was precious little time for anything other than rugby: 'We were either training or playing most days,' he said.

How the New Zealand captain must have craved for the comfort of that victory in Llanelli on this nail-biting night at Eden Park when he was running around, effectively, on one good leg. With a serious foot injury having restricted his training, and with the French nightmare of 2007 at Cardiff coming back to haunt him, we can only wonder what was going through his mind. So also was the television cameraman who zoomed in on the All Blacks captain during a pause in play shortly after the French had scored. Raising his eyebrows with a quick glance upwards, Richie swallowed hard, as if he was registering the fact that things were, again, beginning to slip away. But this time, at Eden Park, he was going to ensure he and his countrymen emerged on top.

Eden Park is a most impressive arena, situated in a pleasant part of Auckland city. Near the main entrance there are two larger than life bronze statues. One of these is of Dave Gallaher, the Originals' captain, and the other is of Michael Jones, commemorating his try, the first ever to be scored during a Rugby World Cup competition (at this same ground, in 1987). Michael, a famous All Black, whose father's ancestors originate from the 'Llandrindod Wells to Montgomery' area in Wales, would know that what distinguishes Eden Park from most other grounds are the underlying values for which it stands.

These are Māori values and their permanent presence at this same stadium today take the form of large carved statues which are found near every major gangway around the ground. Each gives respect to a Māori God, such as Rongomatane (Māori God of Cultivation and Peace) and collectively they explain with a little background information why Eden Park, essentially a sporting battlefield, is such a glorified All Blacks fortress. As an arena, it is also 'underpinned by the values of respect, fairness and, ultimately, peace'. The stadium is also 'a domain of battle where contemporary gladiators clash under the banner of sport with an intensity and ferocity reminiscent of that of the ancestors'.

It is gladdening to see, as well, that in this special ground a Welshman is honoured; for from the ceiling of the International Rugby Hall of Fame in dive-passing pose there is a sculpture of Sir Gareth Edwards in his playing prime.

But on that evening in 2011, Eden Park reverberated to cheers and groans of a nerve-racking final few moments as Richie McCaw and his men rallied to every Māori battle cry and kept the ball amongst the forwards, determined not to surrender their one-point lead. It was not 'pretty rugby' as they say, but it didn't matter.

Victory sparked parties that went on all night. Inside the winning camp at the Heritage Hotel, a member of staff recalled, 'It was a time of chaos, but it was nice chaos, throughout!' Meanwhile, a woman who lives nearby and who I happened to talk to in view of the hotel a year later, will never forget the scenes as thousands of people filled the streets long into the night, flying flags, waving banners, with smiling, happy faces all around.

'And what about the Welsh?' I enquired, referring to fourteen brave men who so nearly conquered the French.

'The Welsh,' she replied, 'played like champions. They were robbed!'

PART XII

A WET WINTER'S NIGHT IN CARDIFF AND THE 'TRY THAT NEVER WAS'

The Legacy of a Scottish Referee

The victory parades and celebrations that followed Rugby World Cup success in New Zealand reflected the craving of a nation for a trophy surprisingly missing from a cabinet otherwise overfull. As for the architect of this success, former Welsh coach Graham Henry, he was seen at the beautiful Waiheke Island, some ten miles from Auckland Harbour, a seemingly new man, at peace with the world, basking in the glory of his latest achievement. I met islander Rick Hillman who would see him from time to time. 'Gee, you're looking more relaxed than in the final, Graham,' Rick said to him one day. 'Yes, Rick, I can sleep walking around now,' was his reply.

Sir Graham could not fail to have looked benignly upon a new-look, innovative and youthful Welsh team which was soon carrying their World Cup performance into Grand Slam glory. Likewise, he would have empathised with a Welsh nation which mourned the semi-final loss to the French and missed out on the ultimate sporting opportunity of a final against the All Blacks at Eden Park. Here was a man who knew better than most the effect of defeat on the people of two fervent rugby nations whose teams he had coached. He understood how defeat got into the soul of the people, a despondency that brought the two countries into line, 'except' as he stated in *Graham Henry: the X Factor*, 'the Welsh have been losing a lot more consistently than the All Blacks over the past couple of decades'!

Rick Hillman, who shares with Sir Graham an appreciation of Waiheke's own rugby team, remembers the All Blacks attending a training camp on the island in the early 1990s when the squad members, having performed their practice drills, went around this popular retreat meeting the people. And it is their willingness to mix conscientiously and often with the team's broad fan base which makes the All Blacks winners off the field as well as on it. New Zealand, being a large country, about the size of Britain, but with only about 7 per cent of its population, has by tradition spread Test matches geographically between the bigger cities, principally Auckland, Wellington, Christchurch and Dunedin. Here one will today see the All Blacks amongst the crowds, fulfilling public engagements or simply walking around town. Undoubtedly this unity and togetherness of the players and supporters for the one rugby cause is a major factor driving success in these commercially orientated days.

Richard Myers is an All Black of the 1970s who played in far less profit-driven times. Richard, a back-row forward who got to meet many of the Welsh when playing against the 1977 British Lions, can look back to an era when the top Test players would turn out not only for their club in a full programme of fixtures, but for their province and as All Blacks. With full-time jobs and so many training commitments, these men had little spare time, yet they still found the opportunity to give talks, to pass on their experience and to promote rugby's cause. 'You can imagine they were big men in the club dressing room,' said Richard, 'having played a Test the week before. They had to set the standards; likewise the rest were striving to keep up, and this worked for everybody.'

Richard speaks glowingly of rugby's great continued fellowship. 'The beauty of the game has always been the social aspect,' he said, and this is evident from the grass roots of the game upwards. 'In New Zealand the All Blacks are invited to one players reunion dinner a year. This year [2012], it is in Dunedin, before the Test match with South Africa.' Richard, who appreciates the innate longing of the Welsh for rugby fame, keeps in touch with Warren Gatland, fully understanding the scale of his task in Wales. 'He told me that a high percentage of people live in the South Wales corridor,' said Richard. '"I've only got to step outside my front door,"' he said, quoting Warren, '"and everyone wants to speak to me. And it's usually to tell me what to do and who to pick."'

Another to know Wales' man at the helm is former All Black Matthew Cooper. Matthew, who was a prolific goal-kicker for the Waikato province, and who emulated the Barry John style of striking the ball, played alongside Warren in the fast and furious battle with Otago in 1992 when Waikato won the National Provincial Championship. Matthew has not forgotten the overall contributions that the young Warren Gatland made to the team, credentials that have since proved invaluable in guiding Wales to higher levels in the world game. 'The input of Warren as a senior player was incredible,' said Matthew, 'he had a lot of theories – and this was back in 1992. On and off the field he created harmony amongst the playing ranks.'

In September 2012, Matthew, as chief executive officer for Sport Waikato, convened a twenty-year anniversary celebration of that great game in the Sky City Function Centre in Hamilton. As the team assembled to be feted by hundreds who attended, Warren was far away, no doubt focussing his attention on the upcoming autumn series of internationals that was to stage the latest game in the on-going Wales versus New Zealand contest. In the run-up to this match, Welsh hopes were understandably high, having also given a most impressive display of rugby on the earlier summer tour of Australia. As usual, Cardiff was packed for the big day, Saturday November 24th, a dark and wet afternoon when the elements were shut outside by the retractable stadium roof. As legendary figures like Sir Colin Meads and J. P. R. Williams met at celebrity luncheons to remember battles of old, the stage was set.

The love of singing and music has enriched the special bond between the two rugby nations throughout the years. In the 1970s the Welsh crowd was accustomed to the sound of *We'll keep a Welcome in the Hillsides* resonating around the ground as the players prepared to run out onto the field. Who could forget the rousing words, stirring to read but enough to 'blow you away', as Sir Colin Meads stated, when sung by fifty thousand voices or more: 'This land you knew will still be singing . . . when you come home again to Wales.' Nowadays we have other favourites, still good rugby selections and there is an open invitation to support the band and sing out loud.

As the players stepped onto the field at the Millennium Stadium amidst fireworks exploding and great puffs of smoke rising into the air, the scene could not have been more different from when Dave Gallaher led his men onto the old Cardiff Arms Park in 1905. There was, however, one definite thread of continuity in this, the twenty-ninth official meeting of the two teams, and it was that both were intent upon outwitting each other in technical aspects of play to gain the upper hand. Just as the two teams had gone to great lengths to steal the 'scrimmage' heel all those years ago they were now hunting for weaknesses in each other's make-up, contingencies in place, determined to seize whatever initiative could be found.

If there was one possible avenue for the Welsh to exploit perhaps, it was to kick towards Julian Savea, the All Blacks' left wing, a newcomer to the team that season. Julian, a brilliant runner, had so far been a revelation. He had scored a dozen All Black tries in his first season, yet, perhaps, he was still unproven under the high ball. If Wales could pepper this young man with some awkward kicks, there might be some gain – rather like the time JPR was singled out for special treatment at Eden Park in 1969. Up went the kick and as the left wing rose high into the air, he made no attempt to catch the ball, but instead palmed it back to Israel Dagg, full back. The next moment, they were both haring upfield on a counter-attack, resulting in Liam Messam scoring in the far corner.

Such attention to detail sets the men in black apart, doing the simple things well, time and again. However, they are not without fault, for Andrew Hore's strong forearm caught Bradley Davies' chin and effectively ended the Welshman's part in the game. This was later proved to be a dangerous act but it was also out of character for both the player and this modern set of All Blacks. But Wales had the last word: a fifteen-man line-out and a heavily packed maul resulting in a rather novel score, one that even their opponents had no answer to.

That day the Millennium Stadium looked a blaze of bright colour and green grass. When peering across the field at the old North Stand of the 1970s, this famous structure brings a sense of perspective to this historic arena, which has changed beyond all recognition over the years. It is to the east of the old stand that we have a most famous piece of turf. It is in this vicinity that Teddy Morgan scored for Wales in 1905 and, not far away, is where Bob Deans either did, or did not, score for New Zealand.

This controversy has stimulated rugby conversations for years, but what we do know, of course, is that a statement appeared in the *Daily Mail* from Bob Deans, confirming the validity of the score and the fact that colleagues Jimmy Hunter and Frank Glasgow would vouch for the accuracy of the comment. But what we also realise is that the man holding on to Deans in this same incident, Rhys Gabe, was every bit as emphatic that it was not a try.

When Deans died only a few years later at the young age of twenty-four, he made a point of reiterating on his death bed that the try was good, but, likewise, when Cliff Morgan[51] interviewed Gabe towards his last days, Gabe was equally adamant that it was not. Interestingly, this next and fuller statement from Gabe in earlier years provides an impression of referee Dallas' positioning at the time of the incident. Here Gabe continues his account having just stated that he had brought Deans to the ground:

> I knew it was touch and go whether I had managed to tackle him before he reached the line. Then, as I lay there gripping him firmly, I felt Deans trying to struggle away from me. Instinctively I clutched tighter. Then I realised why he wanted to wriggle on. He had not reached the line. He was just inches short. I pulled back with all my strength and then the whistle went. The referee had arrived on the spot . . .[52]

This controversial incident is well documented in the official history of the Welsh Rugby Union, *Fields of Praise*. The book states that Ack Llewellyn, who was on duty for Wales as

---

51 Cliff Morgan and Geoffrey Nicholson, *Cliff Morgan the Autobiography: Beyond the Fields of Play* (Hodder & Stoughton, 1996).

52 Gareth Williams, *The 1905 All Blacks Tour of Britain* (www.rugbyrelics.com 2013) and 'Disputed Try', 1905, (www.rugbyfootballhistory.com 2013).

a touch judge, also believed it was a try. This accords with Teddy Morgan's words as they appear in the final sentences of his contribution to E.H.D. Sewell's *Rugby Football* of 1921.[53] In that quote Teddy Morgan can recall 'the white goal line' beneath him. As he climbed 'off Deans' legs', Deans was grasping the ball along with two of the Welsh, the ball now being 'grounded about a foot outside the line.' He added that the referee arrived but had not 'seen what had happened after the tackle.' New Zealand's George Nicholson thought it was a try as well, although Welsh players close to the action and with a good view of events, including Cliff Pritchard and (later) Gwyn Nicholls, said it was not a try.

With the greatest of respect to whoever is correct, the overwhelming effect of the official 'no score' is that it launched the Wales versus New Zealand fixture forward into the future, as no other verdict could have. Of course, the nineteen-year wait for the return match was long and cruel, but that wait added a certain distinctiveness to the fixture. John Sinclair is adamant that the Deans incident was the making of matches between Wales and New Zealand, as he pointed out earlier in the story: 'it was good for the Wales–New Zealand fixture.' Meanwhile, Stephen Berg, today's curator of the rugby museum in Palmerston North, makes an interesting comment about the nation's reaction to the 1905 incident, which is not dissimilar to the Parable of the Lost Sheep:

> It says a lot for the mentality of the New Zealand rugby supporter when you don't hear talk about what the [Originals] team did well. Everybody jumps on the bandwagon about the Wales match in 1905 – but never mentioning that the team scored 976 points, conceding only 59, in 35 matches [at a time of three-point tries].

---

53   As detailed in *Fields of Praise*.

With the incident being a pivotal part of New Zealand's proud rugby history, every single stride that Deans made to the line that day has been explored by his countrymen, culminating in a fascinating and amusing commentary that can today be heard at the New Zealand Sports Hall of Fame in Dunedin Railway Station. There were no radio commentaries in 1905, but one has since been created with the benefit of hindsight, based on New Zealand's understanding of this wonderful 'argument.' And this is a masterpiece that includes the sporting commentary of an unmistakable Welshman and it is a must for rugby lovers to listen to when venturing near to Otago's famous rugby parish.

As for John Dewar Dallas' appointment as referee, we know that this gentleman, a lawyer and player, was not the original choice for the match. He was invited to officiate because George Dixon, New Zealand manager, and the Welsh Rugby Union could not mutually agree on the original candidates. We know that John Dallas had considerable experience of rugby, having captained Watsonians of Edinburgh and having been capped by Scotland in the winter of 1903, less than three years earlier, when they beat England at Richmond to clinch the Triple Crown. That day, Mr Dallas scored one of Scotland's two tries, although it is understood that the Scottish selectors opted for a heavier pack of forwards for the next match and Mr Dallas, a slimmer man, was not capped again. Now, refereeing his first international, Mr Dallas was still only twenty-seven, younger than many of the players, including both captains.

Refereeing an international match in 1905 was a great honour but was also, surely, a lonesome task, especially as this one was headlined 'The Game of the Century' even before it was played! Two touch judges, one representing each team, assisted Mr Dallas, but, of course, he had no army of officials, video referees or citing commissioners as we have today. In his favour was the fact that crowds were more tolerant towards officials of the day, a characteristic perhaps, of greater sportsmanship, or possibly a respect for social rank. Strong pulpit sermons may also have had some bearing on behaviour and certainly Mr Dallas would have played a modest, yet integral, part in the after-match formalities. But, at such a young age, he had little top-class experience with the whistle and it is to his credit that he controlled such a dynamic and passionate match at the Arms Park, which was bursting at the seams.

For certain, some criticism came his way; this was, after all, the biggest match in rugby history to date. George Dixon, for one, thought that there was 'overwhelming evidence' that Deans' effort 'was an absolutely fair try'[54] and questioned Mr Dallas' mobility around the field, implying that he was not well situated to judge incidents when he was far behind play. As noted previously, George Dixon also criticised Mr Dallas' lack of 'buttons or bars' [studs] and suitable clothing, yet when Ben Wathen, a Welsh spectator of that game, was interviewed at the age of ninety in November 1978 by the *Western Mail*, he said, 'I remember the referee wore a dark yellow or green jersey over his long trousers and a cap, like a schoolboy's cap.' That day Mr Wathan had climbed aboard a crowded train from Dowlais and paid 'one shilling admission' near the Angel Hotel ground entrance, and an extra 'penny for a programme'. His viewpoint had been from a bank of earth at the tightly packed eastern end of the ground.

Amongst Mr Dallas' admirers that day was the Welsh official contingent. They felt that he had contained a situation

---

54 Bob Howitt and Dianne Haworth, *The 1905 Originals — The remarkable story of the team that went away as the Colonials and came back as the All Blacks* (HarperCollins Publishers, 2005).

that was potentially explosive and had – by the by – allowed both teams to stake their claim for the historic victory. Indeed, his control of the match was applauded generally and he was considered fully deserving of praise. Complimentary words about his performance also appear at the New Zealand Barbarians Club. As stated earlier this used to be a pleasant little building situated outside Eden Park before being demolished to allow for the stadium's expansion. The club has since been relocated within the stadium complex so that it enjoys a bird's-eye view of the rugby field. As for the words praising Mr Dallas – they are Welsh words again! These appear in a full-page spread of the *South Wales Echo*, dated December 16th 1905, encased in a glass frame and are a tribute from an unnamed Welsh referee:

> Wales won because the referee, Mr Dallas of the Scottish Union, insisted from the outset upon the laws of the game being adhered to. With weak refereeing, the result would probably have been very different – for one saw how the speedy New Zealanders could profit by infringements . . .

Then, after mentioning the tenacious tackling of the two teams, the correspondent paid a further compliment, one that generally refers to a refereeing job having been well done: 'But for a few minor incidents, the best of good spirit prevailed.'

This match was the making of Mr Dallas as a referee. In the following seven seasons he was appointed to take charge of a number of internationals in the Home Nations Championship, including the England versus Wales fixture of 1910. But wherever he ventured in pursuit of rugby, he returned to Aberdeen. His presence in this area nurtured the game's progress and on that cold Wednesday afternoon in November 1935 when the All Blacks beat the local divisional team, the occasion was all the richer for Sheriff Dallas' attendance and full participation in the social proceedings.

In Terry McLean's *The All Blacks*, the great writer refers to a fascinating, yet mildly frustrating, story concerning this 1935 New Zealand visit to Aberdeen, where Mr Dallas had invited one of the players to his home in Queens Gardens, a three-storey terraced house set off the road, with basement accommodation and moat-like steps leading to the front door, every inch a sheriff's residence. It was not uncommon for such acts of friendliness as this to take place because it broke the monotony of the long tour and other players were, doubtless, hosted in like manner in and around the town. As the two men sat beside the fire on this 'bitterly cold' day, Mr Dallas made, what the New Zealander felt, was 'a sort of confession,' giving the impression that he was not ideally placed to view the Deans incident in 1905. 'It was a remarkable experience for me,' said the All Black, who was, tantalisingly, unnamed!

Such uncorroborated anecdotes from an unnamed source take us no nearer to solving the great mystery in absolute terms, although adding to an overall picture that now seems a lot clearer. Certainly, the above story appears to run with the written statement contained in a letter from Mr Dallas within days of the match, referring to his proximity to the incident which had been criticised. This letter, quoted in *Fields of Praise*, was written in response to press suggestions – as well as Mr Dixon's conviction – that Dallas had missed the try:

> When the ball went back on its way out to Deans, I kept going hard and when Deans was tackled, he grounded the ball 6 to 12 inches short of the goal line. At that moment, he could neither pass nor play the ball, and as I passed between the Welsh goal posts my whistle went shrill and loud.

It is true that when I got to the spot to order a scrum, the ball was over the goal line, but without hesitation I ordered a scrum at the place where Deans was grounded. I never blew my whistle at the spot. It had gone before. No try was scored.

Although backing his judgement in this letter, Mr Dallas does not, however, provide a clear statement of his location to Deans as Deans reached for the line. Indeed, there is a hint of a time lapse between the incident and Mr Dallas's arrival on the scene, which, when considered alongside the varying statements provided by those nearest to the action, creates sufficient mystique and intrigue to carry the story to the present day.

John Dewar Dallas died aged 64 on July 31st 1942, a notable figure and well loved. His obituary was glowing and his friends, colleagues and family would remember him for the good deeds he had done. But in the eyes of rugby followers, particularly in New Zealand, he will be remembered for the one action he had left undone. By doing so, or should one say by *failing* to do so, Sheriff Dallas unknowingly sealed a unique and lasting relationship between two rugby nations.

Looking Back to 1905 for Wales's Next Victory

When the Welsh heroes emerged from their beds following rugby's titanic battle of 1905, they did so with the satisfaction of having planted their national flag at the summit of world rugby. This triumph had given pride and self-esteem to their kinsfolk, besides greater status in the wider world. By halting the runaway All Blacks and subduing Kiwi followers in the faraway Pacific Ocean – the Welsh had rightly claimed to be rugby's kingpins. Yet, aside from their on-field achievements, the triumph spoke of the collective efforts of an entire nation who refused to see its men falling short when it mattered most.

On that mid-winter's day leading up to Christmas, 'confidence' and 'belief', two essentials in sporting success, were evident in the hopes and expectations of the Welsh. From quiet country villages to Cardiff's coal-exporting city, the talk was of Wales, Triple Crown holders, being good enough and ready to win. Players had crossed the borders to study their opponents; selectors had sat taking notes in the earlier internationals; tactics had been scrutinised; match reports assessed, and a means of countering the visitors' lethal running and scrummaging determined. When All Black coach James (Jimmy) Duncan predicted his men would be 'too clever' for the Welsh, he underestimated their know-how and grit in the cut and thrust of fierce sporting action. He also misjudged the effect of upbeat journalism on a home crowd in good voice. Yet, Wales had still needed a handsome dollop of luck!

All these years later, the All Blacks employ the same thorough preparations that gained victory for the Welsh in

1905. There will never be a substitute for hard work and good rest – yet, remaining rooted to the causes of good character and family contentment is equally important to these giants of the game, for it gives sporting excellence and off-field diplomacy a chance. Such is the way of these affable, humble men whose respect from a global fan base is unshakeable. When Beauden Barrett celebrated his 100th international at Cardiff in October 2021, it was no coincidence that his family were praised in the after-match presentation of his commemorative cap.[55] Quite simply, the New Zealand Rugby Union recognise the efforts of one's nearest and dearest in supporting elite sportsmen at the pinnacle of their game. Likewise, to please the crowds by participating in fun-training with the children, High Street promotions and autograph sessions, or simply by being accessible to adoring fans, strengthens the bond between the All Blacks and the New Zealand public.

This subject has been the recent study of author James Kerr and the theme of his popular book, *Legacy – what the All Blacks can Teach us about the Business of Life*.[56] Kerr provides an examination of the discipline, mentality, motives, morals and practices of these men, with the purpose of preparing corporate executives, business entrepreneurs, high-flyers and 'the ambitious' for success. In acknowledging this, we have some idea of the task facing Wales's rugby team whenever our 'Three Feathers' tangle with the 'Silver Fern'. If this is not daunting enough, our men have to face the severity of today's pumped-up haka that can take one's breath away. Admittedly, it is a crowd-thriller that we all love to see and cannot do

---

55   Beauden Barrett's 100th Test Capping Ceremony, 2021, YouTube.
56   James Kerr, *Legacy – what the All Blacks can Teach Us about the Business of Life* (London, Constable, 2015).

without, but it is nonetheless a re-enactment of steely-eyed Māori warriors primed for physical battle, set to mysterious chants, war cries, and provocation.

Few can envy the Welsh team facing the haka when possessing no such armoury of their own to respond to the challenge it presents. I suspect it brings embarrassment too, of a kind, because to stand and to glare back, or to remain motionless, or to smile, or even to look away, is hardly the response this spectacle deserves. For certain, none of this behaviour will impress the Māorilanders. So, what is there to stop the Welsh team from singing one of our rousing 'call to battle' renditions and leading the crowd in a beefy blast as our heroes did so emphatically in 1905? On that occasion, it was the singing of *Hen Wlad Fy Nhadau* (*The Old Land of My Fathers*) that won the day, whilst hastening the convention of singing national anthems at sporting occasions. So, is it not time for the dragon to step forward onto the big stage and give the kiwi a little competition?

When reading *Rugby – a New Zealand History*,[57] which is a tome all rugby-lovers and historians will welcome – I was reminded by its author Ron Palenski that the Welsh and New Zealanders entered the field at Cardiff Arms Park in 1905 to the singing of *Men of Harlech*. This thunderous song dates back to the Wars of the Roses and is a favourite amongst male voice choirs because it invites choristers to expand their chests and erupt into the early lines. I know that Ron, who I met in Dunedin in 2012 and with whom I am still in touch, will be humbled to have pinpointed a suitable response to his country's haka that can be used by the Welsh! The thrilling

57   Ron Palenski, *Rugby – a New Zealand History* (Auckland University Press, 2015), 113.

prospect of a full stadium singing this item – or even *Rachie*, another to raise the roof – will bring a new dimension to future All Black fixtures in our capital.

When looking a little closer at the nitty-gritty of the 1905 action, I wish to highlight one well-documented kick downfield by the Welsh which not only resulted in Deans's famous run for the line, but which is still a liability to our Welsh game today. I refer to the kick that All Black Billy Wallace fielded in the second half which allowed him to weave his way through the Welsh defence to put Deans clear. That incident so nearly cost Wales the game, and such ineffective kicking is still our bugbear today. During the recent Six Nations campaign this was all too apparent, and how the French failed to score more than once from our generous gifts remains a mystery. Whilst I appreciate there is a place in the game for good line kicking, grubbers, chipping ahead and more, the 'hopeful and often hopeless' up-and-under brings two questions to mind. Is it not easier to retain or to pass the ball, than to kick it away and struggle to win it back again? And, why put the ball into the hands of strong running opponents (who must be tackled) when to control one's own ball is surely the way to enjoy, score and win matches.

At Twickenham in the Rugby World Cup final of 2015, the 'kick and chase' executed by Ben Smith and Beauden Barrett will forever win applause. I delight in viewing this crucial score for its sheer simplicity, brilliance and audacity. The sight of Ben Smith gathering Australia's knock-on deep inside his own half and punting the ball up-field for Beauden Barrett to chase, epitomises the thrill of rugby's spontaneity when performed well and at pace. As the world knows, Barrett, who had entered the field as a substitute with fresh legs and blistering speed, overtook his opponents, one after another, before toe-poking the bouncing ball onwards for a try. Quick-witted and opportunistic, here we saw seven points in little over seven seconds from a knock-on seventy yards away.

Somehow, the All Blacks make rugby look so simple time and again. Yet, controlling the oval ball is not easy. In difficult conditions on a November evening in Cardiff in 2014, Welsh three-quarter George North was seen chasing a loose ball near the halfway line with the field open in front of him – surely a rare opportunity against the All Blacks. Had George guided the ball towards the goal line, he would no doubt have backed his ability to score. Yet, his swinging right leg missed its target and overran the ball. That night, Wales played defiantly in the manner of our 1905 men. They thwarted attacks, stole possession, hunted for openings and stopped black-shirted endeavours in their tracks. But, as Wales led with twelve minutes to go, that genius Beauden Barrett pounced again. Chipping ahead from near the right touchline, having purposefully struck the right-hand side of the ball to control its direction, Barrett knew exactly where to collect the bounce, and into his grasp the ball shot, as if by magnetic force.

Doesn't this story just epitomise the cutting edge of these All Blacks that is missing from the Welsh team of today? Failure to close out a near-certain victory against Italy in April 2022 when taking a six-point lead and possession into the final minute clearly demonstrates this. By kicking into the open – yet again – Wales allowed fullback Ange Capuozzo to race up-field and present Edoardo Padovani with a try beneath the posts, which was converted for a one-point win. Still, most agreed Italy's victory was long overdue and both their celebrations and the fascinating 'Man of the Match' award tête-à-tête between Josh Adams and Ange Capuozzo brought added sportsmanship, variety and colour to the occasion. Notably, this pleased former Welsh captain and TV pundit Sam Warburton – and I can only wonder if he, too, felt Italy had done Wales a favour that day?

If Italy's bolt from the blue brought Welsh disappointment, it is worth reminding ourselves about Ireland's heartbreak in Dublin on 24 November 2013 when the All Blacks won in injury time. After an outstanding full-blooded display, the Irish led by five points when they were penalised inside New Zealand's half in the last minute. As the visitors tapped and got behind the ball, the Irish, who thus far had only ever drawn against their opponents, 10–10 in 1973, fought for history, honour, headlines and to prevent a last-minute hiccup from blowing away the lot. But, as the advancing All Blacks pounded the Irish defence for an opening, and the high-pitch excitement dropped to a lower frequency, umpteen phases of play paved the way for Ryan Crotty's try in the left corner to tie the scores. With his trusted boot, Aaron Cruden added the winning points on his second attempt, because the first charge had been made early. All around, Irish faces grimaced, and the hearts of TV viewers went out to Irish lock Paul O'Connell whose look of bewilderment said it all.

This shattering end to sporting drama and the Irishmen's later response again serves to remind Wales of the strength of resolve needed to beat the best. It reminds me also of the words of soccer's Terry Venables, a man who knows Wales because he was evacuated to his mother's home in Clydach Vale, Pontypridd, in his youth. When consoling Gareth Southgate, today's England manager, following his penalty miss in a crucial UEFA Euro semi-final against Germany at Wembley in 1996, Venables stated, 'What doesn't destroy you completely, will only make you stronger.' And, so it was for the Irish. From the moment they slunk off the field and regained their energy and fight, they targeted every inch of ground on which the All Blacks stood.

Ireland had already come close a year earlier on a cold June night in Christchurch in 2012 when Dan Carter dropped a late goal for a 22–19 win. Now they would chase the Silver Fern around the world. And what better place to go and settle old scores than Soldier Field, Chicago, packed to the rafters with expectant Irish who possessed a rocket of their own to launch on this Guy Fawkes night in 2016. By the time Robbie Henshaw had scored Ireland's fifth and last try in the seventy-sixth minute, the All Blacks were up against the ropes and falling to the floor. It was a terrific sporting contest and the men of the Emerald Isle had, at last, beaten the unbeatable.

It may seem surprising, but I suspect Dave Gallaher, the 1905 All Black captain whose all-winning men were upended by Wales, had a bearing on that Irish performance. Although he missed his team's 15–0 victory over Ireland at Lansdowne Road only weeks before the crunch Welsh game through injury, Gallaher, born in the village of Ramelton, County Donegal, in the north of Ireland, emigrated to New Zealand's North Island with his family as a five year old. But, in 2005, one hundred years after his famous tour to the British Isles, his connection with Ireland was publicly celebrated when the All Blacks were welcomed to his birthplace premises. There, above the front door on the banks of the river Lennon, All Black legend and then captain Tana Umaga unveiled a plaque in Gallaher's memory, accompanied by crowds and the media.[58]

Furthermore, seven miles down the road in Letterkenny, the

---

58 All Black Rugby Team visit Donegal at Dave Gallaher's Home in Ramelton, Ireland, 2005, YouTube.

town's new rugby field, named the 'Dave Gallaher Memorial Park', saw the visit of All Black Jerry Collins who had the honour of smashing a bottle of Ireland's best on the inscribed stone standing alongside the playing field. It is therefore highly credible that the Irish, intent upon sharpening their own sword, had from that moment onwards embraced the legendary status and sporting tenacity of Gallaher – who died heroically in the First World War – because of his birthplace legacy in this delightful Irish country setting.

For certain, Gallaher, who is remembered in France for the 'Dave Gallaher Trophy' – strengthened the focus of Irish rugby. Only a few years later, they had again toppled the All Blacks on two more occasions – and now, as I write in July 2022, they have just won a test series in New Zealand. This gives Ireland a total of 5 victories inside 6 years – and what an achievement! But, for our Welshmen to play the 'Gallaher way', they really must stop kicking the ball away and build on their success in beating South Africa in Bloemfontein this same summer, 2022.

As we know, another to achieve a unique hat-trick of victories against the All Blacks in quick succession was Carwyn James of Cefneithin, Carmarthenshire. His success with the British Lions in 1971, with Llanelli in 1972 and with the Barbarians in 1973 ensures that his rugby stock will forever be praised. Carwyn was a stickler for keeping the ball away from the heavier All Black packs – and, by virtue of a magnificent display of running rugby in the last mentioned fixture, his players produced an all-time classic. The thrilling occasion is remembered for swift ball handling, changes of direction, sidesteps, feints, dummies, and passes of short, long, and sometimes American football range (but not forward passes, of course) that amounted to seven-a-side rugby played by a fifteen-man team – and, indeed, much like Japan's running game.

Over the past decades, we have been reminded of Carwyn's unique and unflustered preparation for key matches by recordings of him pacing up and down the changing room geeing up his men whilst reminding them of key goals to take onto the field. All were short, sharp one-liners in his usual quiet, soft manner, although he was no doubt inwardly boiling over like the saucepans produced at Llanelli's former tinplate works. These gave rise to the favourite folksong *Sosban Fach* ('A Small Saucepan') and the presence of such replicas on top of the goal posts at Carwyn's beloved former Stradey Park and at today's Parc y Scarlets stadium. For this Barbarians clash we can imagine Carwyn cajoling his men to rise up and make history with typical comments in the manner of: 'Now let's get the job done ... we need a good start ... then keep it going ... win the ball and throw it around ... use every inch of the field ... but deny "them" possession.' Amazingly, all of these were achieved on the day, which started brilliantly when Gareth Edwards's try set the match alight in the second minute. Thereafter, the cheering and singing never stopped.

This day, spectators were treated to an open-air concert. As the teams gathered beneath the North Stand to enter the field, *Sospan Fach* was on maximum heat and letting off steam. Then, *Cwm Rhondda* (but known also as *Guide Me, O Thou Great Redeemer*), *I Bob Un Sydd Ffyddlon* (*Rachie*), *Calon Lân*, and *We'll Keep a Welcome in the Hillsides* followed. It mattered not whether Sid Going was feeding the ball into the scrum, or John Bevan was brushing aside defenders, or David Duckham was running around like a galloping horse – the singing and cheering continued throughout the afternoon. For certain, every player on the field revelled in the atmosphere, but it was the home team who took the gains. At the final whistle, thousands of fans spilt onto the field to hoist their heroes shoulder high as the delightful *Now is the Hour*[59] echoed around the ground for a memorable and touching grand finale. Let us remind ourselves of a few of the words of this Māori favourite because they speak of our special friendship with the New Zealanders:

Now is the Hour, when we must say 'Goodbye'
Soon you'll be sailing far across the sea
While you're away, oh, please remember me
When you return, you'll find me waiting here.

For those who chanced their luck and went along to the Arms Park with a ticket, they really had picked a winner. I was one, standing in the North Enclosure in the midst of excitement, euphoria and bedlam, where some, in sheer delight, simply went berserk. But for those viewing at home, the warm commentary of another Welshman, Cliff Morgan, could be savoured – the same man whose cheeky, deft, darting runs inspired Cardiff and Wales to victories over Bob Stuart's All Blacks in 1953. If the late Cliff, a passionate Welshman from Trebanog in the Rhondda Valley, was still with us today, I feel certain he would share my concern about the loss of some of our beautiful match-day singing.

May I therefore – with Cliff in mind – suggest that we in Wales address this matter. There is surely scope to unite the efforts of the day's band with the back-up of Welsh choirs and choristers, as well as with contributions from leading singing celebrities such as Katherine Jenkins, Bryn Terfel, or indeed from some of Wales's lesser-known talents. This would see us playing to our strengths, an essential practice if we are to

59 www.https:NZ history.govt.NZ/media/sound/NZ's first million-selling song now-is-the-hour – for which we thank Clement Scott, Maewa Kaihau and W.H. Paling & Co for its creation, viewed 28 April 2022.

beat the All Blacks again. No doubt, song sheets and lyrics can be slotted into the official programme, and likewise the media will surely embrace the well-intentioned 'singing spirit' whilst forewarning those attending to prepare their voices accordingly. The message would be simple, 'Let's sing our team to victory' – which is no more and no less than what our predecessors did in 1905. Somehow, I sense this would have gained Cliff Morgan's full approval.

That early evening in Cardiff in 1973 after the two teams had left the field, Cliff, when winding down his commentary, complimented the singing, the players of both teams, the referee Georges Domercq of France and the two architects of the fast-flowing rugby feast, Carwyn James and Barbarians captain John Dawes. He then offered what I consider to be a suggestion to the Welsh contingent that 'a little something extra', as seen that day, would be necessary to beat the All Blacks again.

'And what this crowd has seen today,' he stated, 'has been, not strictly, a treat of running rugby – it has also been *thoughtful* rugby.'

These words were spoken in 1973, a full twenty years after Cliff Morgan had walked off the same hallowed turf with the last men to taste victory over the All Blacks in a Welsh shirt. Had Cliff been with us today, another fifty years later, still without a victory, he may well have wished to say a little more. Cliff's message is subtle and is concealed by his typical eloquence. But I recognise it and I endorse it, too.

~ *finis* ~

345

WALES versus NEW ZEALAND

Dec 16th	1905	3–0	Cardiff
Nov 29th	1924	0–19	Swansea
Dec 21st	1935	13–12	Cardiff
Dec 19th	1953	13–8	Cardiff
Dec 21st	1963	0–6	Cardiff
Nov 11th	1967	6–13	Cardiff
May 31st	1969	0–19	Christchurch
June 14th	1969	12–33	Auckland
Dec 2nd	1972	16–19	Cardiff
Nov 11th	1978	12–13	Cardiff
Nov 1st	1980	3–23	Cardiff
June 14th	1987	6–49	Brisbane*
May 28th	1988	3–52	Christchurch
June 11th	1988	9–54	Auckland
Nov 4th	1989	9–34	Cardiff
May 31st	1995	9–34	Johannesburg*
Nov 29th	1997	7–42	London
Nov 23rd	2002	17–43	Cardiff
June 21st	2003	3–55	Hamilton
Nov 2nd	2003	37–53	Sydney*
Nov 20th	2004	25–26	Cardiff
Nov 5th	2005	3–41	Cardiff
Nov 25th	2006	10–45	Cardiff
Nov 22nd	2008	9–29	Cardiff
Nov 7th	2009	12–19	Cardiff
June 19th	2010	9–42	Dunedin
June 26th	2010	10–29	Hamilton
Nov 27th	2010	25–37	Cardiff
Nov 24th	2012	10–33	Cardiff

* *Rugby World Cup*

Nov 22nd	2014	16 – 34	Cardiff
June 11th	2016	21 – 39	Auckland
June 18th	2016	22 – 36	Wellington
June 25th	2016	6 – 46	Dunedin
Nov 25th	2017	18 – 33	Cardiff
Nov 1st	2019	17 – 40	Tokyo, Japan*
Oct 30th	2021	16 – 54	Cardiff

BIBLIOGRAPHY

John Billot, *All Blacks in Wales* (Ron Jones Publications, 1972).

R. H. Chester and N.A.C. McMillan, *Centenary 100 Years of All Black Rugby* (MOA with Dominion Breweries Ltd, 1984).

Peter Corrigan, *Jonathan Davies Code Breaker* (Bloomsbury, 1996).

Gerald Davies, *Gerald Davies: an Autobiography* (George Allen & Unwin, 1979).

George Dixon, *1905 The Triumphant Tour of the New Zealand Footballers* (David Ling Publishing Ltd, 1999).

Gareth Edwards, *Gareth* (Stanley Paul, London, 1978).

David Farmer, *The Life and Times of Swansea R.F.C.: The All Whites,* (Published with the assistance of the BJ Group, sponsors of Swansea R.F.C., 1995).

Philip J. Grant, *Tommy Vile – a Giant of a Man* (Philip J. Grant, 2010).

Wynne Gray and Wayne Shelford, *Buck, the Wayne Shelford Story* (MOA Publications, Auckland, 1990).

Bob Howitt and Graham Henry, *Graham Henry the X-Factor* (Queen Anne Press, 1999).

Bob Howitt, *Grant Batty a Biography* (Rugby Press Ltd, Auckland, 1977).

Bob Howitt, *75 New Zealand Rugby Greats*, revised edition (Hodder Moa Beckett Publishers Ltd, 2004).

Bob Howitt and Dianne Haworth, *All Black Magic: 100 Years of New Zealand Test Rugby* (Harper-Sports, 2003).

Bob Howitt and Dianne Haworth, *The 1905 Originals — The remarkable story of the team that went away as the Colonials and came back as the All Blacks* (HarperCollins Publishers, 2005).

Barry John, *The Barry John Story* (Collins, 1974).

James Kerr, *Legacy – what the All Blacks can Teach Us about the Business of Life* (London, Constable, 2015).

Heather Kidd & Piri Weepu, *Piri – Straight Up: Cups, Downs & Keeping Calm* (Hodder Moa, 2012).

Bob Luxford, *Johnny Simpson Iron Man* (The Rugby Museum Society of New Zealand, 1998).

Robin McConnell, *Inside the All Blacks* (HarperCollins, 1998).

John McCrystal and Lindsay Knight, *Eden Park: a History* (Phantom House Books Limited, 2011).

Terry P. McLean, *The All Blacks* (Sidgwick & Jackson Limited, 1991).

Bill McLaren, *Rugby's Great Heroes and Entertainers* (Hodder & Stoughton, 2003).

Cliff Morgan and Geoffrey Nicholson, *Cliff Morgan the Autobiography: Beyond the Fields of Play* (Hodder & Stoughton, 1996).

George Nēpia, *Rugby Every Time: George Nēpia's Own Story* (New Zealand Sports Hall of Fame).

Ron Palenski, *Rugby – a New Zealand History* (Auckland University Press, 2015).

Ron Palenski, *Last Post: Rugby's Wartime Roll Call* (New Zealand Sports Hall of Fame, 2011).

David Parry-Jones, *Taff's Acre* (Willow Books, Collins, 1984).

David Smith and Gareth Williams, *Fields of Praise* (University of Wales Press, 1980).

Billy Stead, as introduced by Ron Palenski, *Billy's Trip Home* (New Zealand Sports Hall of Fame, 2005).

Christopher Tobin, *The Original All Blacks 1905–1906* (Hodder Moa Beckett, 2005).

Alan Turley, *Rugby: The Pioneer Years* (HarperCollins, 2008).

Tony Williams, *100 Great Moments in New Zealand Rugby* (David Ling Publishers Ltd 1999).

NEWSPAPERS

The Aberdare and Merthyr Express, The Aberdare Leader, The Aberdeen Press and Journal, The Cambria Daily Leader, The Daily Telegraph, The Evening Express (Aberdeen), The Evening Post, The Herald of Wales, The Llanelli Mercury, The Neath Guardian, The New Zealand Herald, The Otago Daily Times, The Pembrokeshire Herald, The Port Talbot Guardian, The South Wales Argus, The South Wales Daily Post, The South Wales Echo, The South Wales Gazette, The Tenby Observer, The Times, The Sunday Times, The Western Mail and South Wales News

GENERAL SOURCES

Diaries of George Dixon and Stan Dean; Minutes of the Welsh Football Union; Minutes of Swansea Cricket and Football Club Management committee; Official match programmes of New Zealand versus Abertillery & Ebbw Vale (1963), Llanelli (1972) and West Wales (1978).

WEB SITES
(i) Rugby Football History.com, 'The Laws of Football as played at Rugby School, 1845 and 1862,' and Gareth Williams' paper 'The 1905 All Blacks tour of Britain.' (ii) The official site of Aberavon R.F.C. (iii) The official site of Swansea R.F.C. (iv) 'The Greatest Try of All Time, 1973, All Blacks versus Barbarians; and (v) 'This is Your Life, Colin Meads,' Television NZ. (vi) Beauden Barrett's 100th Test Capping Ceremony, 2021, YouTube. (vii) All Black Rugby Team visit Donegal at Dave Gallaher's Home in Ramelton, Ireland, 2005, YouTube. (viii) NZ history.govt.NZ/media/sound/ NZ's first million-selling song now-is-the-hour.